UFO's: The Great Last Days Deception

FIRST PRINTING

Billy Crone

Cover Design:
Chris Taylor

To my brother, Jim.

As I look back on this life,
I am amazed and humbled at the manifold wisdom of God.
What I mean is this.
Of all the people that the Lord would ordain to overshadow me,
via an only older brother,
it was and is you.

Thank you for the sharing of your time,
your patience, your wisdom, and very life in me.
It has proven to be an investment in God's hands,
to help mold me into a responsible man.

At times, you have been more than a brother to me,
but a father figure as well, when I needed it most.
Thank you, Jim.
I love you.

Contents

Preface

Living a life apart from Christ was and is miserable. For me it was a dark, deceptive, and deadly time, partly because of the unfortunate things I got involved in. Due to the hypocrisy I spied in other so-called Christians while growing up in high school and certainly the hardness of my own heart, when I finally became interested in "spiritual things" I was not about to go down the route of Christianity. Instead I went straight into the occult, dabbled in satanism, and then became enthralled with demonic New Age teachings. This unfortunate spiritual journey led me straight into the topic and teachings of UFO's and Aliens. Why? Because when one begins to peel back the layers of lies embedded within the identity of these so-called Space Brothers or Extra-Terrestrials, one discovers a merely cunning repackaging of occult behavior and sinister dark satanic activity custom tailored for our modern skeptical and technological society. What better way to have people actually comingle and communicate with demons then to simply relabel them as Aliens from another world? What more ingenious trickery is it to get people to submit to an occult initiation ritual then by merely calling it an abduction experience? What more of a slick marketing technique is it to redefine actual demonic possession as simply a walk-in, or those who converse with actual demons as mere channelers of the light or a chosen star child working with Extra-Terrestrials to aid humanity in their darkest hour? And who can compete with the ultimate deception of explaining away the Rapture of the Church, next great event on God's prophetic calendar, as merely being a lift-off of people from planet earth by UFO's orbiting the planet as we speak? No wonder the Scripture calls satan "cunning."

What you are about to read is definitely going to take you out of your comfort zone. It's not meant to scare you or frighten you, but rather to equip you on how to effectively and accurately deal with one of the darkest deceptive lies ever to hit our planet; the real identity behind UFO's and their occupants. One last piece of advice; when you are through reading this book will you please *READ YOUR BIBLE*? I mean that in the nicest possible way. Enjoy, and I'm looking forward to seeing you someday!

Billy Crone
Las Vegas, Nevada
2018

Chapter One

The Premise of UFO's

You are about to read what I believe is one of the most sinister plots ever foisted upon mankind. It's a dark, deceptive, and dangerous plan, and it's centered around the topic of UFO's and Aliens. I believe, and I think you will

agree, when you are finished reading this book, that UFO's, and the so-called mystery that surrounds them, are single handedly helping to usher mankind into one of the darkest periods that this planet has ever seen. In fact, we have already been conditioned to accept UFO reports as a common recurrence as shown below.

Michio Kachu MSNBC Interview: "Ninety-Five percent of UFO sightings can be easily identified, it's the five percent that give you the willies."

HLN News Anchor: "Pilots chase them sometimes and can't catch them. There are near misses between these things and commercial aircraft."

General Denis Letty French Air Force RET, History Channel: "And we saw the disk…hovering"

General Denis Letty French Air Force RET. Micho Kachu MSNBC Interview: "These are very hard to dismiss, the handful of sightings."

The History Channel: "A UFO in broad daylight in Paris"
National Press Club: "We suddenly observed a very bright red- orange object. It was oval."

Larry King Live CNN: "UFOs have interfered with missiles."

FIFE Symington: "I saw something that defied logic."

National Press Club: "Reported strange craft, triangular in shape"

National Press Club: "Triangular in shape"

Crowley UFO Sighting: "Mystery craft being seen"

Berlin UFO Sighting: "Dark metallic in appearance"

The History Channel: "Flying Craft"

Richard Vick Witness KCTV 5: "It was an orange orb"

Fox News: "A glowing orb"

Jennifer Waddell 9 ABC new: "A glowing orb"

ABC News: "A giant ball of light"

National Press Club: "A glowing object"

RT Markets: "It could be aliens" – Theories abound on truth behind strange spiral light in arctic sky.[1]

So much so has the media drilled it into our heads that UFO's and Aliens are real, that people, even people of faith, now believe in their existence at an alarming rate, even more so than they do in the existence of God. For instance, polling data reveals how, "More people believe in Aliens than in God," and "More people believe that Aliens have visited planet earth than that Jesus is the Son of God." In fact, "UFO-logy has effectively become a new religion for 21st century," where people now believe that Aliens will save them, not God. Then add to this how Vatican astronomers have said in recent years that they believe there is no conflict between believing in God and in the possibility of

"extraterrestrial brothers." Furthermore, with this kind of religious endorsement from the Catholic Church one begins to understand the mind-blowing results of another survey taken from Pacific Lutheran Theological Seminary. People of various religions were asked about the impact on their faith concerning an announcement of official extraterrestrial disclosure and they actually stated, "Their religion would be just fine, no problem" and "I'd share a pew with an alien any day."[2] Truly something significant and deceptive is transpiring on a planetary-wide scale that I think it would behoove us to get to the bottom of.

Now, first of all, for the record, let me state that I do not believe that all reports and occurrences of UFO's are real. I think the vast majority of them can be explained either by military or governmental aircraft, natural phenomena, or just flat out hoaxes. However, I do believe that some instances are real, very real, and frankly, sinister beyond what most people even want to believe or imagine.

And believe it or not, it's been going on for quite some time. Let's start off our journey by taking a brief look at the history of UFO sightings from around the world, and you tell me if something sinister hasn't been cooking for quite some time now.

Chapter Two

The History of UFO's
Part One

When I decided to write this book, I thought a good place to start my research would be at the infamous Area 51. It is such a well-known hot spot for UFO activity. But what most people don't realize is that UFO activity and accounts of Aliens visiting planet earth have been reported for quite some time now. So let's journey back in time and take a look at the history of UFO sightings from around the world and again, you tell me if somebody hasn't been planning this deception for a very long time.

"Most people today envision UFOs to be exactly as they are portrayed in most science fiction films and books. This is of course a relatively recent conception, that has been stimulated perhaps by our expanding knowledge of outer space, but strange sights appeared in the skies long before space flight, or manned flight of any kind was possible, and in each century these visions took on identities that tell much about the worldview of those who saw them."

"Alexander the Great and his armies, for instance, were harassed by a pair of flying objects in 329 BC. Most of the soldiers fled the scene but some of the hardier men stood their ground and tried to hit the disk with their arrows and with stones from their slings."

"Engraved onto a French token, minted in the 1860s, is a disk shaped flying object that experts say may have commemorated a daytime UFO sighting."

"There were sightings in 1897 of a lighter-than-air ship, that had propellers, port-hole windows, and brilliant search lights that pointed at the ground."[1]

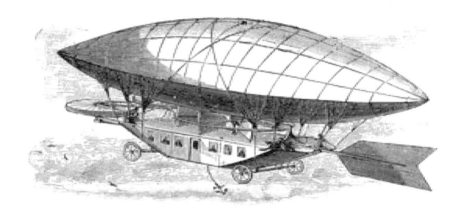

I don't know if you noticed or not, but right out of the gate in looking at the history of UFO sightings, they changed their appearance to the changing technology of the culture. To me, this is your first clue that something fishy is going on here. Let's start with the last one that was mentioned there in the late 1800's, The Mystery or Phantom Airships. This class of UFO's are best known from a series of newspaper reports originating in the Western United States and spreading east during the late 1800's. In fact, airship reports were made worldwide, as early as the 1880s, and they're considered to be the cultural predecessor to modern extra-terrestrial-piloted flying saucer-style UFO claims. Typical airship reports involved unidentified lights, but more detailed accounts reported ships comparable to a dirigible or blimp. Reports of the alleged crewmen and pilots usually described them as human looking, although sometimes the crew claimed to be from Mars.

Now stop and think about that. Why appear as a blimp back then and not the same kind of aircraft people see today? Did your technology really change that drastically and/or did you really travel from Mars on a blimp? Or are you mimicking people's flying technology based upon their generation and then changing it to fit or mimic the next generation's technology that has now become much more advanced? Can you say deceptive?

But let's fast forward a little bit. In 1942, the Hopeh Incident in China was an alleged UFO sighting that was spotted and photographed but was tucked away in a scrapbook. A young Japanese student was going through his father's photographs from the China Campaign and discovered a photo with a strange cone-shaped object in the sky. It showed several people in the street looking up and two pointing up at the object. It is reported that a sidewalk photographer snapped a picture of the strange machine.

Also, in 1942, at the Battle of L.A., Los Angeles, California. was an account of unidentified aerial objects triggering the firing of thousands of anti-aircraft rounds and raised the wartime alert status. It was just three months after the Japanese attack on Pearl Harbor and it was originally assumed to be another air strike from Japan. The identity of the object is still unknown today.

"Los Angeles, California, in the early months of 1942, the city was on edge. The recent surprise attack on Pearl Harbor, had propelled America into World War 2 and the threat of Japanese invasion by sea or by air kept the military on full alert.

Chris Pitman, UFO Investigator: *"Pearl Harbor was a very recent memory for people. People were in high alert. There was a great deal of suspicion, Japanese Americans were being put in internment camps. There were German U-boats in the Atlantic, Japanese submarines in the Pacific and people were very fearful."* *In a well-organized defense operation, air raid wardens and the coast guard were monitoring the pacific shoreline as never before.*

Albert W. Metz: *"The war had started, I was a thirteen-year-old kid and this one night, which was February 1942, the sirens started wailing in the middle of the night. Black out. And we had several black outs before this."*

On February 25th between the hours of 3:12am and 4:15am the 37th Coast Artillery Brigade in Los Angeles fired off a barrage of anti-aircraft shells at an unidentified flying object.

CBS Broadcast: *"We're here on the roof top of the Columbian Broadcasting Building in the heart of Hollywood, we can plainly see the flashes of guns and search lights sweeping the skies in a wide arc along the coastal area."*

Professor C. Scott Littleton, PH. D: *"I think what woke me up initially, was the sound of anti-aircraft guns. I jumped out of bed, my parents were up. My father was an air warden and he figured this has to be the real thing."*

Dorothy Matich: *"My mother was telling my brother and I "Get under the bed! Get under the bed! Stay there!" and of course we got out and we peaked. There was all this firing. It was almost like a Fourth of July"*

Albert W. Metz: *"I started to hear a lot of loud explosions. My brother and I looked out the bedroom window, saw search lights twisting and turning in the sky." But what was the strange UFO that the search lights were focused on? Where had it come from? Japan? Or somewhere from out of this world?*

Could this incredible photograph that was published the next morning in the Los Angeles Times provide the proof? Could ancient astronaut theorists have been right all along?

The lights people described as seeing over the city of Los Angeles

Professor C. Scott Littleton: *"It was practically overhead, and I mean overhead." Retired Anthropology Professor C. Scott Littleton was nine years old and growing up at Hermosa Beach when he spotted the strange object hovering right over his house. "We saw what my mother always called a silver bug. I'd characterize it today as a lozenge, a long oval. It was something I'll never ever forget. In 1942 this is the opinion of what was seen that night in Los Angeles.*

It was caught in searchlight beams and anti-aircraft shells were exploding all around it. It gradually went like this, (motions in a sideways crashing motion), and then began to lose altitude a little bit as it moved over, what had to have been, Redondo Beach. We lost track of it, but the banging continued.

Very quickly afterwards, I saw, we all saw, a flight of planes following the track of the object, going overhead, anywhere from 3-5 interceptors, clearly piston driven, US planes. No one has ever admitted those planes were in the sky. My first thought immediately was a Japanese observation plane. Later, the Japanese records definitively prove that there were no Japanese planes over Southern California that night, or indeed ever."

After ruling out the possibility that a Japanese plane had invaded American airspace, Secretary of the Navy Frank Knox attributed the incident to war nerves. But Secretary of War Henry Stenson quickly refuted this explanation. Defensively declaring that an actual aircraft had been the target of the assault. To this day no one seems to know just what or who was hovering over Los Angeles that night.

"By a process of elimination, the most efficient, and I say this as a scholar. The most efficient explanation is that it was what we call today a UFO. Something not of this world, something that belonged to another technology. If that's true then this event was one of the largest mass UFO sightings in history, over a million people saw it."[2]

Now, let's fast-forward to 1946 and that is where we had the Ghost Rockets in Scandinavia. These were objects that were sighted repeatedly over Scandinavia even to the point where the Swedish Defense Staff expressed their concern.

Interviewer: "You spoke in your presentation about certain events that took place over Scandinavia in the mid-40s. Objects that were seen and what were those objects and what was the interest in terms of defense following that?"

A member of the Swedish Defense Staff*: "In the summer of 1946 there was a massive wave of what became known as ghost rockets, sometimes spook bombs they were called. They seemed to be concentrated in Scandinavia, Sweden. There's no doubt about that, but the fact of the matter is that it was a worldwide phenomenon.*

They were seen as far south as India, there were reports from Turkey, from Greece, and there were other events around the world at this time. But definitely the concentration was over Sweden and for several weeks in the summer of 1946 these things were seen. There were thousands of reports, several thousand reports, and they were often seen like trailing fire.

Sometimes not trailing anything. They were generally described as tubular objects. Very occasionally wing type protrusions were seen but often no protrusions at all, such as would be required to guide a rocket, like guiding veins on a rocket, such as V2. The consensus of opinion at that time was that the Russians were test flying V2 rockets captured from the Nazis. Both the Americans and the Russians had captured V2 Nazi rockets and they were certainly doing some experiments with them.

But 1946, it was far too early for the Russians to have developed anything so sophisticated because these things were diving into lakes, they were seen leaving lakes in some cases, they were encountered by SAAB bombers. There was one craft which actually struck one of them, there was a collision with one of the SAAB bombers."

"The three-man crew was lost, this made headlines, a story in the Washington Post, completely unexplained, and these were not anybody's rockets that we know of. They were not Russian because one of the world's leading aviation historians Bill Gungstun has confirmed in my book.

There is no way that so many sightings could be attributed to Russian experiments and why would you fly them over the middle of Stockholm, it wouldn't make any sort of sense. Besides, they didn't look anything like V2s."

Interviewer: "Were they moving at variable speeds?" "Variable speeds" nods head "Sometimes preceding at a leisurely pace, sometimes at tremendously high speeds, and varying altitudes. So, it remains unexplained."[3]

In 1946, you also had the Angelholm Incident in Sweden. A gentleman named Gösta Karlsson reported seeing a UFO and its alien passengers. A model of a flying saucer is now erected at the site.

Then in 1947 we had the Maury Island Incident in Washington State. A gentleman named Harold A. Dahl reported that his dog was killed, and his son was injured by encounters with UFO's. He also claimed that a witness was threatened by Men in Black. The mystery continues right on up to today.

Like fog on a fall day, a haze of mystery still surrounds Maury Island nearly sixty years after a supposed space ship sighting that's still not fully explained. It's been written about in books, even captured in the comics but outside of hardcore mystery buffs, few people know about what may have happened two weeks before the most famous UFO sighting.

Philip Lipson, Seattle Museum of Mysteries: *"People are always talking about Roswell and very few people realize the first UFO incident was in Pujet Sound."*

A man named Harold Dahl and his fifteen-year-old son were out in a boat salvaging logs just off Maury Island. It was the afternoon of June 21st, 1947 when they saw six large donut shaped objects appear overhead. One seemed to be having problems staying airborne. Dahl says as he quickly brought the boat to shore. The troubled UFO began dropping tons of hot metal and rocks.

The UFO Memorial in Angelholm

Dahl says that his son was even burned on the arm and their dog was killed by the dump of debris. The whole beach was said to be covered with that sludge. No one knows for sure if it had been previously dumped here by a local smelter or if it indeed fell from a saucer in the sky, but it did get the attention of the government. Two air force officers soon arrived, they studied the facts, scooped up some of the sludge, climbed on to a plane and died. Their B25 crashed near Kelso.

Philip Lipson: *"And there's some reports that there might have been sabotage, that there was somebody that was trying to stop them from analyzing it and somehow caused their plane to crash. The Airforce investigation of the crash site was classified, and the site still hasn't been thoroughly investigated by an outside agency. That's part of why the mystery of what happened at Maury Island still* *endures today. "I think they did see UFOs and something dropped sludge on the beach."*

Then in 1947 we had the infamous Kenneth Arnold UFO Sighting in Washington State. Three days after the Maury Island incident, this UFO sighting sparked for the very first time the term "*flying saucer*". While flying near Mount Rainier, Washington, pilot Kenneth Arnold spotted a formation of nine silvery crescent-shaped objects flying in tight formation. He described the disc's movements to a reporter as "like pie plates skipping over the water." In his story the next day the reporter coined the term "*flying saucers*" and the label has stuck ever since then. Later, he estimates their size at 40 to 50 feet wide, their speed at a fantastic 1,200 miles per hour, more than twice as fast as any known aircraft of that day. In fact, here's the actual original radio broadcast immediately after the event took place.

Interviewer: *"Every newscaster and newspaper across the nation has made headline out of it and this afternoon we are honored indeed to have here in our studio this man, Kenneth Arnold, who we believe may be able to give us a first-hand account, and give you the same, of what happened.*

Kenneth first of all, if you'd move up here to the microphone just a little bit closer, we'll ask you to just tell in your own fashion as you told us last night in your hotel room and again this morning what you were doing there and how this entire thing started. Go ahead Kenneth."

Kenneth Arnold: *"Well at about two fifteen I first took off from Jahalus, Washington on route to Yakima, and of course every time any of us fly over the country near Mount Rainier we spent an hour or two in search of the marine plane that's never been found, that they believe is in the snow some place south-west of that particular area.*

That area is located at about ten thousand feet and I had made one sweep past Mount Rainier and down one of the canyons and was dragging it for any types of objects that might prove to be the marine ship, and as I came out of the canyon after about fifteen minutes, I was approximately twenty-five to twenty-eight miles from Mount Rainier, I climbed back up to ninety-two-hundred feet and noticed to the left of me a chain which looked to me like the tail of the Chinese kite, kind of weaving and going at a terrific speed across the face of Mount Reiner.

At first, I thought they were geese because they flew like geese, but it was going so fast that I immediately changed my mind and thought that it was a bunch of new jet planes in formation. Well, as the planes came to the edge of Mt. Rainier flying at about one hundred and sixty degrees south, I thought I would clock them because it was such a clear day and I didn't know what their destination was.

But due to the fact that I had Mount St. Helens and Mt. Adams to clock them by I just thought I'd see how fast they were going. Among pilots, we argue about

speed so much, and they seem to flick and flash in the sun just like a mirror. In fact, I happened to be at an angle from the sun that happened to hit the tops of these peculiar looking things, in such a way that it almost blinded you when you looked at them though your plexiglass windshield.

It was about one minute to three when I started clocking them on my sweep second hand clock and as I kept looking at them, I kept looking for their tails, they didn't have any tails. Well, I thought maybe there was something wrong with my eyes. I turned the plane around and opened the window. Sure enough, I couldn't find any tails on them and the whole observation of these ships didn't last more than about two and a half minutes. I could see them only when they seemed to tip their wing or whatever it was, and the sun flashed on them.

They looked something like a pie plate that was cut in half, with a convex triangle in the rear. Now I thought, maybe they're jet planes with the tales painted green or brown or something and I didn't think too much of it but kept watching them. They didn't fly in the conventional formation that's taught in our army. They seemed to kind of weave in and out right above the mountain top. I would say that they even went down into the canyons on several instances, oh probably a hundred feet.

But I could see them against the snow of course on Mt. Rainier and on the snow on Mt. Adams as they were flashing against a high ridge that happens to lay in between Mt. Rainier and Mt. Adams. But when I observed the tail end of the last one passing Mt. Adams I was at an angle near the Mt. Rainier Summit, but I looked at my watch and it showed one minute and forty-two seconds. Well, I thought that's pretty fast, but I didn't stop to think what the distance was between the two mountains.

Well, I landed at Yakima, Washington and Al Baxter were there to greet me. After I told him what I saw he told me he guessed I had better change my brand, but he kind of gave me a mysterious sort of a look, maybe I had seen something, he didn't know. I just kind of forgot it then and got down to Pendleton and began looking at my map and taking measurements on it and the best calculation I could figure out, and even allowing for error, it would be around twelve hundred miles an hour.

Because making the distance between Mt. Rainier to Mt. Adams in approximately two minutes, it'd be around 25 miles per minute. Now allowing for error we can give them three or four minutes to make it and they're still going more than 800 miles an hour and, in my knowledge, there isn't anything I have read about outside some of the German rockets that would go that fast.

These were flying in more or less a level constant altitude, they weren't going up and they weren't going down, they were simply staying straight, and level and I laughed when I told the men they sure should have had a tail, but it didn't seem to help me much.

To the best of my knowledge, and the best of my description, that is what I saw and like I told the Associated Press I'd be glad to confirm it with my hands on a Bible because I did see it. And whether it has anything to do with our army or our intelligence or whether it has to do with some foreign country I don't know. But I did see it, I did clock it, and I just happened to be in a beautiful position to do it. It's just as much a mystery to me as it is to everyone else who's been calling me the last twenty-four hours wondering what it was."[5]

After Arnold's initial report, UFO sightings in our skies exploded. On June 26, four witnesses including a doctor saw a "huge silver globe" moving along the rim of the Grand Canyon. Two days after that, an Air Force pilot reported a flight of six discs over Lake Mead, Nevada and within days, reports were pouring in from Michigan, Ohio, Oregon, Louisiana, and as far-north even Canada.

Then of course we have, in 1947 the Roswell UFO incident in Roswell, New Mexico. This is the infamous account where the United States Army Air Force allegedly captured a flying saucer. It is reported that they recovered debris from an alien aircraft that was found in the desert of New Mexico and thus began one of the biggest controversies and mysteries in U.S. history, including great suspicion of a government cover-up.

And then in 1948 we have the Green Fireballs in the southwest United States. Objects were reported over several United States military bases and an official investigation followed.

Also, in 1948 the Mantell UFO incident in Kentucky. The US Air Force sent a fighter pilot to investigate a UFO sighting over Fort Knox, Kentucky. Unfortunately, the pilot was killed while pursuing the UFO.

Captain Thomas Mantell

"There is a great scene in the movie Independence Day when the pilot sacrifices his life to bring down an alien mother ship. Well, that was fiction, but nearly sixty years ago a National Guard pilot in Kentucky died in the pursuit of a UFO. Drew Speier is here with the ongoing mystery behind the death of Captain Thomas Mantell."

A mystery indeed, this season it came on the heels of another UFO story that came on the air in the summer of 1947. That's when a UFO allegedly crashed in Roswell, New Mexico. That story of course, well-documented, but this equally puzzling mystery regarding a UFO in the skies above Kentucky just a few months after the Roswell Incident.

In our report, a 1956 government film, addressing this case, a case that will never be solved, because Captain Thomas Mantell, from Simpson County, Kentucky, an experienced pilot and World War Two Ace took the answers to his grave.

It made headlines across the country. January 7, 1948 1:30pm Kentucky State Police receive reports of a UFO near Godman Airforce base. One reports, "It's like seeing one green bright shiny star. I don't know, it appears like a star now."

Four F-51 Mustangs on their way from the Sandford Airforce Base Kentucky are contacted by the tower. "Godman tower to Captain Mantel, investigating an unidentified object in your area." They're wanting to investigate an unidentified object, one to two hundred feet in diameter. One plane returns for fuel and oxygen the three others approach the object.

"Mantell to tower, I see it. Above and ahead of me. I'm still climbing." The planes climb to 22,000 feet too high for World War Two fighters without oxygen. Two planes return to the base leaving Captain Mantel in sole pursuit of the unknown. Minutes later Mantell with another transmission.

"Mantel to tower, it appears to be a metallic object of tremendous size." Captain Mantell kept climbing most likely above 30,000 feet. Radio contact was lost. "Captain Mantell come in, over. This is Goodman Tower to Captain Mantell, come in, over."

Minutes later, less than two hours from the initial sightings, Mantells F51 crashed on a farm in Franklin Kentucky. His watch stopped at 3:16pm, his body still strapped in his plane. By all accounts he passed out from a lack of oxygen, forcing his plane to plunge to the ground.

Today a historical marker sits near the site where Mantells plane went down here in Franklin, Kentucky. In fact, it went down on a farm nearby Joe Phillips farm. His son, a school child then, was one of the first on the scene.

"We heard this real loud boom, ya know, it actually shook the house. Best I remember it was two of them. Like an explosion." William Phillips Jr. was six years old and home sick with his younger sister when the crash occurred.

"We ran to the window and we just happened to run to the right window and see it hit the ground, just as it hit the ground." The news of the incident immediately made the headlines. Newspapers reporting that Mantell had been shot down by a magnetic ray from a flying saucer. The story took on a life of its own. He was the first person ever to die while pursuing an unidentified flying object. The militaries response: "most likely he was chasing a weather balloon."

"I can't see that a balloon could move and outrun a P51. The P51 was the fastest plane the military virtually had in forty-seven." It's a story almost sixty years later, that's still talked about in Franklin Kentucky where Mantell was born and oddly enough died, just a few miles from the Simpson County Tourism Center where he is honored.

Dan Ware, Simpson County Tourism: *"There are many UFO buffs who stop by to ask and see what we got and then want to know as much as they can about the story. It continues to fascinate people even after fifty years."*

"Several years later when they restructured the project. Project Sign was the first one and they were serious. They came to the conclusion that we were dealing with something from somewhere else."

Project Sign later become Project Bluebook because Mantell was a respected pilot and gave the UFO story credibility, the military was concerned.

"If you look in the Bluebook archives, which is the Airforce records, it shook up a lot of military people. After searching all the records and after the Airforce claimed that it was a Skyhook balloon, they had pretty good records on all the launches, but they never could establish a launch date for that day."

Also, there were several reported sightings of UFOs on the day of Mantells death including Madisonville and Owensboro. Newly found documents left off the Bluebook records that showed some of these objects were maneuvering and could not be attributed to balloons of any kind. So, for now this case remains a mystery.[6]

In 1948 we have the Gorman Dogfight in North Dakota. A US Air Force pilot sighted and pursued a UFO for 27 minutes over Fargo, North Dakota. Gorman approached the object to investigate it and suddenly it brightened and accelerated. The object had been traveling "about 250 miles per hour," but as Gorman began the chase, it sped up to "about 600 miles per hour." The P-51 could only travel 400 mph, so the object quickly outdistanced Gorman. It then made a "180-degree turn and came straight at him." Gorman "attempted to crash into it," but as they neared, it veered upward and passed over him.

In 1950 we had the Mariana UFO Incident in Great Falls, Montana. The manager of Great Falls' pro baseball team took color film of two UFO's flying over Great Falls Montana. The film was extensively analyzed by the US Air Force and independent investigators.

The following was recorded August the fifteenth 1950. It was taken in Great Falls, Montana by Nick Mariana. Immediately after we were notified of the sighting we sent an intelligence man to get a record.

Nick Mariana: *"My name is Nick Mariana, for the last six years I've been the General Manager for a minor league baseball club called the Electrics. We play out of Great Falls, Montana and are a farm club for the Brooklyn Dodgers. On August 15th, 1950 at Legion Ballpark in Great Falls, Montana, after a couple of hours in the clubhouse office I went up into the grandstand to call the groundskeeper.*

As I reached the top of the stairway I glanced northward to the tall Anaconda Copper Company smokestack to check the direction of the wind from the white smoke. A force of habit I suppose, because our outfielders use it as an indicator on defensive play. As I looked up I saw two silvery objects moving swiftly out of the northwest.

They appeared to be moving directly south. The objects were very bright and about 10.000 feet in the air. They appeared to be of a bright shiny metal, like polished silver. Both were the same size and going the same rate of speed, which was much slower than the jets which shot by shortly after I filmed the discs.

Suddenly they stopped. It was then that I remembered the camera in the glove compartment of my car. I raced down stairs yelling for my secretary, Miss Virginia Ronnie. The distance from the top of the stairway to my car was about sixty feet and I must have made that in about six jumps. I asked my secretary if she saw anything and she said "yes, two silvery spheres."

I unlocked the glove compartment of my car, took out the camera, turned the telephoto lens on the turret into position, set the camera at F22 picked up the objects on the viewfinder and pressed the trigger. The discs appeared to be spinning like a top and were about fifty feet across and about fifty yards apart.

I could not see any exhaust, wings, or any kind of fuselage. There was no cabin, no odor, no sound, except I thought I heard a whooshing sound when I first saw them. As the film clicked through the camera I could see the objects moving southeast behind the General Mills grain building and the black water tank directly south of the ball park. I filmed the objects until they disappeared into the blue sky behind the water tank."

The Montana film (two objects) was photographed at about 11:30am MST. During the forenoon the surface wind was 25 to 28 mph; it reached 37 mph at 12:30pm. The objects moved almost directly counter to the wind direction. They were not balloons. Studies of the magnified pictures projected, frame by frame, show the motion of the objects to have been steady and horizontal.

They were definitely not free-falling. They were not meteors, bird, not any kind of known aircraft. This is the Montana film projected exactly as it was photographed. The objects are moving against a 25 to 28 mph wind. This is the film in double frame or slow motion. A slight bounce in the movement of the objects as well as the towers perceptible. This is due to the hand-held camera.

The film analyzed frame by frame shows the movement of the objects are horizontal and steady. We will now vary the action and size of the objects and also stop the action from time to time for your study. We have just made a jump cut of the film to an enlarged size and reversed the action. You are now seeing the objects exactly as they were photographed but from a closer perspective.

Pictures taken at the Legion Ball Park in Great Falls, Montana

Analysis reveals that the objects are not balloons nor any kind of known aircraft. The images are very different from those produced by any kind of bird at any distance. The shape, brightness, speed, recto-linear path, steady motion and any separation, rules out any forms of optical atmospheric mirages or cloud reflections.

Comprehensive analysis has eliminated meteors and other known natural phenomenon. The possibility of airplane reflection has been carefully studied and ruled out. "[7]

In 1950 we have the McMinnville UFO Photographs in McMinnville, Oregon. And this is the account where two farmers took pictures of a purported "flying saucer." It is claimed that these are among the best-known UFO pictures and continue to be analyzed and debated to this very day.

Skeptics will often ask why there aren't any better UFO photos available. In fact, there are UFO photos out there that have withstood expert analysis. The best of which come from McMinnville, Oregon, taken on May 11, 1950 by farmer Paul Trent.

Bruce Maccabee, PhD: *"By analyzing the two photos it was possible to determine where Mr. Trent stood, when he took the two photos. To within an accuracy of about a foot or so. And so, if you can imagine looking down from above you can plot where he was standing and where the sighting lines went out.*

They said this object moved to the left, moved southward as you're looking towards the west, it moved slightly between pictures. And in fact, he was standing in one location for the first photo looking this way and then he moved a little bit to the north.

As this object was travelling along he didn't want it to get blocked by the nearby garage, so he moved a little bit to his right and then he looked and took a photo this way and the sighting lines crossed.

Now the overhead wires can be positioned where they were, and the sighting lines did not cross under the wires. So, you know, if it was a model it wasn't hanging straight down under the wires."

The two photographs taken by Paul Trent provided a stereoscopic pair of pictures that gave researchers the data necessary to determine and measure distances to objects within a short range of the camera.

Brad Sparks: *"His altitude or the altitude of the camera also dropped by about a foot. So not only do you have a horizontal triangulation method, but you have a vertical triangulation method. Now when you combine those two methods of distance determination you can determine the distance to every short-range object in those photos.*

And the UFO model, if that's what it was, does not fit. It is not at the close range of those overhead wires that were about fifteen feet away from the camera. They don't fit the location and distance of the garage or the house or the trees that were several hundred feet away in the background."

One of the McMinnville UFO photographs

"There is no indication that this is a hoax, the indications are totally that they actually saw some object flying past their farm and took two photos of it."

Brad Sparks: *"In the 1960s the US Airforce contracted an outside scientific study of UFOs to be conducted by the university of Colorado. The astronomer William Hartman concluded that this was one of the few cases in which all of the geometric, photometric, and photogrammetric aspects agreed that there was an object, extraordinary object, tens of meters in size and metallic in appearance, about a mile away. Which would seem to be consistent with an alien visitation. Even though that's pretty hard to believe."*

Hard to believe, perhaps but in the McMinnville case it's hard to escape the conclusion that a picture really is worth a thousand words.[8]

In 1951 we have the Lubbock Lights, in Lubbock, Texas and these lights were repeatedly spotted flying over the city of Lubbock Texas in a "V" formation with 20 or 30 of them at a time. The sighting was so popular and highly publicized that the photos and story appeared in Life Magazine in 1952. The witnesses included professors from Texas Tech University and they were even photographed by a Texas Tech student as this report shows.

For a few weeks in 1951 people here witnessed a phenomenon of a different sort. A series of UFO sightings that five decades later still defy explanation.

Fox 4 News reports: Beginning August 25th, 1951 and for several nights that followed, a strange line of blueish lights was seen flying swiftly over Lubbock, Texas. This is a classic case for a number of different reasons, including the first group of people who saw the Lubbock Lights, four college professors from Texas Tech university. They attempted to make a study of what they had seen, a scientific study, and were not wholly successful but in the end, they concluded that the Lubbock Lights were under intelligent control.

"You know, we aren't talking about the flying saucer lunatic fringe here, or something. We are talking about professional people who are apparently impressed enough by having seen strange things in the sky to go out and try to observe them under scientific conditions."

Donald Rugulosin is a present-day college professor from Roswell, New Mexico who says comparisons can be made to a more recent incident. On March of 1997 when hundreds of people witnessed a flotilla of flying objects over Phoenix Arizona. Back in 1951 no one in Lubbock had a home video camera but an eighteen-year-old college freshman named Carl Hart Jr. was a budding still photographer who was just about to go to bed when he saw the Lubbock Lights.

Carl Hart Jr.: *"So, I just grabbed my camera and set the exposure to where I wanted and ran outside. I waited and then two more flights came over I took two pictures of one and three of the other. My first process I didn't think I had a thing. It didn't take up much room on the negative.*

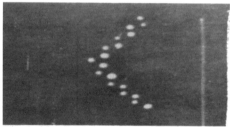 

The Lubbock Lights, photographed at Lubbock, Texas by 19 year old Carl Hart Jr. in 1951. (Credit: Bettman/Getty Images)

Hart took the photos to his boy scout leader who contacted a reporter for the local newspaper which eventually published them but only after Hart endured the first in a series of grillings.

Carl Hart Jr.: *"First, I talked to the people at the Avalanche Journal. Well they were all pretty skeptical and then after they published well first it was the Airforce."*

Local Airforce investigators turn Hart over to higher ups from out of town and eventually to FBI agents.

Carl Hart Jr.: *"Pretty intense questioning, they went over and over my story and I guess they were trying to get me to be inconsistent but apparently they were satisfied eventually."*

Life magazine published a lengthy article in the spring of 1952 and over the years a number of independent studies were conducted. After nearly five decades of intense scrutiny there is no reason to believe that Carl Hart faked anything.

His photos are still among the most remarkable and vexing in UFO history. The government's official report was released in late 1951 and its conclusion, what Carl Hart captured on film were highly reflective duck bellies. "Very clearly, this imaging shows that these are not birds"

Dr. Burleson with advanced degrees in both mathematics and literature is conducting what could be the most intensive computer analysis of Hart's photographs to date.

Dr. Burleson: *"This is in my estimation, the most spectacular, of the photos. It shows a regular flotilla of eighteen large disc-like objects in the sky. I'm inclined to think that these objects may well each have been an excess of two hundred feet in diameter."*

Burleson says the objects heat photograph, display what appears to be structure on the underside which may link them to whatever crashed in nearby Roswell, New Mexico four years earlier.

"It gives clear indication of a cell-like, or beehive type structure underneath. Which is very interesting because it matches nicely with the witness descriptions of the Roswell Object. I think he simply photographed something anomalous in the sky and was treated frankly, pretty shabbily for his trouble."

Carl Hart has never sought fame or fortune from the photos he took, just the opposite.

Carl Hart: *"If it comes up, I would just as soon ignore it. I guess there's a group of people who still feel like anyone who's seen a UFO is kind of a nutcase and I get put in that category part of the time. Part of the people think that anything like that has to be fake, so I get a little bit of that."*

Even the government's analysis, some of it declassified years later concluded there was no evidence of a hoax, that the negatives had not been retouched. That the lights where brighter then stars and that the objects changed position in the formation.[9]

In 1952 we have the Washington D.C. UFO Incident. In July 1952 there was a series of sightings accompanied by radar contacts at three separate airports in the Washington D.C. area. First spotted on an air traffic controller's radar, and they were moving in unusual flight patterns that witnesses called bright orange lights. An Air Force public information officer, Lt. Col. Moncel Monte, confirmed the directive stating, "The jet pilots are, and have been, under orders to investigate unidentified objects and to shoot them down if they can't talk them down." It was further stated that no pilot had been able to get close enough to take a shot at one of the "flying saucers" because they would disappear or speed away as soon as they were approached, sometimes out flying their pilots by "as much as a thousand miles an hour." In fact, the incident was so publicized that even President Truman demanded an explanation.

Strange lights over the US Capital more than fifty years ago. Fox 5's Brook Baldwin investigates UFOs in Washington.

Fox 5 News reports: *"The sky is the stage; the actors are so called flying saucers and they are back on the scene with some new twists."*

July 1952 Air Traffic Controllers at Andrews Airforce base in Maryland pick up ten to twelve unidentified objects on radar. Minutes later, another sighting this time at Washington National Airport. The Air Force sent up two fighter aircraft to intercept the flying objects, according to confidential security information now released to the public.

Dr. Steven M Greer: *"The Airforce did respond in scrambled chats and it was imaged and photographed over. I believe there were nine of them at one point, that were seen in formation."*

Dr. Stephen M. Greer is the founder of the disclosure project. His organization collects information on unexplained sighting from all over the world. Including, the more than two thousand reports from around D.C. in the summer of fifty-two, now known as the Washington Nationals.

Dr. Steven M Greer: *"It's been very hard to bring out the information, without it getting linked instantly to something that ends up being embarrassing.*

The famous photo shows seven bright objects flying near the capitol dome. Radar also picked up four more objects in Deltsville and in Herndon. Facing increased pressure from the public the military held a news conference saying the objects seen throughout the region were weather related and nothing more than quote "temperature inversion".

"We have, as of date, formed only one firm conclusion, with respect to this remaining percentage, and that is that it does not contain any pattern of purpose or of consistency that we can relate to any perceivable threat to the United States." A conceivable threat that made it all the way to the oval office.

Captain Kevin Randall: *"The president got very interested and wanted some kind of a solution."*

Reserve Airforce Captain Kevin Randall has been studying UFOs for years. He has written eighteen books, one of them specifically about the D.C. sightings.

Captain Kevin Randall: *"What the Airforce said, basically, well what it was is temperature inversions. Were their inversion layers over Washington D.C. in the summer of July 1952? The answer is yes there were. Were they of sufficient strength to cause the problems you see on the radar? No."*

"Controversy arises maybe the puzzling objects are from another planet?" Puzzling objects Dr. Greer believes are behind a cover up at the highest level.

"Everyone who I know who are military or intel were told "You didn't see this. You were not in the squadron that went up." The radar operators were told "this never happened." But, something did happen those July nights whether it was alien or not is still debatable. Kevin Randall believes it is only a matter of time before the truth comes out.

Captain Kevin Randall: *"I believe what's going to happen, eventually, is that there is going to be a UFO event that is inexplicable and leaves the evidence behind that we cannot just explain away."[10]*

The sightings as you saw made front page headlines around the nation and ultimately lead to the formation of the Robertson Panel by the CIA. In fact, during the 1950's, so many UFO sightings were reported around the world that the Air Force was publicly forced (at least to save face) to sit up and take notice. They couldn't let the American public think that they weren't interested in what surely posed a threat to National Security. So, they began a series of *"Official"* UFO investigations. The first was *"Project Sign"*, then *"Project Grudge"*, and finally concluded with *"Project Blue Book."*

In 1952 we have The Flatwoods Monster in Flatwoods, West Virginia. Six local boys and a woman reported seeing a UFO land, but they also said there was a bizarre-looking creature that appeared near the landing site itself.

In 1953 we have the Ellsworth UFO Case in Bismarck, North Dakota. This is the account where the U.S. Military investigated a UFO incident in

Bismarck, North Dakota which is now one of the most significant radar-visual cases in the history of UFO sightings. It was witnessed by almost forty-five agitated citizens along with military Air Defense System personnel. The description was of a red glowing light that made long sweeping movements over a period of two nights.

Then in 1955 we have the Kelly Hopkinsville Encounter in Kentucky. This is an account where a group of strange, goblin-like creatures were not only reported to have been seen by a family. But these creatures were reported to have even attacked the family. The family shot at them several times with little or no effect.

"They were simple people, just simple country people, you know, honest-type people. The house was sort of run down and old, just a simple country life in farming and they were just trying to make a living."

"You gonna play him again Billy?" Asked Taylor.

"No, I figure, I know when I'm licked. Besides, I ain't got another dollar." answered Billy-Ray.

When Billy-Ray Taylor left the kitchen to fetch water from the nearby well nothing could have prepared him for what would happen next. As he began to fill up his bucket something unusual in the air caught his eye.

"Come quick, you ain't gonna believe it, something weird just fell out of the sky, a bright light or something. I don't know what! It went lickity-split across the field, right there and then it looked like it landed somewhere down in the gully." He told his family.

"Here he goes again, Billy-Ray, you are not only a bad card player, you are a very bad liar to boot." Said Taylor.

"Why would I lie about something like that?" answered Billy-Ray.

It scared him so that he went inside to tell his family, in disbelief they put him down as a joke and told him to 'don't be doing this no more. You've been doing this all the time.'

"Are you daft in the head Billy-Ray? Trying t'pull a fast one?" Taylor asked.

"Why would I do that?" Billy-Ray answers still breathing hard.

No doubt Billy-Ray's story amused the family. Maybe it was a shooting star. They were not in the habit of taking him seriously and soon they cast it aside as a practical joke. No one even bothered to walk out to the gully on the chance that something was there.

"I don't know maybe it was a shooting star for all I know." Says Billy-Ray.

"I think your brain is a shooting star, son." said Lucky.

"Ha-ha, very funny." Replies Billy-Ray.

Before long, darkness fell over the small Kentucky homestead. At around eight o'clock Lucky's dogs began to bark violently as if an intruder was on the property.

"What in the blazes is going on with those darn dogs, Lucky. I told you to get rid of those varmints. I can barely hear myself think, let alone read a good book." Glennie says.

"Shut your trap there, you be still." Lucky said.

As the men stared out the window they were startled to see a strange glow coming from the fields beyond. Lonnie Langford was only twelve years old when he and the others encountered the mysterious invaders at Kelly. His mother was Glennie Lankford also the mother of Lucky Sutton. She and Lonnie as well as his siblings, Charlton and Mary, would soon become witnesses to the impossible.

There was a houseful of people there and they were all terrified. Instructing the family to stay inside Lucky and Billy-Ray warily walked outside to get a better look at their uninvited visitor.

"What in the name of God is that!" Billy-Ray exclaimed.

As the thing came nearer they could make out what seemed to be a small man only a man unlike any they had ever seen before.

"Everybody, you stay put and don't make a sound. I'll whip your ever-loving hide if you do." Lucky yelled to the family inside.

Lucky and Billy-Ray would take no chances, horrified, they raced back inside and grabbed their shotguns as the others looked on in stunned silence. Back outside the unearthly apparition was moving silently towards them.

"What in God's green earth is it?" Lucky asked.

"I don't think God's got nothing to do with it Lucky. It's getting closer Lucky! It looks just like a little man. I ain't ever seen a little man with ears like that." Billy-Ray yelled.

"A goblin, that's what it is, a goblin, straight out of the pits of hell!" Lucky said.

"What are we gonna do, Lucky?" Billy-Ray asked.

"Shoot it!" Lucky answered.

Gail Cook-Kelly, Resident: *"They didn't hurt him. He kind of rolled up into a little ball and kind of, rolled back down the hill over there, where the ship was." Inside the house, the men were confused and dazed not sure what to do next, while the rest of the family, especially Glennie Lankford and the children, remained vigilant next to the bed.*

"Landagosha Lucky, you're nearly scaring those kid's half to death." Glennie exclaimed.

"For God's sake woman there's a thing out there." Lucky warned her.

"What kind of a thing is it Billy?" Glennie asked.

"The kind of a thing that the Lord never intended to be in this universe. Do you hear me woman? We have got to protect our home. "Billy-Ray told her.

"Oh Lucky, why did you have to go and shoot it? It probably never meant us any harm, you might have killed it!" Glennie said.

"We didn't kill it Glennie. Our bullets sounded like they hit nickel plate or something. It ain't human and what ain't human don't deserve to live."

O.P. Baker: *"My name is O.P. Baker and I was in the house that night and I saw them creatures."*

O.P. Baker brother of Eileen Sutton was thirty years old in 1955, a farm laborer who lived in Hopkinsville at the time, but often stayed overnight at the farm house where the person with whom he rode to work could pick him up more conveniently then they could in town. Today he is the only known adult survivor who was present on the night of the close encounter at Kelly.

O.P. Baker: *"Back then I wasn't going to no church, but I started church and have been going ever since. I remember we all were sitting there bout, I'd say around eight o'clock when we heard a noise up on top of the roof." "Listen mom, listen, there's something up on the roof."*

"I was told that these beings were up on the roof scratching and clawing, trying to get through the ceiling. The children and mothers, that were in the house at the time, were trying to hide, trying to get away from this, they were all scared." One of the kids were saying, "Make it go away, just make it go away, please make it go away!"

"There was one up on top of the house, on the awning, one was scratching on the windows, I mean they were like curious. Wanting to see what's going on. Far as the guns being shot I don't know if it was on the far side of the house or this side I do know that they said they come over."

They say that curiosity killed the cat but, in this instance, the curious just grew more curious as the unknown beings once again immerged from the shadows.

"Well he said that they would come up to the windows and they would just stick to the side of the house like a spider. And he said, it would just kind of peek around the window sill with its head and those big, beady eyes in the window and just stare. "Mama screamed, and I jumped up out of the bed and looked out the window and I saw him. They were about three-foot-tall, had pointed ears, webbed feet and hands, and big round eyes."

"They had great big ears, I mean BIG ears, and you could shoot em' and it wouldn't hurt em."

"And he said they would stare until one of them blew it off the window sill. He said, once you shot it off the window sill, he said you'd run outside and shoot them again. Then by the time I got back in the house and look at the other window and there's another one looking in the window."

"Yeah, I was real scared, I was in the corner of the house on the floor. Everybody was running around the house just panicked. I didn't know what was going on."

"What do you think's going on?" Glennie asked.

"God help us Glennie, I don't know. I just don't know" Billy-Ray answered.

"I think it's demons more than likely Billy-Ray. Hell has indeed come to this little house tonight.' Lucky said.

"I think I killed it Lucky, I couldn't have missed at such a close range." Lib said.

"Lib, why isn't it lying prone to the ground just like any normal human being? You, you do know what happened the first time we shot it?"

"Well, I don't care if it's the devil himself, I'm going outside to finish him off. Him and his minions from the deep dark outer space or wherever he comes from." said Billy-Ray.

"I believe it was a twenty gage they were using, my father had, and I believe Billy-Ray had a twenty-two. JC had another shotgun and as all three are shooting' at these things, none of them could make a hit to actually kill one of these creatures."

Wendell McCord, Glennie Lankford's Nephew*: "One of these green men reached down and got him by the hair of the head."*

"One of the little men had picked him up by his hair and then that's when they started shooting and all the little kids like my age were on the bed terrified. I

can't say for sure, but I do know that there are facts proving that something of a higher power had landed in their back field."

When they made a direct hit on the creatures it sounded as if their bullets had struck the center of a metal bucket.

"They just never could kill one of em'. They just seemed to bounce off. He said, there was a battle, they would get on the window sills, scare the women, they would have to run inside and blow them off the window sills. Then they'd run outside to see where they were, and they'd be in the trees and they'd blow them out of the trees."

After taking a direct hit, the creature seemed to defy gravity as it floated off and landed in a grassy area several yards away. Cautiously the shooters moved towards the spot where they believed it had fallen. To their surprise a luminous glow appeared on the ground where the thing had been.

Dr. Barry Taff: *"These beings, these creatures, whatever they were, wherever they were from, displayed a very unusual intrigue and I guess, curiosity that is uncommon with this type of phenomenon."*

According to the witnesses, the creatures seemed capable of extremely rapid movement when running away and it was impossible to tell whether there were several of them or whether there were only two or three that disappeared from one place and re-appeared very quickly in another.

Most of the offices were reluctant to express any opinions about the reported invasion but all seemed impressed at the evident fright and sincerity of the highly excited family.

A check with neighbors revealed that they were not prone to drinking and no evidence of alcohol was found around the place. All the witnesses told practically the same story with only minor variations depending on what part of the house they were in at the time of the happening.[11]

Chapter Three

History of UFO's
Part Two

Then in 1957 we had the Antonio Villas Boas Incident in Brazil. A man named Antonio Villas Boas claimed to have been abducted and examined by aliens. He also claimed to have had intercourse with an alien woman while he was onboard the UFO ship.

The case of a young Brazilian farmer Antonio Villas Boas took place in 1957, four years before Betty and Barney Hill had their encounter.

Antonio Hunees, Journalist: *"Antonio Villas Boas was a farmer and basically, chronologically speaking would be the first abduction case."*

John Schuessler, Former Int'l Director, MUFON: *"He claimed he saw an object come down out of the sky and land nearby."*

Antonio Hunees, Journalist: *"He reported that he was taken, captured by these two aliens that landed near his tractor." Villas Boas was taken inside the craft and his clothes were taken from him. He was put in a chamber that filled up with a gas that made him sick. Most believe the gas was some sort of disinfectant. A naked female alien entered the chamber and she and Villas Boas had sexual* *relations. He even reported that he was bit on the chin. He was then dropped off back in the field with his tractor and the UFO took off.*

Villas Boas soon began to notice strange marks and burns on his body. He was examined by Alago de Fontes, a professor at the National School of Medicine. Fontes was a pioneer in Brazilian Ufology and a well-connected man, with ties to the Brazilian government and military. Fontes diagnosed Villas Boas with radiation poisoning and declared that he was a good case, a case with merit.

Antonio Villas Boas' claims of abduction are further supported that he never sought fame or tried to capitalize on his experience.

***Antonio Hunees**: "In fact, the case wasn't even written or published until several years after. And he later became a lawyer and went to Brasilia, and never profited from his UFO experience."*

***John Schuessler:** "And he eventually died of a very strange disease and we never did know exactly what, but we did know that he came to the United States and was tested at one of the medical universities in California and after that it wasn't too long until he passed away."[1]*

Then in 1957 we had the Levelland UFO Case in Levelland, Texas and this is the account where numerous motorists reported seeing a glowing, egg-shaped object which caused their vehicle's engines to shut down. When the object flew away, their vehicles restarted without a problem. In 1959 we have Dyatlov Pass incident in Russia. There were several mysterious deaths of experienced skiers in the Ural Mountains that were reported to have been caused by "unidentified orange spheres" and an "unknown compelling force."

February 1959, a group of nine mountaineers embark on a winter trek into Russia's Ural Mountains. Their destination, a mountain named Mt. Otorten, which in the local Mansi language means "Do not go there."

Paul Stonehill, Author, UFO Case of Russia: *"Among them were three experienced engineers, the rest were students. They were all young. I think the oldest was thirty-seven years old. They had conducted other hard treks through the area. They were all experienced, strong-willed, determined people."*

On their fourth night out, bad weather forced the hikers to camp atop an area called Kholat Syakhl, which in Mansi translates to "Mountain of the Dead."

Paul Stonehill: *"It was a very inhospitable, very strange, a very hard place to be. Snow, cold, freezing winds, and very few living things around. They decided that they would spend the night of February 1ˢᵗ in an open area not too far away from the top of the mountain. They didn't want to go back to the forest, one and a half kilometers, because it would take them too much time and they would lose the day."*

Ten days later when the nine adventures fail to show up at their destination military rescue teams search the area. They find the hikers camp abandoned and a tent that is badly damaged. Investigators determine that the tent has been cut and ripped open from the inside and the hikers appeared to have fled the area in only socks or bare feet.

Mikhail Gershtein, Russian Researcher/Journalist: *"This tent had been cut with knives from the interior. It was absolutely obvious that neither animals nor people had approached the tent to break in, meaning that nothing from this earth had approached them."*

Paul Stonehill: *"Something was pushing them to run away without taking any clothing with them, without taking any supplies. They were behaving like they were in a daze, confused."*

The Investigators followed the trail to the edge of the forest but what they eventually find is beyond belief.

Bill Birnes, J.D., Ph.D.: "*All nine hikers died, they were discovered by Soviet troops in various stages of what can only be described as being mutilated. Their bodies were burned, some suffered radiation poisoning, and in one case a hiker's tongue was missing. They had prematurely aged, their skin was orange, their hair had turned grey. What could have explained this?*"

Paul Stonehill: "*Three of them had injuries that could be sustained when somebody is hit by a speeding car. Except the injuries were inside. Their ribs were crushed like eggshells and some of them entered their hearts but there was no effect on their skin. It was like a force was directed at all of them.*"

Mikhail Gershtein: "*An unknown force had hit the hikers and it was very selective in hitting only the hikers. Leaving untouched the snow, the trees, and everything else around.*"

The official explanation was that the nine died from hypothermia, but the chief investigator refused to sign off on the report and instead resigned from the inquiry.

Paul Stonehill: "*When the investigation was taking place by the local officials, one of the people in charge was removed quite quickly from the investigation because he was very thorough and local officials did not want this to come out.*"

Mikhail Gershtein: "*The authorities did their best to cover the whole thing up, it was practically forbidden to mention it.*"

Paul Stonehill: "*At the end, the bodies were buried in zinc coffins, I believe, so nobody could see. But it was enough of the investigation, enough people had seen what had been going on and were amazed at what they found, including the coloration of the corpses when they were found and other things that news broke out and this is one of the most mysterious murder cases in the former Soviet Union. I am convinced it was a murder, but they were not killed by anything we know. They were killed by an unknown force.*"

Years later members of the search party spoke out. According to their testimony, at the time of the incident, strange orange spheres or orbs were seen floating in the sky.

Mikhail Gershtein: *"These observations were from local people who saw some unidentified flying objects during the night of the hiker's deaths. I think there is a clear connection."*

Paul Stonehill: *"Locals know they exist, it's like a part of life. They don't put too much attention to them and they hope and pray that the fire spheres don't bother them."*

"It's not a coincidence that UFOs were reported by these hikers in the Ural Mountains in 'The Place of the Dead, The Do Not Go There' because I believe that many UFO sighting come here from a parallel reality and they come though portals"[2]

In 1961 we have the Betty & Barney Hill abduction in New Hampshire. This is probably one of the most widely publicized alien abduction experiences around. Betty & Barney Hill reported that they had been kidnapped for a short time by a UFO while driving back from vacation.

Betty and Barney Hill might seem like unlikely candidates to rewrite UFO history. Betty was a department supervisor in the state government and Barney worked for the U.S. Postal Service. They were driving home to New Hampshire from a vacation in Canada when their encounter began. As they motored down route 3 in the isolated White Mountains, Betty noticed a curious star in the sky that seemed to be following their car.

The Hills stopped the car as the light got closer to them. Peering through

Betty & Barney Hill Archival Collection

binoculars Barney reported seeing red, amber, and green flashing lights. Panicked, Barney jumped back in the car and started speeding down the road. When the Hills arrived home to Portsmouth, New Hampshire, they realized that the trip had taken two hours longer than expected. Within days of their sighting, Betty Hill began having nightmares in which she and Barney were taken aboard a flying saucer and then medically examined.

The Hills filed a sighting report with NICAP a newly formed UFO research group. Then the emotional trauma from their experience prompted Barney and Betty Hill to seek the help of Dr. Benjamin Simon, a prominent Boston psychiatrist. Dr. Simon used hypnosis to treat the Hills over the course of several months. Betty and Barney Hill said the therapy helped them recover some memories of their missing two hours. Listening to recordings of these sessions brought back even more recollections.

Barney Hill: "I tried to maintain control, so Betty cannot tell I am scared, God I'm scared."

Dr. Simon: "Go right on, you experienced it. It will not hurt you now."

Barney Hill: "I got to get my gun. Oh, they got my gun. Ahhhh!!"

Dr. Simon: "Alright, that all. Alright, just keep breathing and be calm."

Barney Hill: "I put it in my coat and then I get out with the binoculars and then it's there and I look. I look and see something, and I think I am not afraid, I'll shoot it down, so I'm not afraid and I walk, I walk out, and I walk across the road. There it is up there. No! No!" *He screams*

Dr. Simon: "Calm down, calm down it's there, you can see it, but it's not gonna hurt you, go on."

Barney Hill: "Why doesn't it go away."

Barney Hill would later make sketches to illustrate his story.

Barney Hill: "It's very big and it's not that far, and I can see it that it's tilted toward me."

Dr. Simon: "What does it look like now, when you say tilted? Did you see wings?"

Barney Hill: "It looks like a big, big pancake with windows, and rows of windows, and rows of windows."

Dr. Simon: "Rows of windows, like a commercial plane?"

Barney Hill: "Rows of windows, they're not like a commercial plane because they curve around to the sides of this pancake and I look up and down the road. Can't somebody come tell me this is not there?"

During her hypnotic regression Betty Hill described the deeply disturbing events that she said took place inside the landed space craft.

Betty Hill: "And then they rolled me over on my back and they take out a long needle. I see the long needle in his hand and it's bigger than any needle I've ever seen. I asked him what he's going to do with it and he said he's going to use it to hurt me and I ask him, why?

And he said he just wants to put it in my nail. I tell him no, it will hurt, don't do it. And he puts it in my nail and I am crying and it's hurting, and I tell him "It's hurting get it out!" Then the leader, he comes over and he puts his hand in front of my eyes and he said I'll be alright, I won't feel it and all the pain goes away."

Five years later the bizarre experience of Betty and Barney Hill became legendary as a cover story in Look Magazine and a book entitled The Interrupted Journey. It was the first reported alien abduction in the United States.[3]

Their claim of alien abduction was also adapted into the 1975 television movie 'The UFO Incident', and its importance is such that many of Betty Hill's notes, tapes and other items have been placed in a permanent collection at the University of New Hampshire and as of July 2011, the site of the alleged abduction is marked by a state historical marker.

And speaking of abductions by alleged UFO's, before we proceed, let's go ahead and categorize the seven various kinds of encounters with UFO's.

- A Close Encounter of the 1st Kind refers to a person seeing a UFO.

- A Close Encounter of the 2nd Kind refers to a person seeing a UFO with physical effects. (heat, radiation, animal reactions, etc.)

- A Close Encounter of the 3rd Kind refers to a person seeing an actual alien creature.

- A Close Encounter of the 4th Kind refers to a person being abducted by a UFO.

- A Close Encounter of the 5th Kind refers to a person having communication with a UFO/Alien.

- A Close Encounter of the 6th Kind refers to a person being injured or dying from a UFO.

- A Close Encounter of the 7th Kind refers to a person mating with a UFO Occupant/Alien.

But in 1964 we have Lonnie Zamora Incident in Socorro, New Mexico. Lonnie Zamora was a New Mexico police officer who reported a UFO sighting while on duty on Friday, April 24, 1964 near Socorro, New Mexico. His account received considerable coverage in the mass media and is sometimes regarded as one of the best documented, yet most perplexing UFO reports.

It happened in Socorro, New Mexico here just outside of this quiet desert town. A state highway patrol officer Lonnie Zamora was on duty as he had been for the past several years. A black Chevrolet was observed speeding by the courthouse, Zamora put his highway patrol car into pursuit. Lonnie chased the car north on US-85. As he passed this hilly area Zamora heard a roar and something caught his attention. Ten or fifteen seconds passed. Lonnie then calls in to the sheriff's office.

Sheriff: "The time was about 5:45 I recall, and he said, Zamora to 10-44, an accident, and then he said, I'll be hit sticks out of the car, which means he was going to be investigating the possible accident."

Lonnie Zamora: "And I went up this road about a half mile and then I stopped my car and got out, and I looked up and I could see a white looking object in the distance. I thought it was an overturned car at first, but I get into the patrol car and went up closer to it. When I started to get out of the car I heard a big roar. As I got to it I could see what looked like a couple of coveralls hanging from a clothesline. I couldn't see what it was, but it looked like a couple of coveralls."

Sheriff: "Zamora called in, he sounded very excited. He said he watched an object lift up slowly and disappeared into the sky very fast."

Lonnie Zamora: "I went down to where the object had been, and I noticed the brush was burning in several places. The object had left four perpendicular impressions in the ground. I noticed that several bushes where smoldering, but they felt cold to the touch. I noticed what appeared to be a couple of footprints on the ground."

Sheriff: "I knew Lonnie had seen something, the proof was right there."

The incident was very interesting to say the least. It seems to differ from practically all the earlier cases we investigated from one standpoint. The vehicle had left pod marks. There was an insignia observed by Lonnie

New Mexico HP Off. Lonnie Zamora

Zamora on the side of the craft. The insignia was unidentifiable, not American nor Russian. And last of all, the observation of these two people in some sort of suit.[4]

In fact, it was Zamora's account that helped persuade astronomer J. Allen Hynek, who was one of the primary investigators for the Air Force, that some UFO reports were an intriguing mystery. Also, several other independent witnesses reported either an "egg" shaped craft or a bluish flame, at roughly the same time Zamora has his encounter in the same area, some of them, just within minutes. And several other stories appeared in local newspapers in the succeeding days of other sightings of oval-shaped objects, including another landing with burned soil in northern New Mexico.

In 1965 we have the Exeter Incident in Exeter, New Hampshire. Here a UFO was observed by a teenager and two police officers. This sighting remains among the best-documented and best-publicized in UFO history and is even celebrated by an annual event.[5]

In 1965 we also have the Kecksburg UFO incident in Kecksburg, Pennsylvania. There was a mass sighting of a falling UFO followed by a cordoning-off of the crash site. It was reported to be an acorn-shaped UFO that had crashed into the woods and was purportedly taken away by military personnel.[6]

In 1966 we also have The Mothman Sightings in Point Pleasant, West Virginia. A wave of sightings of a strange winged humanoid creature that began to be reported throughout the area and was reported to be connected to other mysterious events that included the sightings of UFO's.[7]

In 1966 there was the Wanaque Reservoir UFO sighting in Wanaque, New Jersey. A UFO was seen in the vicinity of the Wanaque Reservoir in New Jersey that led to traffic jams and overloaded police communications. It shifted colors on a continual basis and reportedly shot down a beam of light towards the ice near the dam and maintained its position for another half hour then flew off to the Southeast.[8]

Wanaque Dam Area, New Jersey 1966

Then another UFO was sighted the next night flying in a zigzag pattern. The mayor, Warren Hagstrom, as well as Chief of Police Floyd Elston and captain Joe Cisco watched the craft for some time. Then two reserve officers, Sgt. Ben Thompson and patrolman Edward Wester also witnessed the craft along with a number of other observers.

In 1966 we had the Westall UFO encounter in Australia. This is the account where more than 200 students and teachers at two Victorian state schools witnessed a UFO that descended into a nearby open grass field. They described it as being a grey saucer with a slight purple hue about twice the size of a family car. After about twenty minutes the object climbed at high speed and departed towards the northwest.

Back nearly forty years, witnessed by two hundred people who say it was kept secret by the military. As Brian Seymore reports more light is being shone on Australia's Westall incident.

This boy came running in saying, "Mr. Greywood, there's these things in the sky, there's these things in the sky!"

"We looked up and we just saw this saucer type thing taking off."

It wasn't a plane, it wasn't a balloon, it was nothing like that."

"A lot of the kids took off towards where it seemed to go."

"All of the students were just running all over the place, hysterical."

"Went to the high school as the tension, the situation ceased."

"My girlfriend and I sat on the fence, climbed the fence, the school boundary and we were crying thinking it was the end of the world."

For forty-four years the story about what happened at Westall has been largely untold, all covered up.

Joy Clarke: "That afternoon our principle called a special assembly and told us all not to talk about it."

Principal: "I was prepped to tell the students that what they'd seen didn't exist." "We were told that we weren't allowed to speak to the media."

You've most likely heard about the best-known UFO encounter that happened in Roswell, New Mexico in 1947, but the fifth greatest UFO encounter happened a world away just south-east of Melbourne in the suburb of Clayton South. It happened at Westall High School Wednesday April 6th, 1966, at recess time about eleven o'clock in the morning. Scientists and UFO experts have long known about the Aussie sighting but until now the details have been locked in our past.

Joy Clarke: "All I knew was what I saw, and it was definitely not any aircraft of the day, by any stretch of the imagination, and it was certainly not a weather balloon."

Victor Zakruzny: "It was amazing and something that I've never forgotten."

Victor Zakruzny was in second form when he says he had a very close encounter. After watching with over 150 other children, a mysterious saucer-shaped craft landed and he decided to approach it.

Victor Zakruzny: "You could feel heat coming off of it, it was pretty warm or hot and then it just gradually lifted, lifted up and went off towards the pines." We are talking about two hundred people and a lot of them were kids too, they're at school, so I mean, I think adults have got preconceptions about what a UFO might or may not be, but kids are a different matter. When you got two hundred witnesses, either there was something strange in the lunch shop that day or there was something else going on."

A news crew interviewed several students at the school right after the event so film maker Chane Ryan tracked down the tape. But oddly there was nothing there. Chane Ryan: "I was absolutely devastated, and nobody had any idea where it had gone."

A teacher saw one of his colleagues who had taken pictures confronted by a man in a dark blue suit.

"It was demanded that she hand over, not only the film, but the entire camera." However, one written account survives in the Dandinon Journal Newspaper, which reported the occurrence, questioned the involvement of the military, and the cover up by school officials.

"The one thing we would really like is that someone ether from the police or the military would come forward and say, yes they were there."

Some of the surviving witnesses are appealing to those with official information to come forward. Incredibly and despite the involvement of the Army, Airforce and Police there is not one single mention of the Westall Incident in any government files.

"You'd ask me if an R&D establishment would destroy evidence, yes of course they would."

"This is happening in the sixties right, and in a lot of countries in the world a lot of governments were concerned about UFO sightings not from the perspective of invasion but mass hysteria."

Documentary maker Chane Ryan has an obsession with what occurred at Westall. He's pieced together and recorded scores of interviews with the school children who are all now in their fifties and sixties.

Paul Smith: "I looked up and I was facing the object in the sky and I just thought, somebody's just got a way of projecting a film of something into the sky. I didn't believe that it was really happening, but my boss turned around and he saw it and we stood there looking at it for several minutes. We crossed and walked down here to this corner. After a while trucks turned up with what looked like army trucks."

Sketch of images by Les Whitmore, from Shane Ryan's Westall 66 Docufilm

Jacqueline Argent: "I was called down to the headmaster's office and there were two men in the headmaster's office, very well-dressed gentlemen, in suits. They were introduced to me in person and I don't know where they came from. But my references now as an adult I would say they were from Asia.

Then we went into "Well I suppose you think you saw a flying saucer." And I was like "No, I didn't say that I said, I think I saw an object" and they said, "And we suppose you saw little grey men." When I came out I think I burst into tears. They were sent by the Australian government and I think it was part of their job to keep everything quiet.

The authorities had found a way to silence the children, but they still had unfinished business with a teacher Andrew Greenwood. He told me that two officers came to his home and threatened him under the Official Secrets Act. They said that he couldn't have seen a flying saucer at Westall because there were no such things as flying saucers. They threatened to tell people he was an alcoholic even though he wasn't.

Jacqueline Argent: "It was their job to squash what was being seen. It was a bunch of kids who saw this, so we'll be able to squash this down."[9]

In 1966 we also had the Portage County UFO Chase in Ohio. In this report, several police officers were said to have pursued a UFO for about 30 minutes.[10] In 1967 we also have Falcon Lake Incident in Canada. This is the account where a UFO's exhaust allegedly burned a man.[11]

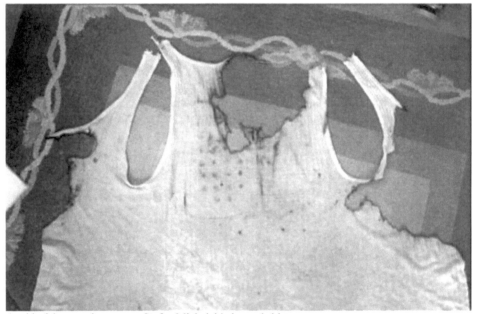

A grid of dots can be seen on Stefan Michalak's burned shirt

In 1967 was the Close Encounter of Cussac in France. This is a story of a young brother and sister who claimed to have witnessed a UFO and its occupants.

In 1967 was the Shag Harbor Incident in Nova Scotia. A UFO was seen crashing into Shag Harbor in Nova Scotia whereupon a Canadian naval search followed. The incident was not only officially referred to as a UFO crash, but the crash left behind a strange yellow foam, that of all things, smelled like burning Sulphur.

The officers wasted no time getting to the scene of the crash, near an Irish moss plant overlooking the harbor.

"When officers first drove into the parking lot of the plant there was already a crowd of locals gathering that were trying to figure out what was happening in the waters of the sound. What they saw when they got there was a pale-yellow light that appeared to be as much as eight feet above the surface of the water and it was moving under its own power.

It was moving in the direction of the ebbing tide, but it seemed to be moving at a greater rate than that and it was trailing a wide path of yellow foam."

"It just looked like a yellow glow, that's all we could see. While we were watching it, there was three RCMP officers and myself and I don't know who else was there just watching it disappear.

It disappeared different that anything I had ever seen. It didn't look like it sank, it didn't look like it went out, I don't know, it just disappeared."

Whenever there was trouble on the water the RCMP relied on local fishermen for help. Lawrence Smith was on his way to bed when he received an urgent phone call.

Lawrence Smith: "We navigated the RCMP boys up through the rocks up to the prospect point wharf and then we opened her up, full speed."

Smith and his crew were the first to get under way. Soon other fishermen raced to the scene joining Smith in the search.

Lawrence Smith: "When we got there, there was no light, no people in the water where we thought there would be for a plane crash and all we found was foam."

Instead of wreckage rescuers encountered a peculiar patch of foam.

Lawrence Smith: "There was a little smell, like Sulphur, burnt Sulphur."

Several local fishermen who had witnessed the foam felt strongly that this was not normal tidal foam. Besides the fact that they are acquainted with the local conditions, there were several key features that made it stand apart. The sparkle, the way it dissipated, the shear amount of it, the density of it implied something quite unusual.

Lawrence Smith: "I had been fishing that area for forty-five years. I have never seen any foam like that ever on the water and if you were motoring out going fishing and you went through something like that you would stop and say, what's been going on here?"[12]

In 1967 was the Schirmer abduction in Nebraska. Sergeant Herbert Schirmer claimed he was abducted by aliens after seeing a blurred white object that came out of what he had at first mistaken for a truck because of its blinking red lights. The white object not only communicated mentally with him, but Schirmer even said it prevented him from drawing his gun. Oddly enough, he also reported that the UFO occupants wore badges that depicted a "winged serpent."[13]

Schirmer description of ship while under hypnosis

In 1968 we have the Minot Air Force Base incidents in North Dakota. This account involves Air Force claims that an unidentifiable craft "buzzed" the air base, specifically the missile silos. The airmen who witnessed this encounter still have not received an adequate explanation.

Across remote stretches of the Northern United States the Airforce kept ballistic missiles and B52 bombers on constant alert. On the night of October 24th, 1968 in Minot Airforce Base in Minot, North Dakota, Airmen First Class Mike O'Connor was dispatched to make a routine repair at one of the missile sites.

Airman First Class Mike O'Connor: "We made our turn to come down the road to the missile sight and out of the corner of my eye I observed, what I thought was a farmer's yard light, but it looked awful bright. As we proceeded down the road the object appeared to lift off the ground and parallel us down the road until we came to the missile sight at which point we got out of the truck and it just kind of hovered there."

Staff Sargent Bill Smith oversaw security for ten nuclear missiles. That night he reported seeing strange objects.

Sargent Bill Smith: "These objects would rise, they would speed up, they would slow down, they would hover. They would dart very quickly one way or the other. We were just not really sure that these were things that we could explain."

The Minot Control Tower diverted a B52 to investigate, Captain Brad Runyon was the B52's co-pilot.

Captain Brad Runyon: "The Air Traffic Controller asked us if we would mind going out to this one area and looking for something. I was curious, and I said, "Well what are we looking for?" and they said "Well, you'll know it if you find it."

The navigator on the B52 Captain Patrick McCaslin suddenly identified an object on his radar screen.

Captain Patrick McCaslin: "I saw a return, faint one sweep, bright the next, large the next, off our right wing three-o-clock at about three miles. At that point I asked the radar navigator to turn on the camera, which would then take pictures of whatever is on the radar screen."

This picture of the radar screen shows the object flying in formation with the B52.

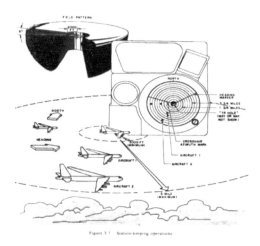

Figure 3.7 Station-keeping operations

Captain Patrick McCaslin: "This thing was climbing out with us and maintaining the same heading we were, that was unusual, but what really watered my eyes, was when this thing backed away and allowed us to turn inside of it."

When the object suddenly disappeared from the radar the Bomber turned back to find it. Co-pilot Runyon was the first to spot what appeared to be a glowing craft hovering near the ground.

Captain Brad Runyon: "When things like that are happening, it seems like time just stands still. My estimate for the overall object was a minimum of two hundred feet in diameter and was hundreds of feet long. It had a metallic cylinder attached to another section that was shaped like a crescent moon.

I felt as though this crescent moon part was probably the command center. I tried to look inside the thing but all I could see was a yellow glow. At that point I was fairly sure that I was looking at an alien space ship; that this was something that had come here from some other planet other than the earth."

Co-pilot and the other crew members of the B52 crew reported their sightings when they returned to the base. According to Blue Books investigation the crew of the B52 and sixteen witnesses on the ground said they saw a UFO that night. In its final report Blue Book concluded that they were all seeing stars.

"None of those pilots saw a star. I know those pilots. I know what their training was. I know how many stars they had seen in the course of their careers. They were not looking at a star. It bothers me that Blue Book blew it off. I don't think that this incident has ever been adequately explained."[14]

In 1969 there was the famous Jimmy Carter UFO incident outside of Leary, Georgia. One evening in 1969, two years before he became governor of

Georgia, Jimmy Carter was preparing to give a speech. When he spotted a strange object that was visible about 30 degrees above the horizon to the west of where he was standing. Carter described the object as being bright white and about as bright as the moon. It was said to have appeared to close in on where he was standing but stopped beyond a stand of pine trees some distance from him. It then changed color, first to blue, then to red, then back to white, before appearing to recede into the distance. He filed a report of the sighting and since its writing, the report has been discussed several times by both ufologists and by members of the mainstream media.

One fall evening in 1969 Georgia Governor Jimmy Carter was preparing for a speech in the little town of Leary, when he spotted a bright object in the western sky. Carter describes his experience.

Governor Jimmy Carter: "There were about twenty of us standing outside of a little restaurant I believe, a lunchroom and kind of a green object appeared in the Western sky right after sun down and it got brighter and brighter and then just disappeared. It didn't have any solid substance to it, it was just a very peculiar looking light. None of us could understand what it was."[15]

In the 1970s we had the Barry DeLong UFO Incident in Maine and this is the account where Sheriff Barry A. DeLong witnessed a UFO and said, "They were hovering about 15 feet from my cruiser, late at night. It had fixed, spinning lights. The craft was a huge oval shape. I knew it wasn't a jet fighter. It slowly started backing off toward Sugarloaf, and then accelerated at a terrific speed.

In 1973 was the Pascagoula Abduction in Mississippi. An alien abduction is alleged to have occurred while the victims were fishing on the Pascagoula River as this interview shows.

Charles Hickman: "In the fall of last year on October the 16th, Calvin Parker and myself were employed at that time by FP Walker and Son's Shipyard in Pascagoula. Sometime during the day on October 11th, we decided to go fishing after work. Something that I do quite often when I'm not working is fishing. So, after we got off work probably about 4:30 I think, we were working nine hours. I came home, and I went to get my fishing gear.

So, we got our bait and went to the river. We tried several spots, but the fish didn't seem to be biting. So, there was one more spot that we were going to try, in the past I had caught fish there a lot of times, the old abandoned Shell Peters

Shipyard. So, we went back up the river to the old shipyard and it had become dark at that time. We did do quite a bit of fishing after dark that time of year.

So, I don't know what had attracted my attention, as I reached around to get more bait, which was sitting behind us. I heard some sort of zipping-like sound, like the sound of steam escaping from a pipe and as I turned around I saw two blue flashing lights, or pulsating lights, I'm not sure, and it seemed like there was some type of craft. It seemed like it was almost down on the ground. In fact, it seemed to be a couple of feet above the ground and it just hovered there.

Calvin had also turned by this time. He was looking at it too, and really, I didn't know what to do. I was just spellbound there for a few minutes and then almost immediately some type of opening appeared on the end, it was towards us which is what I assumed would be the front end. The light had come outside but it was a real, real bright light and three things appeared in the doorway of the craft.

They seemed to just glide out of the craft they never seemed to touch the ground, they just seemed to glide across. It must've been twenty-five to thirty feet from us. Then they just glided over to us. Two of them took me by the arms on either side and one took hold of Calvin. I saw Calvin go limp and I didn't know it then, but he had fainted.

So, they carried me inside the craft. The light was almost blinding inside. In fact, for three or four days after that I had something like a bad welding flash in my eyes. I can't recall, or I can't remember, just what was on the inside simply because the light was so bright that I just couldn't make out what it was, but I didn't see any tables or chairs and the room seemed to be round but of course that could have been because the light was glowing from the walls, the floor, and the ceiling.

They carried me to what I guess what the middle of the room and we just seemed to be suspended there. I couldn't move, I didn't have any feelings, no sensation of any feelings. It seemed something like a big eye, I keep referring to it as an eye because it was about the size of a small baseball, and in the end, it was focused towards me. It was a different color, a different light, and it seemed to come directly out from the wall. It came within six or eight inches of my face and it remained there for a few minutes, a very few minutes.

Then it went over my entire body. I'm assuming it did because when it went down, like this, I was suspended, then the next time I see it, it was coming back up over this way, so I assume it went over my entire body. But it came back in front of my face and it stayed there for a few more minutes and it seemed to just go right back into the wall.

These things, the way they were holding me, weren't as tall as me and they were upright, and I was elevated. I could see, I could move my eyes, the only thing I could move, and I could see that they had released me. I don't know where they went, whether they went outside the craft or another room or compartment, but they didn't come back in front of me. They left me that way for a few minutes, I don't know how long, and then after a while they came up to the side of me and took hold of me again and carried me back outside of the craft.

We were still just gliding. I wasn't touching anything that I know of, and they seemed to just glide out to where they had taken me and put me back down on the ground. Well, when they did, I fell, because my legs were weak, and they just gave way on me and it was at this time that I saw Calvin again. He was standing there, facing the river with his arms out stretched and he was almost in shock. He seemed to appear to me at that time that something was wrong with him.

So, I was trying to make my way toward him, I was crawling. I couldn't get my legs to work, but before I got to him, my strength came back to my legs, I was getting up on my feet, and I heard this sound, like the sound I heard before, the zipping sound. I glanced around, and I saw the blue flashing lights. The craft was just gone, almost instantly. I made it to Calvin, I shook him and was calling to him and it took me several minutes to get to him, so I could even talk to him with any sense. He was going in shock.

These things that came out of the craft were about five, five feet four inches tall and they didn't have a neck. Their head seemed to come directly to their shoulders. They had something that resembled a nose on a face. About where the ears would be, something that was similar to the nose, only a little lower, it seemed to come out almost to a point. Under the nose there was something like a slit for a mouth and it was very wrinkled. It seemed, or it appeared to me to be something like elephant skin.

I don't know if it was a metal or what it was, but it seemed to be very wrinkled with the wrinkles going horizontal. In the area where the eyes should have been it was so wrinkled that I'm not even sure there was eyes. I cannot recall if there were any eyes or not and Calvin says he can't. But, anyway after I got Calvin to where I could talk to him, we didn't know what to do and we were almost scared to death.

October 18, 1973, Charles Hickson and Calvin Parker Jr. recount their experience

We first decided we wouldn't tell anyone but the more we talked about it the more we realized that we had to talk to somebody, the military authorities, if nobody else. So, we called Keesler Airforce Base which is only about thirty blocks south of here and I talked to someone who told me that the Airforce didn't handle those things anymore and that we would have to go through our sheriff's department.

Well, then we hesitated again, because, when you go to people, with something like this, it is just not supposed to happen, and you'll probably be laughed at and ridiculed. We talked it over again and decided we would call the sheriff's department and Sheriff Fred Diamond told us to come on over and we'd talk about it.

So, we stayed there for several hours talking with him and him questioning us and the sheriff promised me that there wasn't going to be any news media or anything about it and that he would get it to the proper authorities if he could find out who the proper authorities were, and have it investigated.

So, we went home that morning. It was morning because they had kept us there quite late with the assurance that there was not going to be any publicity at all. Well, we went on to work that morning and by seven or eight o'clock there were telephones ringing all over the shipyard.

I called Fred Diamond and he said that he doesn't know how the story leaked out of the sheriff's department but by that time the whole world knew about it.

Interviewer: "You said something like an eye ran up and down your body do you think it was examining you?"

Charles Hickman: "Um, yes it had to be some type of examination, it had to be, it appears to me to be and after talking with a bunch of scientists I'm convinced that it was something, that it was some sort of examination."

Interviewer: "Did you communicate with these creatures, these things?"

Charles Hickman: "No, they didn't try to communicate with me. The only sound that they made, and I'm not sure if it even came from them, but there was some sort of mumbling sound, a low mumbling sound from one of them."[16]

In 1975 we have the North Hudson Park UFO Sightings in New Jersey. This sighting is considered to be a close encounter of the second and third kind and is the case that introduced Budd Hopkins to UFO research, a key figure in future alien abduction research. Researcher Jerome Clark cites the incident as one of the best documented, since the story was corroborated by numerous independent witnesses.

And in 1975 we have the Travis Walton Incident in Arizona. This is the incident where logger Travis Walton reported being abducted by aliens for five days. Walton's six workmates claimed to have witnessed the UFO at the start of his abduction. Walton described the event and its aftermath in *The Walton Experience*, which was dramatized in the film *Fire in the Sky*.

The Today Show Reports: *Travis Walton and a crew of six others were returning home after working in the White Mountains of Arizona. What happened on the way home has become one of the best documented cases of alien abduction and a mystery that has remained unsolved to this day.*

On film they can be evil, friendly, or ready for a fight. In the nineties movie Fire in The Sky aliens abduct a logger from Snowflake Arizona while the other crew members look on, but this is no fictional close encounter for Travis Walton, the movie is based on of his personal story.

Interviewer: "What's it like for you to come back to these woods, right off the road where the incident happened?"

Travis Walton: "Well, it seems like just yesterday. In a way, a lot of those memories are just so burned into my mind."
Interviewer: So, tell me what happened that night."

Travis Walton: "We worked till almost dark and we loaded up our equipment and headed out of there. There's seven of us in the truck and we're driving along, and we hadn't gone very far, and we saw this glow coming from the trees and we saw this object hovering there and it was unmistakable."

Illustrations based on Travis's description show the object that made the crew stop in their tracks. Travis was the only one to get out of the truck for a closer look.

Travis Walton: "As soon as I straightened up, bam! I just felt this shock. It's kind of like an electric shock actually but I just blacked out."

The six other crew members witnessed the abduction. John Goulet was one of them.

John Goulet: "To be back out here again like this, I'm actually kind of scared now.

Interviewer: And you said you saw Travis lifted?

John Goulet: When I turned my head, he was crouched down like this and when I looked back he was, kind of like this, all spread out."
Travis Walton

Fearing for their own lives the men fled. They returned to the sight later that evening finding no sign of Travis. A massive search and investigation followed.

"When he didn't show up after the first two or three days we scheduled polygraph examinations for the other individuals who were in the work crew and they all passed."

Interviewer: "So, while all of this is going on, what was happening to you? Where were you? What was going on? What are your memories of how you spent those five days?"

Travis Walton: "My first memory after blacking out was of regaining consciousness very slowly. The instant that I saw these creatures and realized where I was, I just completely went crazy with fear. They had these huge eyes that just seemed to look right into me in this really unbearable way."

Interviewer: "How did you know it was real and not a dream?"

Travis Walton: "Ya know how they say pinch yourself? Well, I was feeling a lot more pain then that so, yeah, it was very real."

Five days later Travis returned.

Interviewer: "And then you woke up where?"

Travis Walton; "I woke up, I was lying face down, outdoors. I could recognize this piece of highway as being outside of Heber. "Ya know I ran down in here and it took all the strength I had left to get to these phone booths."

Travis's incredible explanation gained media attention far from the small town of Snowflake but not everyone believed his story.

Jo Baeza, local historian: "They were treated very badly, a lot of people made fun of Travis and the whole crew."

Interviewer: "Does it bother you that some people don't believe you?"

Travis Walton "It used to bother me a lot more. Anymore? ya know I think the record speaks for itself."

Interviewer: "Has this single event that happened when you were twenty-two defined your life?"

Travis Walton: "Yeah it defined my life for me, regrettably, if I had to do it over again I'd never get out of the truck."[17]

Next, we have the 1976 Allagash Abductions in Maine. Here four campers claimed to have been abducted by alien life forms in the Allagash wilderness.

History Channel Reports:

In the summer of 1976 art students Charlie Fotz, Chuck Rak, and twins Jack and Jim Weiner travelled north from Boston into the wilderness of Maine. For nearly a week the trip was everything they hoped it would be, a carefree escape from city life.

On the fifth day they camped near Smith pond, an isolated, stump-filled swamp. It was the perfect spot for night fishing. It was also the place where their lives would change forever.

Jack Weiner: "There was no moon that night it was real dark, and we didn't want to get lost so what we did was make a big fire, so we could see it and know which way to go to get back to camp later.

Chuck Rak: "And it was quite large, but we cleared around the fire so there was no problem. Its flames were leaping a good three or four feet up into the air."

With their make shift light house aglow, the four men left their camp sight behind. They paddled several hundred yards out into the pond, heading toward a night of fishing they would never forget and one they would later illustrate in their artwork.

Jack Weiner, Jim Weiner, Charlie Fotz and Chuck Rak

Chuck Rak: "I remember paddling leisurely; the twins were in the middle and Charlie was in the front. I remember they were having a conversation and I was focusing on the night, the lake and the water and I began to feel observed."

Jack Weiner: "And then suddenly Chuck Rak, who was at the back of the canoe said "Holy Mackerel, what the heck is that? And I turned around and looked and there was this huge white light that was coming out of the trees. It seemed like it was rising out of the trees. At first, we thought, well it's gotta be an airplane or something, right? So, we watched it for a few seconds and we realized that it wasn't an airplane because it wasn't making any sound at all."

Chuck Rak: "It was strange, very strange, it was a bright, luminous yellow light

and changing from that color in a very fluid liquid kind of a way and we were very, very fascinated that I was in a state of extreme euphoria, I remember just feeling, wow this is fantastic!"

Charlie Foltz: "It was just alive and when it was nearest us about a hundred yards away, it paused and when it paused I said to the fellas, I said "I'm going to shine the flashlight and see what is does."

Jim Weiner: "The instant he flashed his flashlight this thing sends down this beam of light down to us. We are in a sixteen foot Grumman Canoe which in the pitch black of night lit up light a roman candle. We must have looked like this object just waiting to be approached on this lake."

Chuck Rak: "All I can tell you is what was going through my mind, it's just exhilarating expectation, just this is fantastic, this is something we can communicate with. It's attempting to communicate with us."

Jim Weiner: "I was completely shocked, I was especially shocked that it reacted as quickly as it did. Which told us there was some sort of intelligence about it and as soon as this light came out this thing started moving."

Jack Weiner: "And so, we thought, well, this is real, this is really happening, this is not a figment of our imagination. I mean we've got to deal with this situation, now, because within a few seconds this thing is going to be right on us."

Charlie Foltz: "I wasn't even interested in this thing anymore, other than I didn't want to be as close to it as I was."

"I remember paddling as fast as I could and Jack saying 'It's getting closer! It's getting closer!'"

And then it was gone, the next thing they remember they were back on shore.

.

Chuck Rak: "And I thought, well that's it we've lost our chance, we let it slip through our fingers, And I observed it leaving and just gradually faded out."

Exhausted the four men stumbled back to their campsite. There they found the remains of their make shift light house. The fire that they had built to last for hours, the fire that was now just a pile of charred embers. At the time no one gave it much thought. Though later it would play a large role in their sighting.

That night, nothing more was discussed, not the fire, nor the unknown object that had chased them only moments before. Sleep was the only thing on their minds. For years, the friends rarely talked about that strange night. Then in 1978 memories of the sighting began to resurface.

Jim Weiner had developed temporal epilepsy after a car accident and suffered periodic seizures. These fits were often triggered by sleep deprivation and by 1980 Jim was definitely not sleeping well. Vivid nightmares had become a perpetual torment.

Jim Weiner: "All I remember is seeing vague figures isomorphic in shape, but it did not seem human to me. They were around me and they were either doing things with my genitals, prodding me with some types of instruments, there was an extreme feeling of malevolence. I mean I was absolutely, always felt terrified in this situation."

For a time, Jim kept his nightmares secret, then he confided it in his brother. Jack Wieners reaction was totally unexpected.

Jack Wiener: "So, he starts telling me, this, my nightmare on the phone and I go "Holy Mackerel! I've been having the same nightmares what is going on here?"

There was no apparent explanation, but Jim was getting worse, his doctors growing more concerned. Repeatedly they asked Jim what was wrong, that's when he finally revealed the nightmares.

A physiatrist working on the case said it sounded like an abduction experience. The doctor suggested that Jim speak with Ray Fowler a UFO researcher. Jim repeated his story, Fowler took it seriously. Later the other three also underwent hypnosis. Finally, four years after the incident the details of that terrifying August night would emerge.

Charlie Foltz: "I remember suddenly being enveloped in this tube of light and I remember looking up and thinking, 'what the heck is that up there?' like you know 'what's up there?' and that took a few seconds and I looked back again and Chuck Rak's gone."

Jack Weiner: "The last thing I remember is having both hands on the side of the canoe looking out to the water to see if Chuck was in the water and then not seeing him and thinking 'What happened to Chuck?' and then looking up and the next thing I remembered was this intense feeling of, almost like I was, coming apart or something. That's the only way I can describe it and the next thing I remembered I was being on my back in this hazy environment, which is just like this nightmare that I had been having."

All four friends seem to recall a similar traumatic experience.

Charlie Foltz: "I'm lying on my back and I'm disoriented, I'm not sure where I am and as I'm forcing and struggling to get up a face appears and looks straight down at me."

Jack Weiner: "They reminded me of insects, I remember thinking 'My god, these things look like bugs.' They had these large eyes almost like ants have. They could have been goggles for all I know but they had some sort of clothing on, like spandex. I became focused on this things hands and realizing that it was not a hand like ours at all. This one had me by the wrist and he was holding my arm up and I realized that he had something else in his hand, but I didn't like the looks of it and I remember thinking,

Oh boy, here we go, this is it, I have five seconds to live, they're going to cut me open, they're going to dissect me. Whatever, I just want to get out of here. Get me out of here.'"

It would take hours under hypnosis before the four men fully detailed the alien examinations. Later, they recalled the peculiar events that brought them back down to Earth.

Jim Weiner: "They moved us again into this other space, this room, then this area in front of me started changing somehow, some type of machine or something, it was very strange and the last thing I remember thinking was 'Here we go. I don't know what's gonna happen next, but something is happening.'"

Chuck Rak: "Under regressive hypnosis I remember aliens trying to put me in the canoe. There's one of them standing in the canoe over me trying to adjust my position in the back of the canoe and another one was waste deep in the water right next to me. And then, they tried to position Jim Weiner in front of me but he's heavier and they were having a hard time with him and then the other two were beamed right on land and then Jim got out to join them."

As their recollections took shape the four men learned why their roaring campfire had seemed to burn out so quickly. To those who investigate abduction cases it's known as 'missing time.' Perhaps as much as three hours have passed during the abduction from the time the men first saw the UFO till the time they found themselves standing on the beach.

Meanwhile their fire had burned down to embers. Hypnosis had restored their recollections of the 'missing time' with unsparing intensity but now there was no hiding from the memories, no hiding from the trauma of what had apparently happened at Smith Pond.[18]

Chapter Four

The History of UFO's
Part Three

In 1977 there was The Colares UFO Incident in Brazil and this is the amazing account of an island that was actually attacked by UFO's shooting harmful beams of radioactive light at the residents.

It is October 7th, 1997, retired Air Force Captain Nogueira de Hollanda Lima is in his expensive home in Cabo Frias, Brazil. The former pilot and parachutist retired in 1992, but since then has struggled with illness.

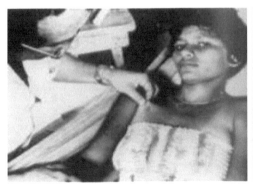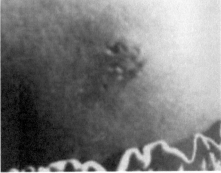

Radiation burns from beams of UFO

Antonio Petit, Ufologist:

"Captain Hollanda had been suffering a chronic depressive disorder since the early 1990s. In my personal view, this depressive process originated from something that he had experienced a long time ago in the Amazon."

Later that night, his daughter climbs the steps to her father's room. She finds a shocking scene; her father is dead. He appears to have strangled himself. Was this a suicide brought on by mental illness or by something more sinister?

Just two months earlier the Captain had given this exclusive interview to UFO researchers Jose Gevaerd and Marco Petit. Both men study and document UFO incidents.

"This object went to Colares and then kept going as if it covered the Amazon in strips. There was an intelligence doing this. Four months into the operation they ordered us to stop."

Some UFO experts maintain that Captain Holanda did not kill himself but was murdered because he said too much about a series of frightening UFO encounters, some allegedly fatal, which took place in the Amazon jungle twenty years earlier.

Carlos Mendes, Journalist: *"He gave eye witness testimony based on his work as a military man who committed one of the most serious operations in the world of Ufology. There is something very strange that the Airforce doesn't want revealed."*

Pinon Frias, Co-Pilot: *"I don't believe it was suicide, Holanda's death is connected to something beyond the normal."*

"He left a very clear message, that we are being visited"[1]

In 1977 we have The Malboeuf Incident in Canada. This occurred when Florida Malboeuf, a 58-year-old woman reported seeing a UFO and two extraterrestrials on the roof of the house in front of her home.[2]

The very next year we have the Emilcin Abduction in Poland. A man in Emilcin, Poland is said to have been abducted by grays." There is now a memorial at the sight.

1978 – Valentich Disappearance – Australia – An Australian pilot contacted air traffic control and reported sighting a UFO just before his aircraft vanished.

Valentich: "Melbourne this is Delta Sierra Juliet, is there any known traffic below five thousand?"

Air Traffic Controller: "Delta Sierra Juliet, no known traffic."

Valentich: "Delta Sierra Juliet there seems to be a large aircraft below five thousand."

Just after halfway through his flight Valentich had been in contact with a flight service center on the ground. Evidence mounted that something was not quite right. The following recreation is based on a transcript on Valentich's exchange with an air traffic controller.

Valentich: "There seems to be some sort of landing light's, as it gets closer it could be one or two lights, I don't know."

"Melbourne this is Delta Sierra Juliet, that aircraft just passed over me at least thousand feet above."

Air Traffic Controller: "Roger, and it is a large aircraft? Confirm?"

Valentich: "An unknown due to the speed at which it is travelling. Is there any Airforce craft in this vicinity?"

Air Traffic Controller: "Delta Sierra Juliet, no known aircraft in the vicinity."

Valentich: "Delta Sierra Juliet, it seems as though it's playing some sort of game up here. He's travelling over me at two to three times at speeds I cannot identify."

Air Traffic Controller: "Can you describe the aircraft?"

Valentich: "Delta Sierra Juliet, as it passes by, it's a long shape…"

Stephen Robey, Air Traffic Advisor: "He wasn't to the point where he was panicking but he was genuinely concerned by what he saw, with what he saw, he was worried, and he sounded confused. Then as he described what the aircraft was doing, now I became a little bit concerned too."

Valentich: "Now this thing's stationary. What I'm doing now is orbiting, and this thing is just orbiting on top of me. It's got a green light and its sort of metallic, like its shining all over. It's just disappeared. Melbourne, you wouldn't know what sort of aircraft I've got up here would you? Is this some sort of military aircraft or what?"

Air Traffic Controller: "Delta Sierra Juliet, is the aircraft still with you?"

Valentich: "Delta Sierra Juliet, now approaching from southwest. Delta Sierra Juliet, I am sitting on twenty-three twenty-four, but this thing's just caught me!"

Air Traffic Controller: "Delta Sierra Juliet."

Valentich: "Melbourne, this strange aircraft is hovering on top of me again, it's hovering, and it's not an aircraft."

Suddenly an identifiable clicking noise came over the radio. The sound lasted seventeen seconds and then silence.

Air Traffic Controller: "Delta Sierra Juliet this is Melbourne"

It's hovering and it's not an aircraft, these were Valentich's final haunting words which inevitably led to speculation that the young pilot encountered a UFO.

However, it was nothing more than speculation until a witness came forward with a startling firsthand account.

Around the time of Valentich's disappearance, the eye witness and his family were returning from an afternoon outing when they noticed unusual activity in the sky.

The unidentified man on the ground: "That's a plane."

The unidentified woman on the ground: "I can see the plane it's the green light above the plane."

The witness has asked that we not reveal his identity.

The unidentified man: "I looked up and I saw this long green light about a thousand to two thousand feet above the aircraft. So, we sat there and watched it for a few seconds and the green light got closer to the plane and I said, 'That planes coming down pretty steep about a forty-five-degree angle. I think it's going to crash.'"

The eyewitness account appeared to support the theory that Valentich had a run in with a UFO. However, the witness did not actually see the aircraft crash at the Bath Straight, the only certainty was that Valentich had vanished.[3]

In 1978 we have the Kaikoura Lights in New Zealand. Here a series of sightings was made by a freight plane that reported how the airplane was escorted by strange lights that changed color and size.[4]

In 1979 was Val Johnson Incident in Minnesota a deputy sheriff spotted a bright light which appeared to have collided with his patrol car and damaged it. The deputy also suffered temporary retinal damage from the "light" that came from the craft.[5]

In 1979 we had the Robert Taylor Incident in Scotland. A forester, Bob Taylor, was pulled by two spiked globes towards a UFO, which stood on a clearing. He lost consciousness and afterwards had trouble walking and speaking. He also was constantly thirsty for several days and once again there was a strange odor.

Occasionally, there is physical evidence to back up reports of close encounters. On the morning of November, the 9ᵗʰ, 1979 forestry worker Bob Taylor walked down this woodland track, outside of Livingston Newtown near Edinburgh.

He rounded a corner and was astonished to be confronted by an unearthly object.

"A huge thing, with a big round dome, a very dark grey color, and had a big flange green all the way around. I could see arms sticking out of this flange and what I took to be blades on the top."

Later he described what he'd seen to a local newspaper artist who drew this sketch.

"As I stood there two balls came out here. I'd say they were about three feet in diameter with about six spikes and they were crawling on these spikes. They came right up beside me, and I remember feeling attacked and at that time was the very first smell, a choking sort of smell and that was it."

He crawled up this path and staggered home to be met on the doorstep by his bewildered wife. He looked terrible when he came in the door and he just stood at the door and I said, "Have you had an accident with your lory?" and he said, 'no I've been attacked.' Then I said, "With what?" and he said, "A spaceship."

And I said, "Oh, goodness me, there ain't no such thing as a spaceship, I'm going to phone the doctor. You must've fell and hurt your head." He looked quite shocked and he was drained, he was right white, and his face was dirty, and he had a red scar, here. His clothes were all dirty and his trousers and then, he told me that his trousers had been torn.

The police had been told and they discovered track marks at the scene of the incident.

Artist Rendition of Taylor Sighting

Sgt. Wark: "When I examined the area, I found two track marks and possibly forty holes in the ground. These are the track marks here and these are the forty holes.

Since then I've photographed the holes. This is a photograph of the hole here. The holes measured approximately four and a half inches. And this other photograph, you can actually see the tread marks correspond to the marks. These markings are tracks, actually inside this area here that's fenced off, and there's definitely no other tracks leading to or from this area."

Det. Sgt. Sterkt Stoff: *"These are the trousers worn by Mr. Taylor, as you can see it is fairly heavy material. We have one there on the left, just below the pocket and one on the right trouser leg, just below the pocket. These marks are consistent with the material having been pulled up while the trousers were being worn."*

"Well I'm pretty certain that, that day I saw a spaceship sitting here."

Det. Sgt. Sterkt Stoff: *"We must accept this story of Mr. Taylor. He is a very highly respected member of the community, a man of high integrity, and not one likely to invent such a story."[6]*

Then we have the 1979 in Manises UFO Incident in Spain. Here it was reported that three large UFO's actually forced a commercial flight to make an emergency landing at Manises airport in Spain.[7]

In the 1980's we have the Hudson Valley UFO Sightings in New York. This is the account where a UFO flap was started during the eighties and continued for several years. Overall, it involved thousands of reports of similar UFO's from a multitude of people.

Dennis Sant a husband and father of five has worked in local government for seventeen years. He is currently the highest-ranking deputy in Putman County. On March 17th, 1983 Sant's home in Bruster was the sight of an extraordinary event.

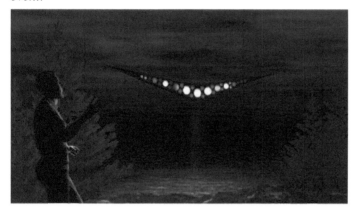

"Oh my gosh, come out here and see this!"
"It was a very large object, the structure of it was a very dark grey metallic almost girder kind of looking."
"What is it?"
"I don't know… Girls! Girls! Come out here and see this!"

The object seemed to be very silent, the lights were iridescent, bright, they stood out in the sky in three dimensions. It looked like a city of lights that just hung in the sky of all brilliant colors. At that time, the girls became very frightened and they ran inside the house. Then my son and I were just drawn underneath it. I felt very good about encountering a visual contact with the object.

We followed the object around to the back yard and at that moment a feeling of fright came upon me. Thoughts started to cloud my mind. Thoughts of the craft touching ground, thoughts of an encounter with an alien being, thoughts of being abducted. All types of fearful thoughts started to enter into my mind and it seemed only to be seconds before the object started to move again but the feelings were overwhelming.

From beginning to end, the nineteen or twenty minutes that I viewed that craft was also a time of self-examination of myself and who I was."

Dennis Sant and his family were not the only ones mesmerized by the extraordinary light formation. A few miles away traffic screeched to a halt on interstate 84 as a mysterious object hovered overhead. The Hudson Valley sightings had only just begun.

Officer Andy Sadaf: "I was sitting there looking at it and I wasn't afraid, I was just amazed, I was in awe of it. I didn't know what it was."

Officer Andy Sadaf a ten-year veteran of New Castel Police who is also an instructor of criminal child abuse procedures.

On March 24ᵗʰ one week after Dennis Sant's sighting Officer Sadaf was working routine traffic patrol.

Officer Sadaf: "I was working a 4pm to midnight tour and assigned to set up some radar to look for speeding cars. I had the radar set up and I looked up into the sky and saw, coming from east to west, there was a series of lights and at first, I thought it was a plane. It was quite a distance, quite far away but it was really quite large.

As I recall, there were mostly white lights but there were green lights also. It was alternating green and white lights. It approached my vehicle and as it approached my vehicle it stopped, and it seemed to hover. There was no sound and I'm looking at this thing and thinking, what is it?"

"When I put my head out the window and I'm looking up at it, it was huge. The thing that I recalled the most and that I was amazed that there was no noise. There was no humming, there was no engine, no low sound to it, it was absolutely silent."

Just seconds later the eerie silence was broken, another eye witness report.

"Can you please send someone else, I'm observing something incredible" (from the police radio).

Officer Sadaf: "Unit five to base, I'm seeing it too, it's hovering above my car. It's heading toward town, I'm following it." "About the time we started to transmit over the air was about the time it started moving again and it moved very slowly, almost floated and we followed it. We followed it up until it disappeared off into the hills.

I guess I was mostly curious as to what it could be, ya know. Excited to try and figure out, 'well, maybe it's this, or maybe it's a government thing but I wasn't frightened of it no. There really wasn't time to be frightened of it. I was spending most of my time trying to figure out why there was no noise coming out of this thing."

Ed Burnes, Computer Engineer: "It was truly a flying city, if that's what you want to call it, I mean it was huge"

Computer Engineer Ed Burnes is a retired senior manager for IBM. At the time of the sightings Burnes handled the company contracts in Japan and South America.

On the night of March 24th, at virtually the same time Officer Sadaf was perusing the mysterious object. Ed Burnes was driving home on the Taconic Parkway ten miles north of Sadaf's location.

Ed Burnes: "Out of nowhere I got a lot of static on the radio and I thought maybe I was on the wrong number and I went over to turn the dial again and that's when I looked up and saw this craft. It was a triangular chevron ship and the back of that chevron had to be as large as a football field at least. It was one solid piece off a chevron shape and there was no noise. It seemed so close to the ground. It seemed like I could have thrown a rock at it maybe."

Ed Burnes pulled of the highway and joined a group of motorists by the side of the road. All were gazing skyward, seemingly dumbstruck.

Ed Burnes: "It was so shocking, this one fellow that I was talking to never did answer me a bit."

"Isn't it incredible. Have you ever seen anything so huge?"

Ed Burnes: "They were just staring at this thing and I remember the size of his eyes where so huge and he never did answer me at all. It seemed like I talked for an hour, but it was probably only a minute, but I was so excited about it I wanted to share whatever I was feeling at the time."

"Where was it from? I'm not in to astronomy. Mars? I mean I'm not into the solar systems but what I had witnessed that night was not from this planet."[8]

In 1986 was the Japan Air Line Flight 1628 Incident in Alaska. A group of UFOs' flew alongside Japan Air Lines Flight 1628 for fifty minutes above Northeastern Alaska. The objects were not only huge, but one of them was actually detected by military radar.

"It involved an investigation by the FAA, this is an official government investigation, of the sighting itself." -Bruce Maccabee, Retired Optical Physicist, United States Navy.

The events from that night were captured on tape.

"Japan Air 1628 Heavy, Military radar advises they are picking up an intermittent primary target behind you. In trail, in trail, what say you."

The Boeing 747 cargo jet was on a routine flight from Paris to Tokyo, cruising at six hundred miles per hour, at an altitude of thirty-five thousand feet. It heads towards Anchorage Alaska to refuel. Suddenly at 5:11 pm, Captain Kenju Terauchi, a pilot with twenty-nine years flight experience, sees three large, fast moving, unidentified objects two thousand feet below them. The largest object is described by Captain Terauchi as resembling "a shelled walnut". Captain Terauchi describes the main craft as being twice the size of an American Aircraft carrier.

Bruce Maccabee, Retired Optical Physicist, U.S. Navy: "The co-pilot said there was something solid there, like you were seeing an oncoming jet with its lights on, except it wasn't an oncoming jet."

"The 747 was nothing compared to this big flying saucer."

After several minutes of observing the UFO, the pilots realized that the objects are now matching their speed of six hundred miles per hour, tracking them. The

Captain reports that the objects are "making moves that are impossible for any man-made aircraft to perform".

Then without warning two of the smaller crafts suddenly rise and shoot right in front of the pilot's window. The objects come so close to the airplane that Captain Terauchi says, "the intense glow make his face feel warm."

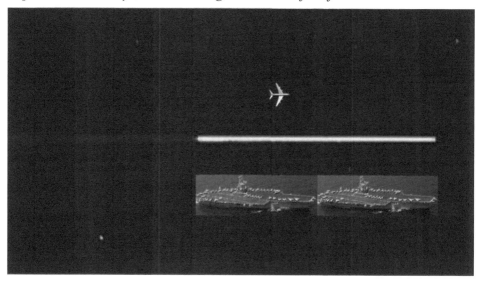

"All of a sudden they appear and they're traveling right in front of the aircraft. They're sort of wobbling back and forth as they move. They seem to be only one thousand maybe two thousand feet in front of the aircraft and travelling at six hundred miles per hour."

At that very moment the radio signal to Anchorage goes dead, leaving the aircraft flying blind, a horrifying catastrophe just seconds away, but the UFOs rise, and veer left.

Japan Air 1628: "Japan Air 1628: Request deviate from object. Request heading two four zero."

AATCC: "Japan 1628 Heavy, Deviations approved as necessary for traffic."
Japan Air 1628: "It's quite big. Right in formation."

In his official FAA report Captain Terauchi says, "We had to get away from that object."

AATCC: *"Japan Air 1628, Sir, do you still have the traffic?"*
Japan Air 1628: *"It disappeared.... Japan 1628."*

AATCC: *"Japan Air 1628 Heavy, I understand that you do not see the traffic any longer?"*

Japan Air 1628: *"Affirmative"*

Moments later an urgent message from Elmendorf Air Force Base the unidentified object now appears on their radar.

ROCC: *"Yeah, this one dash-two again, we have confirmed there is a flight size of two around your one five five zero squawk, one primary return only"*

AATCC: *"OK. Is he following him."*

ROCC: *"It looks like he is, yes."*

AATCC: *"Okay standby"*

The phrase flight size of two indicates that JAL 1628 has uninvited guests with possible hostile intentions.

AATCC: *"Japan Air 1628 heavy, Military Radar advises they are picking up intermittent primary target behind you, in trail, in trail, what say you."*

Immediately after this confirmation the FAA requests that the Airforce scramble jets.

AATCC: *"Do you have anybody to scramble up there? Or do you want to do that?"*

ROCC: *"Well we're going to talk to your liaison officer about that."*

AATCC: *"It's starting to concern Japan Airline. He's making a 360 now and it's still following."*

ROCC: "Yeah okay, we're calling the military desk on this."

Though the military desk took no action, Japan flight 1628 was able to land safely at Anchorage Airport at 6:20pm. Extensive media coverage from around the world help make this incident one of the most widely reported UFO cases in history. While the JAL case continues to inspire debate about the nature and intent of the object that tracked the 747, to this day the case remains a mystery.

"The Japan Airline 747 had a saucer going around it. The papers mysteriously disappeared from the FAA office."[9]

In 1989 was the Voronezh UFO Sightings in Russia. These sightings not only included eye-witness accounts of UFO crafts but also of mysterious 9-foot tall beings that exited the craft. This event was not only witnessed by a multitude of adults, but school children as well and the Russian newspapers even carried the story.

In September of 1989 something happened in the village of Voronezh two hundred miles south of Moscow that caught the attention of the world press. For several weeks strange lights were seen over the city. Then on September the 27th it was reported that a space craft landed in one of the city's public parks from which three alien giant figures emerged. Nothing remotely like this had happened in Voronezh before.

Before coming to America in 1990, Ukrainian journalist Paul Stonehill covered the Voronezh story for the international press.

Paul Stonehill, Journalist/Author: "Top Voronezh researchers of anomalous phenomenon who include scientists, geologists, and also, some military people went to the sight immediately thereafter. They were on the sight on the 3rd of October studying and collecting specimen."

The encounter became a media sensation on national television and in the international press. Drawings of the landings done by the children that were there capture the event vividly.

"It attracted the attention of the media around the world because it was effectively endorsed by Tass and Soviet news agency, who up until that time had certainly not given any credence at all to this kind of story."

Paul Stonehill: "They had the chance to talk to many eye witnesses, adults as well as kids, policemen, school teachers, students, scientists who had witnessed similar or even differently shaped UFOs. The underlying theme was that the giant-like beings exited from the strange-looking craft, did some research throughout Voronezh and were able to get back to their craft and fly away."

"For once we had had a genuine, large number of people all correlating with one another, describing the appearance of these giants. So, it was not a case of you simply believe a witness or you don't. Here you could not fail to believe them because there was so many of them talking in concert."

Lt. G.A. Mateveyev, Policeman: "I was standing not far from the main road at the south park and I saw this flying object at the approximate height of two hundred to two hundred-fifty meters."

Capt. C.H. Okuney, MLOT: "It stayed at the same height and did not move horizontally. I was very interested by all that because it could not have been any kind of metrological balloon."

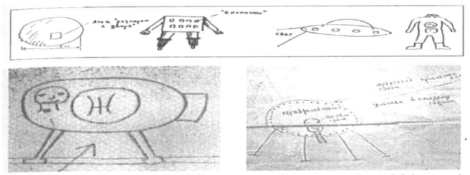

Sketches of the UFO's and robots/beings drawn by some of the witnesses. The top-left drawing of the UFO and robot is by sixth-grader Roma Torshin and the top-right is by Genya Blinov. (credit Hesemann/Jacques Vallee)

Albert Korchagin, Metal Worker: "There was a squeaking sound, perhaps some drilling tool was operating, like it was boring a hole in the ground."

Katusha: "The creatures started coming out, they didn't look too much like humans, they were much taller than humans."

"They did have shoulders, but I didn't see the head"

"He was huge, really huge, bigger than we are. He was a mighty figure."

In 1989 Sergei Makarov was one of the school children who was in the Voronezh park.

Sergei Makarov: "I remember a crowd that gathered around the place. Everybody was scared, everybody turned tail. I was absolutely flabbergasted."

Dennis Murzenko was also one of the boys in the park on that day in September 1989.

Dennis Murzenko: "I saw some traces there and also a strange man. Awkwardly, he looked like any other man, only he was huge, a moment later he suddenly disappeared."

"I had no doubt that the UFO and the giants existed because I saw them, but sometimes when I look back it seems sort of like a fairytale."

Then in 1989/1990 we have the Belgian UFO Wave in Belgium. This series of sightings lasted from 1989 into the 90's, with a massive amount of eye-witness accounts on the very first night. The unknown objects were tracked on radar by the Belgian Air Force and described as black triangles with bright lights that would change color. The Belgian Air Force still offers no explanation for the objects even though photographic evidence exists.

"The Belgian UFO sightings were in the late 1980s and continued into the 1990s"

We've all heard of The Bermuda Triangle, a mysterious area over the Atlantic Ocean where ships and planes have been said to simply disappear. Well welcome to the Belgian Triangle where a huge object suddenly appeared in the sky.

"Belgium is such a small little country and you can imagine that in this small little country hundreds of people seeing this enormous large triangular object." Film maker James Fox has studied UFO sightings for many years.

James Fox: "There was an extremely large triangular shaped craft that could maneuver silently in the night sky, very slow, very low. The Belgian craft was witnessed by hundreds of people including police officers."

With something that large hanging over them the Belgians didn't waffle. They sent in military jets.

James Fox: "They scrambled the F16 jets."

"They locked the radar on it, it showed up triangular on their radar."

James Fox: "But every time the F16 jets would close in on it the object would completely outperform them and was gone. They couldn't get close to it."

Phil Embrogno: "The object dropped from ten thousand feet to five hundred feet in a few seconds. Wow. That's not just super technology, that's Star Trek."

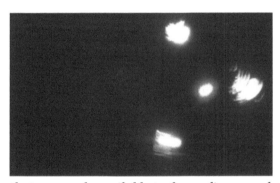

Perhaps the answer lies in this photo.

James Fox: "There was a pretty impressive photograph taken of the craft that was analyzed and you can see the structure in between the lights."

Phil Embrogno: "The picture that was made available to the media was enhanced by photographic computer techniques, but it was basically what the witness saw and what the witness described. Yes, it was probably one of the better UFO pictures that show structure."

So, just what was that giant triangle? Investigator Phil Embrogno decided to trek on over to Belgium to find out for himself.

Phil Embrogno: "I talked to the witnesses who saw the object that night. I can tell you that they were telling the truth from my point of view and once again we see over the years that UFOs are becoming less and less shy and are showing themselves to more and more individuals."[11]

In 1990 we had The Montreal UFO in Canada. This is when more than forty witnesses, including police, observed a UFO above downtown Montreal for more than three hours.[12]

In 1991 we had Space Shuttle Discovery Incident and a video taken during mission STS-48 shows a flash of light and several objects that appear to be flying in an artificial or controlled fashion. NASA explained the objects as ice particles reacting to engine jets. However, researchers analyzed the movement of the objects and found five arguments that the footage could not depict ice particles. Also, the flash of light that preceded the abrupt change in the course of the objects was analyzed and it was concluded that the exhaust plume from one of the shuttle's reaction control system rockets could not have produced the flash of light. The objects appeared to have a definite structure consisting of three lobes arranged in a triangular pattern.[13]

Then in 1993 we have the Kelly Cahill Incident in Australia, East of Melbourne's Dandenong foothills, Kelly Cahill and five others observed a flying saucer that appeared shortly after midnight. They were also confronted by tall, slim, black aliens with glowing red eyes.

Kelly Cahill was a mother and housewife with no interest in spaceships or aliens. But now she's using technology to reconstruct images of her own encounter.

Kelly Cahill: "It does give the idea of the lights there but ya know, the brightness of the lights gives the good impression, but the color doesn't seem quite right."

(c) John Auchett 2001 - Phenomena Research Australia

Cahill pointing to abduction location

Kelly's account starts in August 1993.

Kelly Cahill: "My husband and I were driving up to my girlfriend's place in Mombock which is Dandenong mountains we were driving Belgrave-Helem Road and it was just on dusk. I saw what I thought was round orange lights in the field. It just looked unusual to me."

Later that night while retracing their route home Kelly noticed something unusual.

Kelly Cahill: "About a kilometer or so in front of us about twice the height of the treetops we could see this object, which at first, I thought was a blimp, it had the shape of a blimp, but it was light. As we got closer to it the light seemed to separate, and it was sort of this row of round lights and they were orange.

It appeared like there were silhouettes standing in these round orange lights, like people, but you could only see the black outline. I just said to my husband, "Look, there's people in there." And the minute I said that it shot off to the left of us and within one or two seconds it was gone completely.

About a kilometer or two farther down the road as we kept driving I came across, at least what I thought was a screen or wall of light across the road and my heart started racing and the adrenaline was sort of pumping through my body and I'm thinking, 'We just saw this back down the way, we are in for, ya know, a close encounter, then the next instant, nothing. I seemed to have covered a fare distance that I don't remember covering. There might have been possibly close to a kilometer that I don't remember actually traveling, there was no light, there was nothing blocking the road."

Kelly says it wasn't until weeks later that she remembered actually getting out of the car that night.

Kelly Cahill: "Then I saw that there was another car that had pulled up a hundred meters down the road; then I walked around the front of the car to where my husband was standing on the other side and we started walking across the road together. As we were walking across the road I looked down and saw that the other people were getting out of the car and starting to walk as well. So, I was quite happy that there were other people there who were seeing the same things we were, and we walked along there to where the fence is. Right out in front of us is this huge craft."

"I was totally awestruck, ya know, it was science fiction coming to life. There wasn't any fear then, there was just total awe."

"We stood here, side by side, my husband and I for about thirty to forty-five seconds. Then this tall dark being just appeared in front of the craft and he was followed by about another seven or eight that appeared straight behind him."

"I felt this energy go through me. It was unlike nothing I've ever experienced before in my life; it was like some sort of low level frequency that came in waves, but it was so dense that I could physically feel it going through my body and that feeling absolutely terrified me. It was like, I can't even explain the horror that I felt, just feeling this and I began screaming.

The minute I did the eyes on these things lit up and they came charging across the field, half way across they split up into two groups, some of them headed off down there and the rest came directly towards us. I felt this blow to my stomach and the next thing you know I'm somewhere back here on the grass, it literally lifted me off my feet."

"I thought I was gonna die, I thought 'If I don't get up not, I'm gonna pass out and I'm gonna die, I'm never gonna come back to consciousness' so, ya know, I pulled myself up into a sitting position and when I sat up I couldn't see anything, and it was like there was just black in front of my eyes."

Kelly's not the only one who saw these images that night. For the first time ever, independent witnesses have given the same account of a close encounter. Even though Kelly has never met Jane, Glenda, and Bill from the other car she saw, she has seen the sketches they drew for UFO researchers.

Kelly Cahill: "They've drawn the same circles of light around the top of the craft with these blue lines coming down ending in a semicircle on the ground. They've also drawn a tripod underneath which is something I didn't see that night. It becomes very clear then that we were all looking at the same thing and it was not your average saucer shaped craft."

"Basically, the second party were able to draw sketches of the beings very similar to the ones that I had and they're not your usual little grey things that you see in media propaganda."

"I found a small red colored equilateral triangle underneath my navel which in reality provided only a minor curiosity at the time. It was oddly geometric, and I

did wonder how something like that could get on me that looked like a burn, without me feeling it."

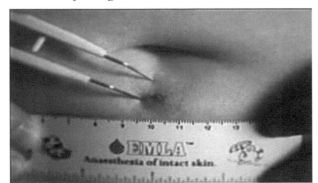

At UFO conferences where Kelly is now a keynote speaker she added strength to her own story by showing photographs of the physical marks left on one of the other women.

"We were all left with triangular marks under our navels but the marks that were actually photographed, the first one came from Glenda which is a series of three small red dots along the inner thigh and both Jane and Glenda were marked with these dots, I wasn't, and Glenda had a ligature mark around her ankle along with severe bruising, it looked like she'd been strapped down to something."

UFO researchers have also reported finding physical traces at the sight where all witnesses said the encounter happened, particularly in respect to where the craft landed.

Kelly Cahill: "Inside that semicircle was a triangular formation of three points about meters apart which correspond with the tripod that was drawn underneath the girl's craft."

To this day Kelly still doesn't know exactly what happened to her that night. Her most vivid memory is the fear that she felt.

Kelly Cahill: "I think a lot of people might have experienced the fear in a nightmare where you're being chased or something like that, and it's a terror that you feel that sometimes can wake you up or whatever but it's absolutely horrifying when you're dreaming it and that's exactly what I was feeling while I was totally awake. That sort of terror and actually having to feel it when you're conscious and physically awake and feel it as a reality is like a living nightmare, it's like a nightmare come to life."[14]

In 1994 was the Meng Zhaoguo Incident in China. Meng Zhaoguo claimed to have been abducted and forced to have intercourse with a 10-foot-tall, six fingered, female alien with braided leg fur.[15]

In 1996 we have the Varginha UFO Incident in Brazil. This is the account where not only were multiple sightings made of a UFO but there was an alleged capture of aliens.

A.J. Gevaerd, Founder and Editor of the Brazilian UFO Magazine: The Varginha case is probably the best, well documented case we have in Brazil and probably in the world. You know over eighty witnesses came forward; first hand witnesses came forward during the first weeks and they are still coming after it happened during all these years we still keep getting witnesses that tell us pieces of the big story that we know comprises the capture of at least two alien creatures in the city of Varginha.

We know for a fact, because we have it all documented, plus the witnesses have confirmed and cross confirmed that one alien was captured in the morning of that day, which was a Saturday about 10:30am by the fire department and some personnel from the army. Another creature was seen on the same day but middle of the afternoon by three girls. It was them who called the attention of the entire

city to the fact that there were strange creatures being seen because one was seen being captured in the morning, it didn't draw too much attention but in the afternoon, when the girls saw another creature then they spread the word to everybody 'we saw the devil', that's what they thought they saw.

That night, of the Saturday January 20,1996, that second creature, probably the same one seen by the girls was also captured by a police car, actually a military police car with two policemen inside. The one who was sitting in the passenger seat was Marco DeCharez and he was lucky enough to be the one who spotted the creature and grabbed it with his bare arms, bare hands, got back to the car, put the creature on his lap and took it hostage.

Twenty-five days after that he died on February 15th of some bacteria attacks proving that his immune deficiency system was absolutely destroyed and army personal kept it all secret for lots of time, until the UFO researchers started protesting along with the press and created so much pressure that eventually information was released.[16]

In 1996 we had the Space Shuttle Columbia Incident. Another video has surfaced, this time taken during mission STS-80 of Space Shuttle Columbia while in orbit. It was analyzed and showed different unusual phenomena including a number of fast moving objects near the shuttle that appear as bright streaks, and two slow moving circular objects. One comes into view from the left and then remains stationary while the other one appears out of thin air and moves off to the right.[17]

Then in 1997 we have the Phoenix Lights Incident in Arizona where lights of varying descriptions, most notably a V-shaped pattern, were seen by thousands of people for about three hours, in a space of about 300 miles, from the Nevada line, through Phoenix, to the edge of Tucson.

The case of the Phoenix lights began on an evening in March of 1997.

"Late breaking, you're watching news 15 at ten. Do these lights belong to visitors from outer space? Hundreds of people from across the valley think it's a distinct possibility. Good evening I'm Marc Baily"

"And I'm Robin Sewell, thanks for joining us. We start our broadcast tonight with those strange dots of light that were the talk of the town."

As reported multiple UFOs were sighted throughout the Phoenix Basin. Numerous eye witnesses were already outside looking up into the night sky hoping to catch a glimpse of the Hale Bob Comet. Michael Tanner is part of a team of investigators received roughly eight hundred reports of eye witnesses regarding the Phoenix Incident.

Michael Tanner, UFO Investigator: "Between 8:15 and 8:45 we had enormous crafts at varying altitudes come right through the center of the valley of Phoenix led by a formation of orbs that were clearly visible through most of the state."

Here are some of the eye witness reports:

"It passed right in front of us, right above eye's length. My estimate of the size of the craft from the nose as it passed us where we live to the end of the wing as it passed in front of us was over five-thousand-feet long."

"It's coming across the sky and as it's moving it's blocking and unblocking the stars, there is actually a shape."

"It was actually five lights that were in a V one in front and two on each side and it was a perfect triangle."

"The object we saw, if we opened up a newspaper you could not block out the object that we saw."

"People say, ya know, you saw a B-2 Bomber, my response is we could land all forty of our B-2 bombers on the wing of that craft."

"He says "You're not gonna believe what I saw." and I said, "Yes, I would, that's all that's been on the news all night long, is this craft."

Reporter: "Explanations have been tossed about, that they were flares, that they were planes flying in formation. Well, Mark and Robin we checked with the FAA today and we checked with Sky Harbor and we check with Luke Airforce Base and there's been no official explanation of those strange bright lights last night."

Truck driver Bill Greiner was driving South on I-17 towards Luke Airforce base. He witnessed several fighter jets scramble to intercept two UFOs directly overhead.

Bill Greiner: "I pulled my truck alongside the west silos which faces Luke Airforce base, it was like right there and I was here unloading. Everything was completely quiet, it was really eerie. There was one right over the base and then there was another one out toward Wickenburg and these things were just hovering. They were huge orbs, but they didn't make no sound or nothing, they were just hovering right there over the base.

Suddenly, I heard a lot of roaring coming out of Luke Airforce base and here come these two fighters coming out and they must've had the burners on cuz there were these huge flames coming out of the back of these things. They ripped right around the back of me and shot right towards those things, then they disappeared on them and they were just gone."

Reporter: "The military says the lights over Arizona last night were flares but the people who saw the lights say that they couldn't have been flares."

In central Phoenix in what is known as the Sunnyslope area, the Lay family was coming home in the early evening to watch for the Hail Bob Comet when they witnessed a very large craft fly directly over their house.

The Lay family's account of the incident: "When the craft went over I really focused on the light. The tip of the craft was right out in the street and the arm is going by, and the end of the arm is at least to that mountain over there, it was six/ seven hundred feet away with these huge lights set inside of it."

"I looked inside and it's wavy like when you look down the street on a hot day in Phoenix above the streets and it's wavy and you see everything kind of distorted and that's what it looked like up inside the middle of the craft."

"And it just skimmed by and didn't make a sound, not even a sound."

Further eyewitness testimony came from Stacy Roads and her daughter Emily who both saw a giant craft fly over their car.

Stacy Rhodes: "It was gunmetal black, it wasn't shiny, it wasn't invisible, it was more of a dull blueish- black color."

Emily Rhodes: "And we both just stayed there and looked at it for a couple minutes and it was completely silent."

Mike Fortson spotted the same craft from his back yard in Chandler a suburb of Phoenix.

Mike Fortson: "When you're looking to the north towards Phoenix proper the lights of the city of Phoenix, Tempie, and Scottsdale, and all these, will form a grey background, and this was a black object coming through a grey background. We had no trouble at all seeing this vehicle."

"We knew is wasn't ours because it was just too dog gone big. As a matter of fact, profoundly massive is a better way to describe it. We don't really have words in our language to describe something that large, it was huge."

Councilwoman Francis Barwood was approached by a reporter who complained about the lack of response from local government regarding the sightings.

Frances Emma Barwood, Councilwoman (ret): "What this reporter said was that they had gone to every level of government, including the city of Phoenix and nobody would talk to them, that this object went from north of Prescott and called in all the way down to Tucson and then was also seen in Wickenburg and nobody would give them any answer. They were either told that they were not gonna talk about it at all, or that there was nothing; that nothing happened."

Responding to mounting pressure from his constituents, Governor Phyfe Symington held a press conference.

"Oh, I'm gonna order a full investigation into this through DPS and we are gonna make all the necessary inquiries and we are gonna get to the bottom of it; we are gonna find out if it was a UFO."

Later that day Governor Symington held an unscheduled live press conference to announce that they had discovered the source behind the Phoenix lights.

"And now I'll ask officer Stein and his officers to escort the accused into the room so that we all may look at the guilty party and this just goes to show that you guys are entirely too serious."

Geraldine Greiner: "I think everyone pretty much laughed at it. I thought that it was really disgusting, it was dismissing everything people had seen and said. Just like, we're all loony toons. I just thought that was a really improper attitude for somebody in his position."

"Nobody in state, local, or federal, military, nobody wanted to talk about it. They didn't want to interview witnesses. They said it didn't happen. They said it didn't concern them. There was one councilwoman Francis Barwood, she's the only one who spoke up and said, 'why don't we investigate?' and then when it came time for her election she lost. Then everyone, in the press, the media she was trashed really bad."[18]

Then we have a UFO incident in 1997 over the Mexico City Skyline UFO. An amateur with a digital camera captured footage of a UFO passing behind and above several buildings.

UPN reports: Now for the first time in its entirety, you are seeing the Mexico City saucer just as we first saw it. We haven't enhanced or manipulated the footage, we haven't removed anything. Translation is being withheld because of the nature of the language used. Let's just say the shooter and his friend are very excited.

In order to get to the bottom of this incredible flying saucer footage. We went to the exact location where the saucer had supposedly been hovering. We were looking for answers, for eyewitnesses, anyone who may have had a part in the mysterious sighting on that day. Anyone that is, who would be willing to talk about it.

Eyewitness to event: "And at last I found the place. This is real, the place exists, the buildings, and then I found not one witness but 12 witnesses, some of them where just under the object, others who saw it far away. Others did not see the object but remember that their animals went absolutely crazy that same day."

Interviewer: "You presented this video at first without knowing where it was, why? Because you wanted to flush people out? You wanted people to come out and say, yeah I know where this is."

Eyewitness: "Exactly, and it happened just one day after. It worked, and for me it was very important because I say I found the place, and it physically existed. This was not a photographic trick."

Another eyewitness to the August 6, 1997 saucer was thirteen-year-old Cassandra.

Interviewer: "Can you show me where you were standing when you saw it?"

Cassandra: "It was in the middle of those two buildings. I was scared."

"Was it wobbling floating?"

Cassandra: "At first it was still, it was wobbling, but then when it got balance it shot out toward the corner of the building and then it disappeared."

As the interview progressed Cassandra told us that the object had been spinning and that she thought she saw windows. She also revealed that right after the sighting she told her father about the UFO, but he had not believed her."

Eyewitness: "We have found twelve witnesses. It we want to look for more we could find more."

We continued to look. We questioned those familiar with the area where the saucer had apparently been taped. We looked from every possible point of view. We heard that there had been a sighting about a mile north in the wealthy suburb of Boscs Los Lomas. There we met Annie Lask, a young woman who had been on the roof of her house on August 6th and she told us that the saucer in the video had hovered directly over her.

Interviewer: "And how high above you was it?"

Annie Lask: "Like 20 meters. The outer rim was spinning really fast and hissing. When I realized that there was this weird thing on top of my head I tried to take a picture. I turned up and it wasn't there. But there was like this mist, like a purple mist, or maybe haze."

After the saucer left her standing in a purple staticky haze Annie Lask does not remember getting down from the roof.

Annie Lask: "Since that day I have constant headaches like every day. Really strong headaches, my eyes burn so bad."

"They still do?"

Annie Lask: "Yes. Since that day."

Allison Holloway interviewed David Froning who is a propulsion engineer and thirty-year veteran of McDonald Douglas.

Allison Holloway: "What's your best guess of what this is?"

David Froning: "I think it's an intelligently controlled craft. It looks like it's being propelled by what we call field propulsion. A propulsion, or mode of propulsion that we ourselves have not fully developed yet."

"What if the pilots of this ship realized when the person shooting the video had them locked on, "Holy smokes someone can see us now" and they revved up their engines and got out of there."[19]

And in 1998 we have the Somerset Incident in the UK. An amazing sighting of a UFO was videotaped in Somerset with amazing results.

In the southwest of England just outside Somerset there was another sighting, it was captured on video tape.

Rod Dickinson: "Got it, got it, yeah I think it's coming this way. Yeah, I can see it. Amazing."

David Kingston: "The UFO that you saw originally was spotted approximately about two hundred yards to the left of the Arial mast and I suppose it was probably about five hundred feet up. It was very low in the sky."

David Kingston: "And this is a British communications tower?"

Rod Dickinson: "This is a radio communications tower, they got three military masts on there and it sends out. One is navigational signal which is used for aircraft, the other two arrows are near the top we're not sure but there is a pulsed frequency that comes from them."

David Kingston: "The actual UFO from the time it was first seen by Rod

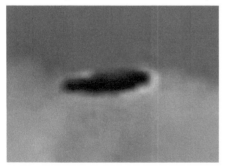

Dickenson who did the filming, it lasted approximately twelve minutes. So, it was quite a long period of time for a daylight sighting to occur."

We took this tape to be analyzed by Lucas Films Special Effects Division Industrial Light and Magic in San Rafael, California. Here we met with Bill George an academy award winning special effects supervisor. Over the last twenty years his special effects have been featured in films like Star Wars the Phantom Menace. He analyzed this film to determine its authenticity.

Bill George: "There are several things that I see when the footage is running that tells me this was actually there when this was filmed. First of all, it's the shake, the shake. If you were to give me a background plate of just the sky and say, 'we want you to take this image of a flying saucer and match it in', that's something that's technically very difficult to do, because you have to match, putting the two elements together, you would have to match the shake.

Now certainly we have computers that can track that but this, this is just all over the map. A couple other cues that tell me this is actually there when it was being filmed was that it is going in and out of focus with the background because the camera is trying to compensate and trying to focus, probably some sort of autofocus.

So, the background is going in and out of focus along with the object. There are these dark things flying through the frame and if someone was to have put those in there they would have to composite it in there behind the birds, it would be a technical problem."[20]

In 2000 we have Southern Illinois UFO. Between 4:00 and 7:00 am, six people, including police officers, observed a large, triangular object a few hundred feet over St. Clair County in Illinois. The object glided silently and slowly to the southwest over several small towns before vanishing near the town of Dupo. The object, studded with several bright lights, was as tall as a two-story house and as long as a football field as this actual 911 distress call reveals.

At the regional 911 center located in Belleville all conversations are recorded. This tape begins with a radio dispatch from an operator 911 operator Tina Joaquin.

Tina Joaquin: "We just received a call from Highland PD in reference to a truck driver who just stopped in and said there was a flying object in the area of Lebanon. It was like a two-story house, it had white lights and red blinking lights and it was last seen Southwest over Lebanon. Officer could you check the area?"

An officer on patrol in the city of Lebanon, Illinois responded to the dispatcher's query.

Officer: "Did they say if the truck driver was DUI or anything?"

Dispatch: "She said he was serious."

Officer: "Just a quick question. If I happen to find it, what am I supposed to do with it?"

After searching for two minute the officer radioed the dispatcher.

Officer: "Be advised, there's a very bright, white light east of town; and it keeps changing colors. I'll go over there and see maybe if it's an aircraft. It doesn't look like an aircraft though."

Dispatch: "That's affirmative. It's not the moon and it's not a star." Officer: "If you would, would you contact Scott Air Force Base and see if they have anything flying in this area please?" Dispatch: "Well, whether it's a plane or not, its heading westbound now. Matter of fact, if Shiloh officer looks up, they can probably see it by now."

Six miles Southwest a call came from another police officer this time in Shiloh, Illinois.

Shiloh officer: "25/50 I see something, but I don't know what the heck it is…"

Thirteen miles southwest in Millstadt another police witness reports a similar sighting.

Millstadt officer: "Cencom, 60/04"

Dispatch: "Go ahead…"

Millstadt officer: "I've got that object in sight also."

Dispatch: "Are you serious?"

Millstadt officer: "It's huge."

Dispatch: "Does it look like a... What does it look like to you?"

Millstadt officer: "It's kind of V shaped." (Twilight Zone Theme)

Dispatch: "Really."

A moment later a fourth police witness in Dupo, Illinois contacted the dispatcher.

Dupo officer: "When I first saw it with the open eye you could see the different colors. Now it just appears to be white."

Dispatch: "Is it very large?"

Dupo officer: "It's hard to tell. It's pretty far off in the distance. This object was above me about 500 feet. It was huge!"

There were no more calls to the dispatcher. Whatever it was if indeed there was anything, vanished into the night skies over Illinois, but police are trained to be reliable observers and four different officers from four different departments all reported seeing something that they could not explain."[21]

Chapter Five

The History of UFO's Part Four

In 2001 we have the New Jersey Turnpike Incident. Several people including police officers stopped their cars along the New Jersey Turnpike to view unexplained light formations in the night sky as mentioned below.

Fox 5 News Reports: One observer: "Oh my goodness, it was a whole row of them."

This amateur video shows what hundreds of people saw around Carteret, New Jersey early Sunday morning, objects yet unidentified, that seem to be flying.

Natatili Stanford: "At first I was like scared cuz I didn't know what was going on but first thing that came to my mind was UFOs. First, it looked like stars but no, couldn't have been."

Make no mistake, the Carteret police department got jammed with calls about the lights and even patrolmen saw this strange occurrence.

Officer Scott Zdep: "About fifteen to twenty lights in the sky, I have no idea what they could be."

Some people who saw the lights already have their minds made up.

Roy Kolakowski: "I don't know what it was. They changed forms, then they dropped off slowly. I don't know what it was, I'm not saying I believe in aliens, but UFOs, that was it."

Astronomers say that there are some major solar storms that are happening right now, which light up the atmosphere, known as the Aurora Borealis but they are not usually seen as pinpoints of light and so the speculation continues as to what they actually were.

Fox 5 New Reporter Harry Martin: "Well as far as we could determine there were no parachutists at that hour, it wasn't a satellite, it's certainly not the space shuttle, but just in case something did land, there is an unofficial mug shot that has been released and I emphasize unofficial mugshot of what may have landed, as he holds up a mugshot of a green alien. We are live in Carteret. Back to you."[1]

In 2004 through 2006 we had the Tinley Park Lights in Chicago Illinois. This encounter includes a series of several mass UFO sightings in Tinley Park and Oak Park, Illinois, suburbs of Chicago. Witnesses to each event reported seeing three silent, self-luminescent objects which red or red-orange in color were and spherical in shape, hanging in the night sky. They moved slowly in "formation" for approximately 30 minutes at low to intermediate altitude and were visible from the ground for approximately 12 miles in any direction.

It was a quiet summer evening in the suburbs of Chicago until some residents noticed that the aroma of grilling burgers and brauts were not the only thing wafting through the night sky.

Tomas T.J. Chapman: "We were at a block party, my sons and I and my one son Justin said, "Look there's a UFO!" and I turned around and I'm like "What in the world are these things, I've never seen anything like this before, never."

Tomas T.J. Chapman grabbed his camera and began filming the strange objects. Sam Moranto, UFO investigator: "I believe it was around 10:30, people were starting to see a configuration of three illuminations in the sky in a pattern of an isosceles triangle or some variation thereof."

Tomas T.J. Chapman: "I got it! I got it on tape!"

Tomas T.J. Chapman: "And as I was shooting, this thing started rotating into a triangle right above the house. We didn't know if these were three separate crafts or if they were tied into each other."

The block party went from barbequing and horseshoes to debating a possible UFO sighting.

Tomas T.J. Chapman: "What is it? We started thinking, is it helicopters? No, it didn't make any sound. Is it flares? No, there's no smoke involved plus flares just give off one color."

T.J. decided to go straight to the experts and contacted UFO investigator Sam Moranto.

Sam Moranto: "When I saw the footage, I knew what we may very well be dealing with is something genuine."

TJ and his block party companions weren't the only ones to report strange things amiss in the night skies over suburban Chicago.

Sam Moranto: "What's nice about a mass sighting is you cut cross the demographic of a community. We have doctors, lawyers, aviation personnel, we have ex- military personnel, people in almost every cut of life imaginable and all of them agree that what they saw that night was something they can't put their finger on."

But the Tinley Park Triangle was not through mystifying the populous.

Tomas T.J. Chapman: "I was fortunate to film a commercial airline cutting in front of them."

Sam Moranto: "That's why this is very good footage, we actually have a plane in the air and we can see that these illuminations, these fields of light, are as big, or possibly three times larger or more than the actual jet. That's pretty conclusive."[2]

In 2004 through 2005 we have the Mexico Mass UFO Fleet Sightings in Mexico. These sightings, also called "The Quiet Invasion" happened in broad daylight and started with a formation of just seven objects. They all emitted a white luminosity and had a spherical form. Some of the objects would leave formation and start performing individual maneuvers and seemed to be controlled by an intelligent force. After filming the seven UFO's for approximately fifteen minutes, suddenly there appeared an enormous fleet of UFO's, 100 to 200 of them, flying in perfect formation, contrasting with the blue sky and white clouds. These sightings are considered to be one of most important pieces of UFO evidence and another fleet of UFOs was filmed later.

And in 2006 we have the Chicago O'Hare UFO Sighting, where a group of United Airlines employees and pilots claimed sightings of a saucer-shaped unlit craft hovering over a Chicago O'Hare Airport terminal before shooting up vertically and punching a hole in the clouds. Authorities initially denied having received reports of it and then later tried to explain it away, as this rare behind the scenes news footage exposes.

(Off Air) Jim: "Oh, hey Jon."

Jon: "Hey Jim, how are you?"

Jim: "Well fine thanks, how are you?"

Jon: "Busy with this UFO stuff."

Jim: "Oh my god, did you see it hit the Fox crawl Monday night?"

Jon: "It's everywhere, CNN, and this is my fourth appearance today."

Jim: "Really?"

Jon: "MSNBC every network."

Jim: "Oh, my goodness that is…"

Jon: "It's worldwide, Australia, everywhere."

Jim: "That's how I'm gonna start off, I'm gonna say, well Jon the response has been out of this world. Well, congratulations, where's the latest on the investigation with the FAA then? Or by this time tomorrow is going to prove a lot."

Jon: "United is now acknowledging that they were approached by employees, so they've done that flip flop and I'm trying to locate photos of this. I'm told there might be photos."

Jim: "Oh really? Wow, that would be cool."

Jon: "I'm told that the story on CT has almost a million hits."

Jon: "Yeah, it's the most read story in the history of CT.com."

Jim: "You've got to be kidding me."

Jon: "No, I got an email yesterday from Phil D. and it's on their history of the website."

Jim: "Wow. Well, incredible, incredible. So, does the possibility exist that you might get the pictures in for tomorrow?"

Jon: "No, no, no I am told that the pilots on that plan that was being pushed back, I said in the story that they opened the windows and stuck their head out and now I'm being told that one of them had a digital camera and snapped some pictures."

Jim: "Wow."

Jon: "So, United's not playing ball with me and FAA, I've expanded my foyer to include the flight plan, which might include the pilot's names. I'm trying to work with the union as well."

Jim: "Are they still going by weather phenomenon?"

Jon: "FAA, because of the federal holiday, I haven't talked to them much but yeah they haven't changed their story. I've heard from other people since then and that explanation just doesn't wash."

Jim: "And they haven't gone out of their way to say anything otherwise, so far?"

Jon: "No, ya know, they say it was November 7th, they're moving on, doing their daily thing."

Jim: "Well I tell ya what, all the people that saw it must be feeling a little invalidated right about now."

Jon: "Oh yeah I'm getting tons of emails from other people outside the airport and at O'Hare who either sighted that same object or saw the hole in the sky and said, "What is that?".

Jim: "Really? Wow. Okay, so what did it look like again for the folks that saw it. It was a saucer-like object hovering over the United Terminal, right?"

Jon: "Yeah, directly over gate C17 and it was stationary in the sky, dark grey metallic, I guess they saw certain shapes, no lights, and it was there for some minutes and when it disappeared it just streaked through the clouds with such energy that it broke a big, a blue hole in the overcast and the hole remained there for several minutes until the wind drifted and pushed the clouds back together."

Jim: *"So, the blue was the sky, wow."*

Jon: *"Yeah the blue was the sky but otherwise the entire skyline was cloudy and overcast. An airplane just doesn't react like that, it slices through and doesn't disturb the atmosphere."*

Jim: *"Do you have any other interviews set up after this Jon?"*

Jon: *"Yeah, I'm going back on the radio stations, a couple radio stations this afternoon and then Headline news has a show at three o'clock."*

Jim: *"I'll have to watch them. Okay, Australia, what other international?"*

Jon: *"I mean all over Europe. I'm hearing from people in Ireland, they say that.*

Jon: *"We hear about what's happening in O'hara (laughs). As well as serious researchers at major US universities that have attempted to do their own investigations but when they go to the government to get information they get stonewalled. So there really is this universal feeling that the government knows a lot more than it's willing to tell."*

Jim: *"Man, okay. I think it's so cool that I was the first one to get to talk to you about it."*

Live News Story

Jim: *"The UFO O'Hare story that the Chicago Tribune exclusively broke on New Year's Day is garnering attention around the world. Joining us to talk about it once again is Jon Hildevitch who broke the story. Jon the response has been well, out of this world."*

Jon Hildevitch: *"Yes, it has been astronomical Jim every major country it seems people have written in, both those who claim they have spotted UFOs during their life as well as serious researchers. I mean in just the last two days this is my email"* (Holding up a huge block of piles papers).

These are the serious emails, the one from kooks who say they were brought aboard spacecraft I put in a circular file. So, it's just a story that has legs and people are fascinated by the thought and I think there is some belief that there are advanced life forms that are visiting us here on a regular basis."

Jim: "You've been contacted now in the last few days, by several country's but that also includes serious researchers here in the U.S. I've got to tell you, I got a call from my dad in California Monday night and he was like "What is up with the O'Hare UFO story?" and I said "Where did you see that? Where did you read that?". Well it's on Fox networks crawl on the bottom, it's just amazing how much this is garnering."

Jon: "Yeah it really is and worldwide attention as you say and from people who have made observations themselves, like on November 7th, the date of this incident, people both at O'Hare and outside the airport, who have either seen this grey, disc shaped metallic object themselves or they saw that huge hole in the sky that the object created when it vanished."

Jim: "Let's go over that one more time. What did people see when it all of a sudden vanished right through the clouds over the United Terminal? And how has the FAA been reacting the last few days too? Is there any new ground on that?"

Jon: "Okay, well the object was hovering in a stationary position about 1,500 feet above the United terminal for some minutes and then when it left, it just burst through this thick cloud layer, creating this large open space of blue sky on an otherwise overcast day.

It took some minutes for that opening to close up when the clouds drifted back together. It's just extremely unusual according to the witnesses. Airplanes usually just don't react like this, they slice through clouds and they really don't disturb the atmosphere that much except with the wing tips and such.

The FAA is still pinning this to some sort of weather phenomenon. Like some lights from the Airport and the overcast sky somehow got together and created this image but weather experts, astronomy expert's others that I've talked to say that that's bonk. The explanation just doesn't wash.

United on the other hand after denying that they got any reports from employees about the sighting is now, yes indeed their employees did approach them immediately because of concerns about safety."

Jim: "And to reiterate Jon, the witnesses who originally came to you were all seasoned credible professionals like pilots and so."

Jon: "They're pilots, they're senior managers, they're mechanics, and others, so they're very truthful about what they're saying, and we are trying to locate photographs if they do exist of this incident."

Jim: "Jon, we know that you have other interviews to do today with other countries, so we'll let you go and keep our eyes to the sky. Thanks."
"Thank you, Jim."

(Off Air) Jim: "This is just incredible. Isn't it amazing what really garners people's attention for several reasons I suppose."

Jon: "Yeah"

Jim: "How cool. I can't wait to see in a week where this stands."

Jon: "I'm still amazed that I'm getting requests for interviews."[3]

In 2007 we have the Islington Incident in London where several UFO's were spotted over north London in the inner-city district of Islington. The police started receiving phone calls only minutes after the objects appeared and one witness stated this.

"I just picked up my son from nursery in Bredgar Road. I had just come out of the door when I noticed what was going on in the sky. There were a group of them, 10 to 15 of them, moving together. I thought for a while that something was happening in the center of London. Bombs and planes crossed my mind.

But I realized very quickly that they didn't look like any aircraft I'd seen before. They were coming from the north and moving south. And then they kind of stopped and they were hovering. There was no sound. They seemed to fade away and I saw more coming and then they stopped. It lasted about 10 minutes."

Another witness stated that, "He was picking his daughter up from school and he saw many people looking up in the air. Traffic had stopped, and people were staring. He said he saw between twelve and fifteen orange lights traveling across the sky. Then they would stop and then they went upwards. The following is a piece of actual footage from another witness.[4]

Also, in 2007 was the New Delhi Incident in India where two UFO's were detected near the Indian prime minister's residence.

Then in 2007 the Alderney Sighting in England took place when airline pilots on separate flights spot massive UFO's off the coast of Alderney in the English Channel.

About two months ago Captain Ray Bowyer a man with more than twenty years flying experience under his wings, so to speak, saw something extraordinary which later made those headlines as he flew at four thousand feet near Guernsey and so did quite a few of his passengers, and so did the pilot of another aircraft that was flying nearby. Captain Bowyer is here now to tell his story.

Interviewer: "Thank-you for coming in and thank you for speaking up because I know from private conversations I've had over the years with commercial pilots certainly from the cockpit, they do see things, and they tend not to report them because they don't want to be laughed at or have their careers jeopardized. So why did you decide to speak out about it?"

Captain Bowyer "Well, I actually didn't decide to speak out about it, it was the press that asked my company, the company I work for, would I mind doing an interview and the company being a very forward-thinking firm had no objection. In fact, pretty much actively encouraged it, so that's how it happened."

Interviewer: "Well, how did the press get hold of it then, did passengers? –"

Captain Bowyer: "I don't know."

Interviewer: "You weren't the only one that saw this phenomenon, were you?"

Captain Bowyer: "No, I wasn't."

Interviewer: "There were some passengers as well as another pilot."

Captain Bowyer: "Yes."

Interviewer: "We got an artist impression done up this afternoon on our computer paint box. Is that kind of what you saw?"

Captain Bowyer: "Ummmm...no."

Interviewer: "Hahahaha. Okay well why don't you describe it to us."

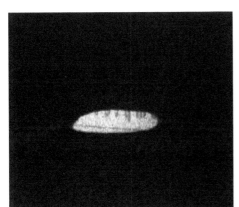

Captain Bowyer: "Well it was a brilliant yellow object, with a brightness you got there about two thirds from left to right. There was a graphite grey section, if you want to call it a fuselage, if you're looking into it."

Interviewer: "And how big was it?"

Captain Bowyer: "Difficult to say once again, but I'd say from fifty miles away, any object from fifty miles away must be pretty enormous."

Interviewer: "What about a mile long?"

Captain Bowyer: "It's possible."[5]

In 2008 to 2009 we have the Turkey UFO sightings in Istanbul. Over a four-month span in 2008, a night guard at the Yeni Kent Compound videotaped one or more UFO's over Turkey at night time. Many witnesses confirmed the two and a half hours' worth of video, leading the authorities to dub it as the "most important images of a UFO ever filmed."

2;20 AM Jun 12, 2008

"This is amazing man! Light is moving."

The UFO's returned once again in 2009, and Dr. Roger Leir was fortunate enough to be behind the camera.

4:59 am May 15, 2009

The following is an excerp from Dr. Leirs's presentation at the 2010 Ventura County UFO Festival in Ventura, California.

"There was a bright full moon and below the moon there was this little bright spot and we didn't know what it was, and we were filming out over the water. There were no structures in the water, there were no oil platforms or ships going by and we zoomed in. This camera has a 200mm lense and an electronic doubler, so we were able to get very tight on the leading edge of the craft.

The craft, you have to realize, is being lit by the moonlight, as I said there was this very bright moon. And then, right at the front on the craft there appeared to be three windows, viewing ports, whatever you want to call them, and standing in these viewing ports were your typical bumper sticker greys and I saw this, I looked through the camera myself.

Fortunately, we recorded it, and that video went to the university in Istanbul and went over extremely intense scrutiny by the Turkish government and then the video was also sent to the UK and several other countries for analysis. By the time all that had been done, it already had been on the internet. It could absolutely not be suppressed from the public."[6]

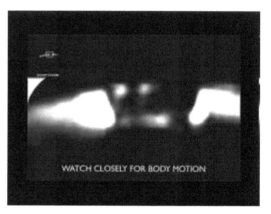

In 2008 in South India we have a UFO Sighting. In India Several UFO's were not only seen and filmed in South India, but they also appeared and disappeared at will. [7]

In 2008 we have the Moscow UFO Sightings. Different people including the state-owned media reported sightings of several orange UFO's.

In 2009 we have scattered U.S. sightings of UFO's that were reported all over the United States.

Also, in 2009 we have the BBC UFO Sighting in Northern England. In this case a UFO was captured on BBC camera.

BBC News Reports: *"Were you watching your tv yesterday around five past nine in the morning? Did you catch the morning headlines, and did you spot* *something suspicious in the screen behind me? Have a look, is it a bird? Is it a plane? What is it? We don't know. Perhaps you can help and if you can, please do and remember, don't have nightmares."*

And in 2009 we have The Ural Abduction in Russia. Once again in the Ural Mountains there was another reported not a death this time but an alleged disappearance of an 11-year-old girl by a UFO.

Again in 2009 we have the Blue Spiral UFO Sighting in Norway. A strange blue spiral shaped UFO appeared over the skies in Norway.

The Early Show reports: *"Scientists from all over the world are trying to figure out what caused a mysterious blue light to spiral in the sky over Norway on Wednesday."*

"As far as UFO sightings go this one is as good, or as weird, as it gets."

"A light appearing high in the arctic sky baffling those who saw it and exciting a lot of comment."

Sheila MacVicar: "Early Wednesday morning this appearing in the sky over Norwegian sky. A blue light, small at first and growing into a spiral and then disappearing into what appeared to be a black hole. In the northern community of Konderlite and on a Norwegian military base phones snapped, video cameras rolled, and bloggers got busy."

RT Moscow Reports: *"Tonight, Norwegian authorities are investigating strange lights seen in the Artic sky. The spiraling white lights were seen for several minutes Wednesday morning. Locals say the lights appeared to be bigger than the moon.*

Thousands of Norwegians bombarded the Metrological Institute to ask what that light could have possibly been. Some thought it could have been a meteor, others a black hole, and some even thought it was aliens."

In 2009 we have the Hole in the Sky UFO in Moscow. An odd-shaped cloud structure appeared in the sky over Moscow.

RT Beijing reports: *People have been baffled by an unexplained circle of light seen hovering high over Moscow in Wednesday evening. Scientists have rejected* *claims of UFO activity saying that the white cloud was no more than an optical*

illusion.[8]

Then in 2010 was the amazing Spiraling White Light UFO in Australia. Another spiraling UFO appeared.

A strange spiraling white light was spotted in the early morning sky over Sydney. It has even skeptical witnesses wondering if it was a UFO. The unusual sight was recorded by hundreds of people from Victoria north to Queensland.

"It appeared just before six o'clock this morning, a spiral in the sky around a bright light. Malcom Richardson saw it move from west to east disappearing into the sunrise.

Malcolm Richardson: "It was actually rotating and giving off a vapor, a glowing vapor in a spiral, it was getting bigger."

He was not alone early morning surfers, farmers, truckers grabbed their phone cameras, still cameras, and web cameras.

"It was just the most astounding thing, I was just looking out the window trying to just see if it's come back or not."

From central Queensland to Melbourne all along the East coast people shared a close encounter. *"This thing was moving at a rapid rate." "I thought wow gee that's so unusual." "I was just dumfounded."[9]*

In 2010 we also had the Turkey UFO Sightings part 2. Over a six-month span in 2010, there were a massive amount of UFO reports and many of them were recorded digitally as a photograph or on video. Analysis of the material showed that many of the sightings or recordings were not natural or manmade objects like Venus, a satellite, or a bird, etc.

In 2010 we also had The Morhping UFO Sighting in Japan. This amazing footage was recorded of a UFO that morphed and released other, smaller UFO's from itself.[10]

Also, in 2010 we had the Zhejiang Incident in China. The Chinese News Agency reported how airport authorities stopped passengers from boarding planes, and that outgoing flights were grounded for about an hour in Hangzhou, Zhejiang capital, after an amazing UFO was spotted. Incoming flights were rerouted to other airports as people watched in total amazement.

CCTV News reports: Some unexpected guests apparently have paid an unexpected visit to Hangzhou. The city known as paradise on earth, may have attracted the attention of some celestial visitors.

Reporter: "At around eight o'clock in the evening and unidentified flying object was spotted hovering in the sky above Hangzhou's Zhejiang Airport. In the next hour the airport was shut down."

Airport employee: "We received orders to shut down the airport until skies cleared."

Reporter: "As a result, outgoing flights were grounded, and inbound flight were directed to nearby airports. Normal airport operations resumed about two hours later. Residents near the airport have taken two photos of the object. The one in daylight reveals a clear comet-like tail and the other one taken at night features a glowing object with a thick golden light. Aviation authorities are still investigating the phenomenon and no further details have been released."

ABC News Reports*: "UFO in China skies forces Zhejiang Airport to stop operations on July 7th. Outbound flights were grounded after an unidentified flying object was detected by a flight crew. The incident has captured the attention of Chinese media. Theories about the UFOs identity are burning up on the internet as well, they include everything from a hidden US bomber to an elaborate man-made hoax. For now, the UFO continues to be a mystery. A spokesman from China's Civil Aviation Administration confirmed ABC news that the matter is under investigation."*

Fox News Reports: *"Some Chinese residents are on edge this morning after another apparent UFO sighting here, it's the second one in two weeks. The first sighting was on July 7th and an airport had to be shut down."*

2ⁿᵈ Reporter: "Alright that's a UFO if I've ever seen one."

"The airport apparently had to be shut down after people saw twinkling lights above the airport terminal. Seventeen flights had to be diverted and this last one happened just two days ago, and people say they saw four lantern-like objects forming a diamond shape in the air, hovering in the sky for over an hour. Aviation experts say they don't know what it was, it wasn't a plane.[11]

In 2011 we had the West Bengal Incident in India. A glowing round object was witnessed making a speedy descent near the West Bengal-Bihar border early in 2011.The alleged UFO left the pilots of five aircraft baffled and triggered widespread speculation about UFO's.

Then in 2011 we had the Lee's Summit UFO Sightings in Missouri. This is when a metallic disc-shaped object with pulsating red, green and blue lights was seen by six different eyewitnesses.

Also, in 2011 we had the Strange Sky UFO's in Russia. Strange flying phenomena also appeared in Russia throughout 2011.

Also, in 2011 we have The Jerusalem Sighting. This is the infamous sighting that created quite a stir.

__The Today Show Reports__: "An unusual sight over the city of old Jerusalem making the rounds on the internet. This YouTube video was reportedly taken along the promenade of Armen Handsewn at about one in the morning. The man who posted it says he was there with a friend when a bright light appeared in the sky and descended on the Dome of the Rock.

The light appears just to hang in the skyline, then an energy burst of some kind and the light goes sailing back. It's hard to see in the darkness but it then appears that blinking red lights are hovering in the sky above, then just disappear. Midnight fireworks in a cloudy sky, or UFO flying over Jerusalem? Theories abound, is it real or a hoax? One thing is for certain the video has the web world buzzing."

In fact, so convincing was the footage that several papers picked up on the story. One article stated this.

"Several videos posted to YouTube last week appear to show a strange ball of light hovering above a Jerusalem shrine before disappearing into the night. The videos show a circular object descending slowly over the holy city's iconic Dome of the Rock before flickering and shooting skyward like a rocket. Similar clips have been seen before and debunked as hoaxes. But this latest sighting had been proving more difficult to dismiss as it was recorded from four different perspectives.

Adding to the mystery is the fact that flying over the Dome of the Rock landmark – an ancient Islamic shrine – is forbidden. Last week, former Ministry of Defense UFO investigator Nick Pope said, "If these are real, they are some of the most incredible videos ever shot."

Then apparently this sighting was followed by several other amazing sightings also caught on video throughout the world, another article shared this in response.[12]

"Yohanan Vargas, a UFO expert in Mexico, reported on Sunday that an increase in UFO's over Mexico occurred the day after the Jerusalem Dome of the Rock UFO Orb.

According to Vargas, a flotilla of UFO's appeared in the northwestern part of Mexico over the city of Los Mochis. Dozens of people reported through the Twitter network.

In the first UFO sighting, there was reported the presence of strange lights in the sky that moved very slowly and in formation. A UFO witness was able to capture video with an iPhone of a UFO "fleet" where there are white areas that had a reddish halo perfectly protruding from the black sky.

Later, there was a UFO fleet videotaped in France that had the same characteristics as those reported in Mexico.

In fact, one researcher stated, "UFO interventions will then accelerate, not so much over our cities, but dispersed over our continents with sightings increasing in duration. The intent of these interventions is to increase mankind's acceptance of the alien phenomena so that hopefully, we will be prepared to accept a face-to-face encounter and communicate, perhaps as early as next year.

The sightings of UFO's have so increased that one article shared this sobering statistic, "UFO evidence is breaking records already in 2011 for more UFO sightings than at any time in human history.

Thus far in 2011, there's been more UFO sightings worldwide than at any time in previous years, say a host of well-known optical physicists and prominent UFO investigators in the United States, at the European Union, in China, Russia, Australia and the Middle East.

Moreover, leading international scientists and detailed UFO reports by the United States, Great Britain, France, Russia, China and other world governments and that include detailed analysis over 50 years – are calling on the United Nations to review all UFO evidence and produce a "systematic scientific investigation" to make first contact now."

And that's precisely what experts, officials and world leaders are saying is coming soon.

Fox News reports:

"With us now from Washington is Stephen Bassett, founder and executive director of the Extraterrestrial Phenomena Political Action Committee. Last time he was here he was running for Congress and was unsuccessful in that venture, but I will ask you today sir, the Mexican military says, hey we took these pictures, these are UFOs, what was that, do you know?"

Stephen Bassett: "This is significant for two reasons Shepard, one this was released by the Defense Ministry of Mexico. This is a message sent to the United States government, that Mexico and many other governments are losing patience with our government's intransigence in ending this embargo.

Other messages have been sent by France in 1999 with the Cometa Report and by the United Kingdom when they released a substantial number of documents regarding the Bentwaters case in 2000. Many countries know about the extraterrestrial presence, but they defer to the United States regarding the timing of which that disclosure would take place but they're simply losing patience."
Shepard: "How do we know this, by the way?"

Stephen Bassett: "Well, we know it by paying attention. I've been following this now for ten years. I call it the politics of disclosure, the disclosure process. Hundreds of government witnesses in this government have come forward and other governments are putting pressure on our government.

The media hasn't covered it thoroughly enough. If it did it would learn about some of the things I'm mentioning here. We would also learn about thousands of the photos and videos that have been taken over Mexico by Mexican citizens."

Shepard: "There's absolutely no doubt about that, since 1991 there have been thousands of videos and pictures of discs but never anything like this. Taken by sophisticated cameras on board military vehicles."

Stephen Bassett: "Oh, there's been plenty."

Shepard: "But not as clear and widespread as this and government confirmed in this way. I'm just saying that these are unusual in a way."

Stephen Bassett: "Oh no it has happened many times before, it's just that this is the first time it's been released. Believe me, there is evidence like this in the archives of every first world government in the world, but they released this publicly in a news conference in Mexico City, that is the difference."

Shepard: "Studies have been done that 'clearly indicate the likelihood of extraterrestrial explanation' but there are people out there, I'm hoping there are millions of people at the moment, who are saying, this is nutty, why do we even talk about such things?"

Stephen Bassett: "The polls show otherwise Shepard, CNN, Times, Reuter polls over the last ten years, consistently, fifty percent of all Americans believe that an extraterrestrial explanation accounts for these sightings up to as many as ninety percent of Americans believe the government is outright lying. The polls are unambiguous, year after year.

In fact, if you could talk anonymously, even in Congress, about fifty percent of Congress is already confirmed, convinced that an extraterrestrial presence explains these phenomena. Disclosure is at hand and is very close and the American people need to prepare themselves very soon for an announcement from our government that there is in fact an extraterrestrial presence and it has been engaging this planet and human race."[13]

CNN News Reports:

Wolf Blitzer: "There is a group gathering here in Washington, to talk about their UFO sightings, but this apparently is no crackpot convention. Former high-level government and military officials are among those sharing what they've seen in the skies. Our national correspondent Gary Tuchman is here, he's watching all of this unfold. Gary what is this conference all about?"

Gary Tuchman: "Well Wolf it's most interesting, a panel discussion within the Belt Way about what might be taking place in the Milky Way and beyond. Have extraterrestrials visited us here on Earth? Well, fourteen men from seven different countries participated in a panel discussion to discuss why they believe UFOs have visited Earth.

These aren't guys they just picked up off the streets. The panel includes former governor of Arizona Phyfe Symington who's one of many Arizonians who say they saw UFOs back in 1997 during an episode that is popularly referred to as the Phoenix Lights."

Phyfe Symington: "We want the United States government to stop perpetuating the myth that all UFOs can be explained away in down to earth and conventional terms. Instead, our country needs to reopen its official investigation that it shut down in 1969."

Gary Tuchman: "Also participating was a retired US Airforce Captain who said he and his passengers saw a huge flying disk. Also, retired Peruvian Air Force Pilot who says he came within three hundred feet of a circular UFO flying at sixty-three thousand feet and then there was a retired US Air force security officer who while stationed in England was summoned to a downed aircraft in a forest."

Pettis Deneen: "When we came up on the triangular craft there were blue and yellow lights swirling around the exterior as though they were part of the surface. The air around us was electrically charged and we could feel it on our clothes, our skin, and our hair."

Gary Tuchman: "While Pettis Deneen's says the craft took off he never saw any beings inside or outside the UFO. He says he took pictures but inferred they were purposely over exposed by the government."

Wolf Blitzer: "There have even been UFO reported sighting right here in the nation's capital. There was a flurry of them back in July of 1952, when the Airforce investigated but was never able to solve or prove anything. Take a look at some of these headlines, 'AEHIAL WHATSITS BUZZ D.C. AGAIN!' 'Air Force After D.C. Saucers', 'Jets Ready to Chase Lights, Jets Ordered to Hunt Down Flying Saucers'. There was a lot of hype, a lot of excitement about UFOs back in 1952."

Fox News Reports:

Bill Hemmer: "Now the United Nations is getting ready for a contact with the aliens from outer space. This is Mazlan Othman she's out of Malesia and she will be planet earth's first interstellar diplomat."

Bill Hemmer: "This is Michio Kaku, she is a theoretical physics professor, also a host of the Science Channel Series Sci-fi Science Physics of the Impossible, which is doing very well by the way. Nice to see you."

Michio Kaku: "I think it's a little premature for us to announce our presence in outer space until we know their intentions, I mean they may view us as lunch, in which case maybe it's a good idea to keep ourselves a little bit obscure for a while."

Bill Hemmer: "And as someone said that if they're looking for intelligent life they don't want to start in the United Nations."

Bill Hemmer: "The Vatican now, a five-day conference on aliens. Father Jonathan Moore is Fox News contributor, back with us. Father Moore, how are you? What a great movie that was."

Father Moore: "A great movie, Drew Barrymore and off she went."

Bill Hemmer: "Did the Vatican find alien life?"

Father Moore: "Ya know as sensationalistic as that question sounds it's really not that far off from what we've seen in the news over these last few days. The pictures of what might have been Pope Benedict standing on the roof The Sistine Chapel, looking for UFOs, that the type of images that this news conjures up. What is exceptional is that the Vatican was taking very seriously what science might tell us about the possibility of extraterrestrial intelligent lifeforms, that is what the conference was about. I can't tell you that the Vatican found any alien life, I don't think that is what they were looking for, but they were taking very seriously this issue."

Biller Hemmer: "You know the history just like we do, they've come a long way since Galileo four-five hundred years ago. What do you think it says about the church that it's actually looking at this issue?"

Father Moore: "What it says is that although there have been some inglorious moments of relationship of faith and science, the Vatican and not just Catholics, the Christians in general, they brought thirty of the best scientists, the astrobiologists, cosmologists, the astronomists to tell the philosophers, the theologians what they already know about the possibility of something that could happen.

Now what they are trying to do is to get out ahead of the story. To get out ahead and say, what if we were to find life outside of this planet? What does that tell us about the doctrine of original sin of Adam and Eve? Their point here is that we have to allow science to lead us in what is their field without going into it with an ideology like, we know that God doesn't exist."

Bill Hemmer: "That's a great point, now you as a Roman Catholic priest, you're open to science, so you say, is that correct?"

Father Moore: "Without a doubt, and not only open, but we have to respect science in its own field."

Bill Hemmer: "How would it change the churches teaching then? If you consider for a moment, if you determine there is an extraterrestrial life there."

Father Moore: "One thing that would be fascinating not only extraterrestrial life, but if it were extraterrestrial intelligent lifeforms, that would definitely make us go back and say, maybe our understanding of perennial truths needs to be updated."

Bill Hemmer: "I think that's an interesting explanation and I think also that if it were to be determined, that would be an earthquake, would it not?"

Father Moore: "It would be, and especially if the Vatican were involved in accepting that."[14]

Radio Broadcast

Art: "Hello, you are on the air."

"Hello Art?"

Art: "Yes"

"Hi, I don't have a whole lot of time...um..."

Art: "Well, look let's begin by finding out whether you're using this line properly or not."

"Area 51"

Art: "Yeah, that's right. Were you there an employee or are you there now?"

"I am a former employee"

Art: "Former employee"

"I was let go on a medical discharge about a week ago. And... and... (Sobbing). I've kinda been running across the country. I don't know where to start, they're gonna, they'll triangulate on this position really, really soon."

Art: "So, you can't spend a lot of time on the phone, so give us something quick!"

"Ok, ok, what we're thinking of as Aliens, Art, they're extra-dimensional beings that an earlier precursor of the space program contacted. They are not what they claim to be. They have infiltrated a lot of aspects of the military establishment. Particularly the Area 51. The disasters that are coming, the government knows about and there's a lot of safe areas in this world that they could begin moving the population to, now."

Art: "But they're not doing, they're not doing anything?"

"They are not! They want those major population centers wiped out so that the few that are left will be more easily controllable."

(Sobbing...) loosing transmission... loosing satellite... transmission lost.

Backup system now up and running.

Art: "In some way, something knocked us off the air and now we're on a backup system now."

Different caller: "The government or??"

Art: "I don't know."

"It has to be something though."

Art: "Well did you hear, now you tell me because you were listening."

"That was awful strange."

Art: "There was a really weird guy on the air when it went off?"

"Yeah…a real weirdo."

Art: "Sort of sounding paranoid schizophrenic."

"Yeah like crying and everything."

Art: "And how far into the conversation was it when it went off?"

"Just a couple, about fifteen or twenty seconds., I'd say."

Art: "Well, you guys really missed the call then and I got to say that somebody didn't want you to hear it."

"Cuz all of a sudden I'm hearing Mark Fermin or something."

Art: "The broadcast went immediately to a backup tape while we figured out what blew up here."

Art: The transmitter was cut off suddenly for some unknown reason. I've never seen it do this in all the years, all the years that we've been on the air, I've never seen the transmitter in this way just simply fail, like massively fail a massive heart attack."[15]

And then as if that wasn't enough, we are now being told that these events are occurring to prepare us for the emergence of a world leader. Can you say the anti-Christ and false prophet? Here's what the articles states.

"What do these phenomena mean? Who is creating them? What is their significance at this time of crisis and change? According to Benjamin Creme,

artist, author and lecturer, these are the many signs or miracles which herald the emergence into public life of Maitreya, the World Teacher.

According to Benjamin Creme's Master, the UFO in Jerusalem was one of the four 'stars' seen around the world since December 2008 that herald Maitreya's open emergence. Many now expect the return of their awaited Teacher, whether they call him the Christ, Messiah, the fifth Buddha, Krishna, Kalki Avatar or "the Imam Mahdi."

In fact, here's Benjamin Crème heralding this news to a press conference.

Benjamin Crème: "Many of us have been affected by the crisis happening in the world today but something wonderful is happening even as we speak. Everybody on Earth without exception is longing for, seeking, aiming for, consciously or subconsciously, for unity, a sense of unity."

What if cooperation could truly replace competition in every sphere of life. According to British author Benjamin Crème, Maitreya, a teacher of extraordinary stature is here in the world to inspire us to make the fundamental changes that will usher in an unprecedented golden age of brotherhood and justice.

Benjamin Crème: "This is indeed a unique time in the whole history of the world. So, we have to reassess the meaning about the purpose of life. The lead in this respect will be given by Maitreya himself. Maitreya and his group of apostles have created hundreds and hundreds of signs for humanity to show that something tremendous is afoot and these are known throughout the world as extraordinary, seemingly impossible happenings but happenings which happen.

The latest of these signs pointing to the herald of Maitreya is a new star-like object which has appeared all over the world. It looks like a star, only bigger and brighter and nearer, tremendous brilliance and changing color and moving but it appears as a star. When Jesus was born two thousand years ago, a star appeared in the heavens, which according to the Christian teachings guided three wise men from the east to Bethlehem, the holy land, where they followed it every day and it stopped over the birth place of Jesus.

That star which, the star of Bethlehem, it was a space craft sent by the spiritual hierarchy to guide the three wise men and act as a sign. This has been repeated today in which our spiritual hierarchy have arranged with our fellow humans in this solar system to have four such space craft, huge, enormous entities, which are posted throughout the world so that wherever you are you see a star, one star, which acts as described.

But what Maitreya really desires is an open discussion on the media worldwide about the star, what it is, because people don't know what it is, they see it, they report it, but it's an amazing object. Is it a UFO? Well in a sense it is a UFO, but it is a very specific one, it is the star and the first so called crop circles which have been created for years all over the world especially in the south of England.

These are created by our space brothers from the other planets but mainly of Mars and Venus and the first crop circle created this year, many weeks ahead of the date that they usually appear is this, if you can see it, a star, that's the photograph of the first crop circle. It was made by a spacecraft in a few seconds I suppose, as they all are, hundreds of meters long and is to remind us that need to know that this is the star, the herald of Maitreya, who is entering into public work.

What will Maitreya talk about on television? Obviously, he will talk about the need for peace, the need for justice in the world, but how do we get justice? Maitreya says there is only one way to achieve justice in the world, to see the world as one, brothers and sisters of one humanity and to share the resources of the world. Sharing is the key, only sharing will produce the trust needed to end war forever.

When we have sharing, we automatically have justice. When we have justice, we will have peace. Freedom, justice, sharing, and peace all go together, one comes out of the other, they're all part of the same divine plan for humanity. This is indeed a unique time in the whole history of the world."[16]

Now add to this deception the wild and otherworldly behavior of the Vatican and the Catholic Church. First, the Vatican has not only bought into the lie of evolution, but as mentioned in the earlier interview, right now they're in a desperate search for extraterrestrials and they are preparing themselves to be the official spokespeople for when the Aliens do land!

The Vatican and the Catholic Church are so serious about this that they have an actual entity called V.O.R.G. or the Vatican Observatory Research Group. This group has a couple of the world's most powerful telescopes on the top of Mt. Graham in Arizona looking for extraterrestrial life. One is called V.A.T.T. or the Vatican Advanced Technology Telescope and the other, they have one-quarter interest in, is called LUCIFER. It stands for Large Binocular Telescope Near-infrared Utility with Camera and Integral Field Unit for Extragalactic Research. It's the most powerful telescope in the world and is reported to get better images than the Hubble Telescope. It's also infrared so it can pick up things that other telescopes can't. And if that wasn't freaky enough, the highway that goes up to Mt. Graham used to be known as the Devil's Highway or 666. So, the question is, "Why in the world is the Vatican searching for extraterrestrial life?" Well, believe it or not, it's because they believe these so-called E. T's are going to be our new Savior and usher in peace to our planet. Here's their own words.

Father Gabriel Funes, Jesuit Priest and head of the Vatican Observatory, stated that, "Extraterrestrial life may not have experienced a 'fall', and may be 'free from Original Sin' and therefore remains in full friendship with their creator. This makes it possible to regard them as 'our brothers.' Therefore, if they're unfallen, they must be closer to God and have a better understanding of the Gospel and of the Godhead and of the nature of God.

In fact, Funes went on to say that he'd not only be willing to baptize an alien into the Catholic faith, but that "They [aliens] are coming here and they're going to baptize us into their faith and it is going to require us to make changes to our knowledge and understanding of the Gospel. Everything we think we know about the Gospel is going to have to be thrown out."

Another prominent Vatican astronomer, is Guy Consolmagno and he too not only says he would baptize an Alien but, "Only if they asked" and then qualified, "Any entity, no matter how many tentacles it has, has a soul." He then later says that, "These non-human forms are described in the Bible as "angels" and "very soon the nations of the world will look to Aliens for their salvation." "We fell, they didn't."

And what of those who resist? Father Gabriel Funes stated, "To not believe in the existence of Aliens and be willing to accept their morally superior dogma, that is going to be the true heresy of the future." In other words, you will be a new heretic if you are unwilling to accept this morally superior and new form of the Gospel.[18]

The Bible clearly warns us about turning to another Gospel, even if it's supposed to come from a so-called angel!

Galatians 1:8-9 "But even if we or an angel from heaven should preach a gospel other than the one we preached to you, let him be eternally condemned! As we have already said, so now I say again: If anybody is preaching to you a gospel other than what you accepted, let him be eternally condemned!"

Is any of this belief getting anywhere in the Vatican? Yes! Both Consolmagno and Funes have been leading advisors to Pope Francis about extraterrestrial life, and apparently their influence is working because Pope Francis just recently came out and said he'd be willing to baptize and alien as well as this news report shares.

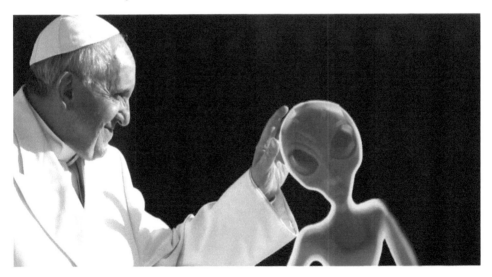

Pope Francis reiterated his view Monday that everyone has the right to be baptized and apparently that invite extends even to Martians. The Pontiff described the hypothetical situation during morning mass. According to Vatican radio Francis said, if for example, tomorrow an expedition of Martians came and some of them came to us and said I want to be baptized, what would happen? In other words, if God prompted the Martians to come to earth, find the Pope, and

say we want in on this Catholicism thing the Pope would probably say OK cool, but probably in Latin.[19]

The Vatican would also have you and I believe that Jesus is really a descendant of alien life and that Mary's virgin birth was actually a direct result of an alien abduction. They are calling Jesus a "star child" and that He was genetically engineered to save us at His First Coming and now the aliens are here again to save us from earth catastrophes coming as a kind of pseudo Second Coming, a Second Saving. This doctrine is called "many Christs" and that's exactly what the Real Jesus warned about in the last days!

Matthew 24:4-5 "Jesus answered: "Watch out that no one deceives you. For many will come in my name, claiming, 'I am the Christ,' and will deceive many.""

So just how close are we to this last days deception? Well, a Professor at the Vatican University, a Father Giuseppe Tanzella-Nitti, said, "Very soon there is information coming from another world, and once it is confirmed it is going to require a re-reading of the Gospel as we know it." And a Vatican spokesman Monsignor Corrado Baldacci said, "There is an Alien presence on earth now." It was reported that Pope Francis is, "Preparing a major world statement about extraterrestrial life and its theological implications and wants to be ready with a statement about 'First Contact.'" And Hollywood, of course, is helping us visualize how that would go.

From a movie:

The space ships have landed. The priest and his niece are watching. He says, "There are living creatures out there." She tries to tell him, "They're not human. Doctor Forester said they are some form of advanced civilization." He replies, "If they are more advanced than us they should be nearer the creator than us." As he ponders what is going on he says, "No real attempt has been made to communicate with them you know." While tugging at his arm she says, "Let's go back inside Uncle Matthew."

He turns to her and says, "I've done all I can, you go back." She turns to go back to the rest of the people watching the alien crafts. He turns to the alien ships and proceeds to walk towards them. He starts to recite "Though I walk through the valley of the shadow of death I will fear no evil," His niece is watching as he gets closer and closer.

As he walks they start coming towards him. She is screaming for him to stop and come back to safety but he doesn't heed her cries. He keeps walking, holding his Bible, and still repeating the Lord's Prayer. The ship sees him getting closer and closer when suddenly a blast comes out of the ship and disintegrates the priest into dust.

One researcher stated, "So what would happen someday if 'aliens' showed up and claimed that they seeded life on this planet, guided our evolution and are now here to lead us into a new golden age? And what would happen if the Catholic Church gave those aliens their stamp of approval?" Yes, I wonder what would happen but as bizarre at that sounds, this is exactly what is going on at the Vatican right now. Yet, they're not the only ones. Even former Presidents like Bill Clinton are getting in on this otherworldly deception. He appeared on the Jimmy Kimmel show and said basically, "When Aliens land on planet earth, it will bring peace to the planet!"

Jimmy Kimmel interviews Bill Clinton*:*

"President Bill Clinton is here with us. So, if I were President, and I won't be, let's be honest. The first thing I would do after putting my hand on that Bible and taking that oath to serve the country is, I probably wouldn't even finish the oath, I would run to the White House, I would demand to see all the classified files on UFO's. Because I would want to know what's been going on. Did you do that?"

The President replies "Sort of, I think it was at the beginning of my second term, we had the anniversary of Roswell."

Jimmy asks, "You waited that long?"

Then the President replies, "I did. Well, I did, and there's also Area 51. Do you remember there was a great sci-fi movie where there was an alien kept deep under the ground at Area 51? So first I had people go look at the records on Area 51 to make sure there was no alien down there. Then when the Roswell thing came up, I knew we'd get zillions of letters, so I had all the Roswell papers reviewed, everything."

Jimmy then asks, "If you saw that there were aliens would you tell us?"

President answers, "Yeah".

Jimmy asks, "You would?"

President says, "Yes I would, what do we know now. We live in an ever-expanding universe, we know that there are billions of stars and planets out there. So, it makes it increasingly less likely that we are alone."

Jimmy asks, "Oh, you're trying to give me a hint that there are aliens?"

President answers, "No, I'm trying to tell you I don't know, but if we were visited someday I wouldn't be surprised, I just hope it's not like the Independence Day movie, like a conflict. It may be the only way to unite this incredibly divided world of ours. If they're out there, we better think about all the differences among people on earth. They would seem small if we felt threatened by a space invader, that's the whole theory of Independence Day. Everybody gets together and makes nice."[20]

When, not if, Aliens land, it will unite the whole planet together and all our problems will go away. Everybody gets together and makes nice. The Aliens can save us! The Vatican and the Catholic Church, the Pope, Priests, Presidents, world leaders, individuals, news media and news outlets, and even Hollywood are all basically saying the same thing when it comes to UFO's and Aliens. It's almost like we're being prepared for something. I wonder what it is?

Chapter Six

The Bible & UFO's

Before we answer the question we just left off with, let me back up a little bit. As I share this with you, what you need to know is that I'm not only familiar with this topic on UFO's and Aliens now as a Christian, but as was stated in the preface, even before I became a Christian, I was well versed in this phenomenon. I've been to conferences talking about UFO abductions, I've read the books, many books on UFO's, I've had some strange encounters myself, and even talked with and interviewed various people having various encounters themselves. I share this not to toot my own horn, so to speak, but to share with you this point. It's only after becoming a Christian and reading the Bible that I began to see their true identity and what we are being prepared for. And folks, let me tell you, it's not a pretty picture. UFO's, I truly believe, are one of the most deceptive lies ever to hit this planet. As we shall see, they are clearly demonic in nature, as was alluded to in some of the historical sightings, yet so few, even Christians, have a clue of what's really going on, let alone what our world is headed for, and what these so-called space brothers have planned for our planet.

So let's begin to answer that question. "Just exactly what are we really being prepared for by all these sightings and accounts of UFO's and Aliens in our history and throughout the media? Are they benign entities or are **UFO's: The Great Last Days Deception**?" To answer that, let us know turn to the Bible and see what it has to say about this issue.

Believe it or not, Jesus Christ, out of love, clearly told us in the Bible exactly what was going to happen in the last days, which I personally believe we are in. And yet here's the irony. People have been trained to either scoff at the Bible and/or just flat out not even pick it up, so as to not discover the truth themselves, including the truth about UFO's and Aliens and who and what they really are. So, let's do our homework and see what Jesus said about the last days and hopefully answer the question, do UFO's play any part, specifically, in that time frame. First of all, speaking of those days, Jesus said flat out you don't want to be there. It was going to be the worst time in the history of mankind full of deceit, deceit, deceit. So much so that if God had not shortened the time frame, nobody on the planet would survive. It's a horrible time and you absolutely don't want to be thrust into that period of deception! Here's what He stated.

Matthew 24:3-11,21-27 "As Jesus was sitting on the Mount of Olives, the disciples came to him privately. "Tell us," they said, "when will this happen, and what will be the sign of your coming and of the end of the age?" Jesus answered: "Watch out that no one deceives you. For many will come in my name, claiming, 'I am the Christ,' and will deceive many. You will hear of wars and rumors of wars but see to it that you are not alarmed. Such things must happen, but the end is still to come. Nation will rise against nation, and kingdom against kingdom. There will be famines and earthquakes in various places. All these are the beginning of birth pains. Then you will be handed over to be persecuted and put to death, and you will be hated by all nations because of me. At that time many will turn away from the faith and will betray and hate each other, and many false prophets will appear and deceive many people. For then there will be great distress, unequaled from the beginning of the world until now – and never to be equaled again. If those days had not been cut short, no one would survive, but for the sake of the elect, those days will be shortened. At that time if anyone says to you, 'Look, here is the Christ!' or, 'There he is!' do not believe it. For false Christs and false prophets will appear and perform great signs and miracles to deceive even the elect – if that were possible. See, I have told you ahead of time. So, if anyone tells you, 'There he is, out in the desert,' do not go out; or, 'here he is, in the inner rooms,' do not believe it. For as lightning that comes from the east is visible even in the west, so will be the coming of the Son of Man."

Here we see, the very first thing out of Jesus' mouth to indicate when we are living in the last days, is that it is going to be a time that is characterized by not only deception, but great deception, massive lies, that we cannot even dream of. That's how cunning and deceiving they are. He said they're promoted by false prophets and false Christ's or messiahs, and that is exactly what these UFO occupants are doing and claiming to be, as we will see in just a little bit. But the point is this. The last days are such a time of great deception, such a powerful delusion, that it even comes close to deceiving the elect, if that were possible. That's how strong of a deception it is. Therefore, we're warned, according to Jesus, according to the Bible, that we need be on our guard so that no one deceives us. That's how big, that's how powerful these last days lies really are. We need to be on our guard, so we don't fall for it as well, even as a Christian. This is also what the Apostle Paul warned about elsewhere concerning this period of massive.

2 Thessalonians 2:1-4,8-12 "Concerning the coming of our Lord Jesus Christ and our being gathered to Him, we ask you, brothers, not to become easily unsettled or alarmed by some prophecy, report or letter supposed to have come from us, saying that the day of the Lord has already come. Don't let anyone deceive you in any way, for that day will not come until the rebellion occurs and the man of lawlessness is revealed, the man doomed to destruction. He will oppose and will exalt himself over everything that is called God or is worshiped, so that he sets himself up in God's temple, proclaiming himself to be God. And then the lawless one will be revealed, whom the Lord Jesus will overthrow with the breath of His mouth and destroy by the splendor of His coming. The coming of the lawless one will be in accordance with the work of satan displayed in all kinds of counterfeit miracles, signs and wonders, and in every sort of evil that deceives those who are perishing. They perish because they refused to love the truth and so be saved. For this reason, God sends them a powerful delusion so that they will believe the lie and so that all will be condemned who have not believed the truth but have delighted in wickedness."

So that's the question. What is this lie that the Apostle Paul is talking about here in the last days? What lie is so powerful that we are warned about it over and over again and it's so powerful that even the elect has the potential to be deceived by it? Well, believe it or not, many researchers believe this lie could very well be linked with the UFO phenomena that is occurring all across our planet and their appearance is going to play a major part in this last days deception mentioned here. This lie is so powerful, so seductive, that people will eventually do what it's designed to get them to do, to sign allegiance with and even worship the antichrist himself in the 7-year Tribulation. This, as we shall see in a moment, is just what so happens to be on the slick agenda of UFO's and Aliens. They are duping people into believing this last days lie so they will worship the antichrist and prepare them to enter into the 7-year Tribulation that will be the worse time in the history of mankind according to Jesus. This is why I unashamedly state that these entities are clearly demonic in origin. But let's not rest this on my own personal opinion. Let's now turn to the hardcore evidence and see why **UFO's** really are **The Great Last Days Deception** and you tell me, when you take a look at the facts presented here, that we're not dealing with a satanic agenda here.

Chapter Seven

The Lies of UFO's

The **1ˢᵗ reason** why UFO's are clearly demonic in origin is because **They Lie Like Demons**.

John 8:44 (Jesus speaking about the devil) "He was a murderer from the beginning, not holding to the truth, for there is no truth in him. When he lies, he speaks his native language, for he is a liar and the father of lies."

First of all, from a Christian perspective, we know that the whole belief in Aliens, a higher evolved race, is a lie because the Bible says Jesus died for humans on earth, not aliens from another world. The Bible also says that Jesus died one time on the earth, not several times for several planets, or different places across the universe. It's a completely unbiblical belief as this researcher points out.

"Are there extraterrestrial life-forms out there? The question of life on other planets is a hot topic in our culture today. Science fiction movies and television shows often depict strange creatures from far-away planets. But these ideas are not limited merely to science fiction programming. Many secular scientists believe that one day we will actually discover life on other planets. There are even projects like the Search for Extra-Terrestrial Intelligence (SETI) that scan the heavens with powerful radio telescopes listening for signals from intelligent aliens.

Many Christians have bought into the idea of extraterrestrial alien life. But is this idea really biblical? The Christian should constantly examine ideas in light of Scripture and take "every thought into captivity to the obedience of Christ" (2 Corinthians 10:5).

2 Corinthians 10:5 *"We demolish arguments and every pretension that sets itself up against the knowledge of God, and we take captive every thought to make it obedient to Christ."*

The idea of "extraterrestrial life" stems largely from a belief in evolution. Recall that in the evolutionary view, the earth is "just another planet"—one where the conditions just happened to be right for life to form and evolve. If there are countless billions of other planets in our galaxy, then surely at least a handful of these worlds have also had the right conditions. Extraterrestrial life is almost inevitable in an evolutionary worldview.

However, the notion of alien life does not square well with Scripture. The earth is unique. God designed the earth for life.

Isaiah 45:18 *"For this is what the Lord says, he who created the heavens, he is God; he who fashioned and made the earth, he founded it; he did not create it to be empty, but formed it to be inhabited, he says: "I am the Lord, and there is no other."*

The other planets have an entirely different purpose than does the earth, and thus, they are designed differently. In Genesis 1 we read that God created plants on the earth on Day 3, birds to fly in the atmosphere and marine life to swim in the ocean on Day 5, and animals to inhabit the land on Day 6.

Human beings were also made on Day 6 and were given dominion over the animals. But where does the Bible discuss the creation of life on the "lights in the expanse of the heavens"? There is no such description because the lights in the expanse were not designed to accommodate life.

God gave care of the earth to man, but the heavens are the Lord's. From a biblical perspective, extraterrestrial life does not seem reasonable.

Psalm 115:16 *"The highest heavens belong to the Lord, but the earth he has given to man."*

Problems are multiplied when we consider the possibility of intelligent alien life. Science fiction programming abounds with races of people who evolved on other worlds. We see examples of Vulcans and Klingons—pseudo humans similar to us in most respects but different in others.

As a plot device, these races allow the exploration of the human condition from the perspective of an outsider. Although very entertaining, such alien races are theologically problematic. Intelligent alien beings cannot be redeemed. God's plan of redemption is for human beings: those descended from Adam. Let us examine the conflict between the salvation message and the notion of alien life.

The Bible teaches that the first man, Adam, rebelled against God (**Genesis 3**). As a result, sin and death entered the world.

Romans 5:12 *"Therefore, just as sin entered the world through one man, and death through sin, and in this way, death came to all men, because all sinned."*

We are all descended from Adam and Eve (**Genesis 3:20**) and have inherited from them a sin nature (**Romans 6:6, 20**). This is a problem: sin is a barrier that prevents man from being right with God (**Isaiah 59:2**). But God loves us despite our sin and provided a plan of redemption—a way to be reconciled with God.

After Adam and Eve sinned, God made coats of skins to cover them (**Genesis 3:21**). He therefore had to kill at least one animal. This literal action is symbolic of our salvation; an innocent Lamb (Christ—the Lamb of God) would be sacrificed to provide a covering for sin (**John 1:29**). In the Old Testament, people would sacrifice animals to the Lord as a reminder of their sin (**Hebrews 10:3**) and as a symbol of the One to come, the Lord Jesus, who would actually pay the penalty for sin.

The animal sacrifices did not actually pay the penalty for sin (**Hebrews 10:4, 11**). Animals are not related to us; their shed blood cannot count for ours. But the blood of Christ can. Christ is a blood relative of ours since He is descended from Adam as are we; all human beings are of "one blood."

Acts 17:26 *"From one man he made every nation of men, that they should inhabit the whole earth; and he determined the times set for them and the exact places where they should live."*

*Furthermore, since Christ is also God, His life is of infinite value, and thus, His death can pay for all the sins of all people. That is why only the Lord Himself could be our Savior (**Isaiah 45:21**). Therefore, Christ died once for all (**Hebrews 10:10**).*

When we consider how the salvation plan might apply to any hypothetical extraterrestrial (but otherwise human-like) beings, we are presented with a problem. If there were Vulcans or Klingons out there, how would they be saved?

*They are not blood relatives of Jesus, and so Christ's shed blood cannot pay for their sin. One might at first suppose that Christ also visited their world, lived there, and died there as well, but this is antibiblical. Christ died once for all (**1 Peter 3:18; Hebrews 9:27–28, Hebrews 10:10**). Jesus is now and forever both God and man; but He is not an alien.*

*One might suppose that alien beings have never sinned, in which case they would not need to be redeemed. But then another problem emerges: they suffer the effects of sin, despite having never sinned. Adam's sin has affected all of creation— not just mankind. **Romans 8:20–22** makes it clear that the entirety of creation suffers under the bondage of corruption. These kinds of issues highlight the problem of attempting to incorporate an antibiblical notion into the Christian worldview.*

Extraterrestrial life is an evolutionary concept; it does not comport with the biblical teachings of the uniqueness of the earth and the distinct spiritual position of human beings. Of all the worlds in the universe, it was the earth that God Himself visited, taking on the additional nature of a human being, dying on a cross, and rising from the dead in order to redeem all who would trust in Him.

The biblical worldview sharply contrasts with the secular worldview when it comes to alien life. So, which worldview does the scientific evidence support? Do modern observations support the secular notion that the universe is teeming with life, or the biblical notion that earth is unique?

So far, no one has discovered life on other planets or detected any radio signals from intelligent aliens. This is certainly what a biblical creationist would expect. Secular astronomers continue to search for life on other worlds, but they have found only rocks and inanimate matter. Their radio searches are met with silence. The real world is the biblical world—a universe designed by God with the earth at the spiritual focal point, not an evolutionary universe teeming with life.

When it comes to extraterrestrial life, science is diametrically opposed to the evolutionary mentality. We currently have no evidence of alien life-forms. This problem is not lost on the secular scientists. It has been said that the atomic scientist Enrico Fermi was once discussing the topic of extraterrestrial life when he asked the profound question, "Where is everybody?"

Since there are quite possibly multiple billions of planets in our galaxy, and since in the secular view these are all accidents, it is almost inevitable that some of these had the right conditions for life to evolve. And if some of these worlds are billions of years older than ours, then at least some of them would have evolved intelligent life eons ago.

The universe should therefore have countless numbers of technologically superior civilizations, any one of which could have colonized our galaxy ages ago. Yet, we find no evidence of these civilizations. Where is everybody? This problem has become known as the "Fermi paradox."

This paradox for evolution is a feature of creation. We have seen that the earth is designed for life. With its oceans of liquid water, a protective atmosphere containing abundant free oxygen, and a distance from the sun that is just right for life, earth was certainly designed by God to be inhabited. But the other planets of the universe were not. From the sulfuric acid clouds of Venus to the frozen wasteland of Pluto, the other worlds of our solar system are beautiful and diverse, but they are not designed for life.

*In a way, a belief in extraterrestrial life has become a secular replacement for God. God is the one who can heal every disease. God is the one in whom all the treasures of wisdom and knowledge are deposited (**Colossians 2:3**). God is the one who can answer the fundamental questions of our existence. God alone possesses the gift of eternal life (**John 17:3**). It is not surprising that the unbelieving scientist would feel a sense of cosmic loneliness, having rejected his Creator.*

But we are not alone in the universe; there is God. God created us for fellowship with Him; thus, we have an innate need for Him and for purpose. Although human beings have rejected God, in Adam and by our sins as well, our need for fellowship with Him remains.

*When I think of the majority of intelligent scientists who have studied God's magnificent creation but have nonetheless rejected Him and have instead chosen to believe in aliens and millions of years of evolution, I am reminded of **Romans 1:18–25**. God's invisible qualities—His eternal power and divine nature—are clearly revealed in the natural world so that there is no excuse for rejecting God or suppressing the truth about Him. The thinking of man apart from God is nothing more than futile speculations.*

Exchanging the truth of God, such as creation, for a lie, such as evolution, and turning to a mere creature such as hypothetical aliens for answers is strikingly similar to what is recorded in

Romans 1:25 *"They exchanged the truth of God for a lie and worshiped and served created things rather than the Creator, who is forever praised. Amen."*

But when we start from the Bible, the evidence makes sense. The universe is consistent with the biblical teaching that the earth is a special creation. The magnificent beauty and size of a universe, which is apparently devoid of life except for one little world where life abounds, is exactly what we would expect from a biblical worldview.

The truth is not "out there;" the truth is in there—in the Bible! The Lord Jesus is the truth. So, when we base our thinking on what God has said in His Word, we find that the universe makes sense."[1]

John 14:6 *"Jesus answered, 'I am the way and the truth and the life. No one comes to the Father except through me.'*

But even if you didn't want to look at the lie of Aliens and UFO's from a Christian perspective at this point, consider this, the whole belief of UFO's and aliens is all based on another lie called evolution. Think about it. The whole premise of aliens is that they're a higher evolved race, right? But wait a second, logically, if evolution is not true, and it's not, then how can these things have ever evolved into a higher race in the first place? And for those of you who don't realize just how big of a lie evolution really is, let me just give you a little teaser of some good ol' fashioned common sense and logic when it comes to this so-called belief system that is supposed to be based on mathematics, science and hard facts. It's not! Let's look at the impossible odds of evolution that takes place.

Logic of the Honey Bee:

Evolutionists believe that all of life evolved purely by chance with no outside help, including a tiny little seemingly simple honeybee. Well, let's observe this belief logically by comparing the tiny little brain of a honeybee to NASA's huge Cray computer, which by the way was built and designed by a team of engineers.

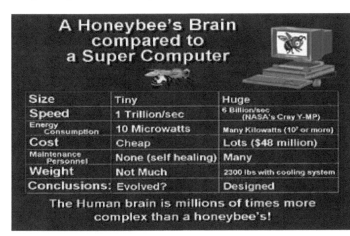

A Honeybee's Brain compared to a Super Computer		
Size	Tiny	Huge
Speed	1 Trillion/sec	6 Billion/sec (NASA's Cray Y-MP)
Energy Consumption	10 Microwatts	Many Kilowatts (10^7 or more)
Cost	Cheap	Lots ($48 million)
Maintenance Personnel	None (self healing)	Many
Weight	Not Much	2300 lbs with cooling system
Conclusions:	Evolved?	Designed

The Human brain is millions of times more complex than a honeybee's!

First, there's the size. The Cray computer is huge while the honeybee's brain is obviously tiny by comparison. Next, there's the speed. The Cray computer can process six billion calculations per second and granted that's pretty fast, but the brain of the honeybee can do about a thousand billion per second, which means that it's brain is about 166 times faster than a Cray computer.

A honeybee can fly one million miles on one gallon of honey!

Then there's the energy consumption. The Cray uses many kilowatts, but the honeybee only uses 10 microwatts. That's pretty efficient, wouldn't you say? In fact, honeybees not only make honey, they fly on honey. That's their energy source. And a honeybee can fly a million miles on one gallon of honey. Let's see you invent a machine that gets a million miles per gallon. Our Heavenly Father did! He's pretty smart, isn't He?

Next, we have the cost. The Cray computer costs 48 million dollars but the honeybee's brain is pretty cheap. We splat them on our windshields all the time. Then we have the maintenance issue. Many people have to scramble when the Cray breaks down, but nobody fixes the honeybee's brain. He heals himself. Let's see you invent a computer that fixes its own problems and replaces its own hard drive when it needs it. Pretty amazing isn't it? Then we have the weight.

Obviously, the honeybee doesn't weigh much and thus its brain weighs even less. But the Cray computer weighs 2,300 pounds. So, what's the logical conclusion of this comparison? The Cray computer is huge, it's slow, it's inefficient, it costs a lot of money, you have to baby sit the dumb thing, and it was designed. There isn't anybody with half a brain that would say, "The Cray computer came from an explosion in an electronics factory," would they? And yet we have the honeybee's brain which is faster, more efficient, energy efficient, cheap, and evolutionists say it evolved. I don't think so![2]

Logic of Mt. Rushmore:

Now let us apply some logical questions to the formation of the world's largest rock group, on Mount Rushmore. Ask any evolutionist these logical questions. "Do you believe that there is any way these faces of Washington, Jefferson, Theodore Roosevelt, and Lincoln could have appeared on this rock by chance? Do you think the wind did that? Or do you think erosion did it? Or how about exfoliation? Or what about thermal expansion of the rock?" If you ask them what caused those faces to appear on Mount Rushmore, they would obviously say that they were designed by someone. And of course, they were, by an artist named Gutzon Borglum. But then ask them this question, "Do you believe that the men represented here happened by chance?" If they believed in evolution, they would have to say "yes." And then say, "Now, wait a minute, you don't think that their face could appear on a rock by chance, but you do think that their whole complex anatomy, with 50 trillion cells, could happen by chance?"

And then ask them, "How many years would it take for these figures to appear on the side of this mountain by chance? Millions of years? Billions of years? Given 100 trillion years, could these figures eventually form on the side of the mountain?" Obviously, the evolutionist would say it's impossible no matter how much time you give it. But then ask them. "But isn't that how you say we got here after billions of years of chance, even though we're incredibly more complex than the faces on Mount Rushmore?"

So, the logical conclusion is that just the faces on Mount Rushmore had to be designed, how much more then was the human body designed?

And speaking of rock heads, while evolutionists will refrain from saying that the faces carved on the rock of Mount Rushmore happened by chance, they really do believe we all came from a rock. Don't believe me? I like what one guy said in response to the scoffer of the Bible who mockingly said, "Oh yeah, if evolution isn't true, you mean to tell me that the Bible's account is true? That all the dogs in the world came from two dogs on Noah's ark?" Let's listen to his response.[3]

Researcher: "I was asked to preach at this college in Boston one time and this preacher called all colleges and universities around Boston. I got my charts out and said, 'now folks I believe the Bible', nobody cared. I said, 'I believe about 6,000 years ago God made everything, the earth is not millions of years old and 2,000 years ago Jesus came'. I gave them the basic Bible story.

Then I told them what they believe, because most of them don't know what they believe. You have to tell them. 'You guys believe that 20 billion years ago, there was a big bang, where nothing exploded and that explains everything, 4.6 billion years ago the earth cooled down, made a hard-rocky crust, it rained on the rocks

"4.6 billion years ago earth cooled down and formed a rocky crust."

for millions of years turned them into soup and the soup came alive, three billion years ago. And this early life form found somebody to marry, boy now that's a good trick, and something to eat of course and slowly they evolved and everything is here today'.

One of the professors got upset about this time, I seem to do that to them. He said, "There are hundreds of varieties of dogs in the world." I said, "Yes sir, you're right about that." He said, "Do you mean to tell me that all these dogs came from two dogs off Noah's ark? Do you believe that, ha ha ha?"

I said, "Sir, would you look at what you are teaching your students. You're teaching your students that all the dogs in the world came from a rock."

I had one lady come to me after a debate one time, she was steaming down the aisle, boy she was mad. I could tell, I'm in trouble now. I stood there quivering in my boots, you know.

She walked up, and she said, "You know, tonight you said that we came from a rock. We do not believe that." I said, "Calm down for just a minute." I said, "Do you believe in evolution?" She said, "Yes I do, I'm a professor here at the university." I asked her, "Well, can you tell me where we came from?" She said, "We came from a macromolecule."

I said, "Where did that come from?" She said, "From the ocean, from the prebiotic soup." I said, "Where did that come from?" She said, "It rained on the rocks for millions of years…" And you could see it was slowly dawning on her.

"I do believe we came from a rock, don't I?" I said, "Yes, you do. Hey, be careful, whatever you do, don't step on grandpa, whatever you do.[4]

Odds of Single Protein:

Now let us journey even further in the land of common sense. It has been calculated that any event with a value of 1 in 10 to the 50th power will never occur by chance. If it did, it would be a miracle. So, now that we know the threshold of an event being mathematically impossible, let's look at the odds of a single protein ever coming into being. World famous astronomer, Sir Frederick Hoyle, decided to calculate the probability of a single bacterium coming into existence by chance from some sort of primordial soup. Prior to this project Hoyle was a firm believer in the spontaneous generation of life but after this project, he changed his opinion 180 degrees. He calculated that the probability of the spontaneous generation of just the proteins of a single amoebae was 1 chance in 10 to the $40,000^{th}$ power. Now remember, any probability greater than 1 in 10 to the 50th power is mathematically impossible. That is, it can never occur unless by a miracle. Therefore, thinking that just even the proteins of a single amoebae let alone the amoebae itself spontaneously generating itself is absolutely ridiculous.

In fact, it has been said that this kind of thinking is about as reasonable as if you were to say that given enough "time" and "chance" that a Scrabble factory could explode enough times, until the letters eventually land to perfectly spell out the book "War and Peace." Or, that a tornado can whip through a junkyard leaving behind a perfectly formed Boeing 747. In fact, if you do the math, the odds of a person winning a state lottery every single week of their life from age 18 to age 99, is more likely than the spontaneous generation of just the proteins of a single amoebae! That's why Sir Frederick Hoyle concluded after his research that, "The likelihood of the formation of life from inanimate matter is one to a number with 40 thousand zeros after it. That is enough to bury Darwin and the whole theory of evolution. There was no primeval soup neither on this planet nor on any other. If the beginnings of life were not random they must therefore have been the product of purposeful intelligence."[5]

Odds of Single Bacteria:

Sill not enough? So far, we've seen the odds of the so-called spontaneous generation of just proteins. But this does not take into consideration the so-called "chance formation" of DNA, RNA or the cell wall that holds the contents of the cell together! Believe it or not, a Yale University physicist named Harold Morowitz has calculated the odds of this. He demonstrated that the "chances" of single bacteria somehow "coming to life" is 1 in 10 to the $100,000,000,000^{th}$ power! And remember, any probability greater than 1 in 10 to the 50th power is mathematically impossible! That number is so big that it would require several hundred thousand blank books just to write the zeros of that number out! Not just you, but you and your entire extended family are more likely to win the lottery every week for 100 years than it is for single bacteria to form by chance! And keep in mind that our bodies have an estimated 50 trillion cells which all have to be in existence all at the same time and all have to work properly at the same time in order for life to function. And this is just one human body. If you want to procreate then you need two human bodies at the same time, one male and one female, and of course they have to be interested in each other. And we all know it's hard enough just to get married! And it was these mind-boggling odds that led Robert Cheaper to conclude this.

"The improbability involved in generating even one bacterium is so large that it reduces all considerations of time and space to nothingness. Given such odds, the time until the black holes evaporate and the space to the ends of the universe would make no difference at all. If we were to wait, we would truly be waiting for a miracle."[6]

I'm telling you, this is the tip of the iceberg! We have 42 DVD's and 5 companion books in our ministry exposing just the lie of evolution and we don't copyright them and you can give them out as much as you'd like. We do this with all our media including what you are reading today. We deal with the topic of Intelligent Design in our study called, "**An Intelligent Design**" which shows that all of creation implies an Intelligent Designer, namely God. Then we expose the myth of our being here for millions and billions of years as evolution would have you believe, and we cover that lie in the study called, "**A Young Earth**." Then we play a game and ignore all the evidence of an Intelligent Design which implies a Designer and we give the evolutionist all the time in the world they need for something to so-call evolve, and we put it to the test. Does evolution and its various mechanisms even work? No! It not only doesn't work, but we actually quote the evidence from the evolutionists themselves who admit that it is a lie, that it doesn't work, and they know it doesn't work, but they continue to promote it because they don't want to give credence to the Bible. We cover that in our study called, "**A Special Creation: Exposing the Lies of Evolution**." Then we provide geological, archaeological, and even scientific evidence that the Flood of

Noah really did happen including the discovery of a highly advanced technological society just like the Bible talks about in the study called "**In the Days of Noah: Giants, Ancient Technology, and Noah's Ark**." And what's amazing is people find this incredible technology buried in the dirt and say, "Well, it must have been from UFO's! This incredible technology. It was aliens that left it here." No, the Bible says it is the left over remains from the pre-flood world, Noah's society, that was super intelligent, and they had the ability to do things that we can't even come close to duplicating today. It has nothing to do with UFO's, but they have to come up with anything they can think of just to discount the Biblical account in the Bible. And finally, we deal with the big topic of dinosaurs and the Bible. What really happened to the dinosaurs and what in the world are human remains doing mixed in with dinosaur remains? We deal with that and much more in our study called, "**The Truth about Dinosaurs**."

So, here's the point. All these studies clearly expose the lie of evolution, even more then what you just read, which should lead to the logical conclusion. If evolution can't take place on this planet, then it cannot take place on any planet. And if evolution can't happen here, then logically, it cannot happen anywhere. Which means the whole premise of higher evolved aliens coming here from across the universe is also a lie. In fact, it's such an obvious lie that even the secular Ufologists admit it.

News reporters are all gathered for the questions and answers.

Interviewer: "Describe what they look like."

Sgt. Clifford Stone: "I could but it would probably take a whole lot of time. The reason I state that is when I got out in 1989 we had cataloged 57 different species.

You have individuals that look very much like you and myself, that walk among us, and you wouldn't even notice the difference except for some of the things that, they might be able to go ahead, even in the dark room and touch an object and identify what color that object might be.

They would have a heightened sense of smell, sight, of hearing, of the situation is that you have several types of what we normally call greys, there are at least three types of greys. There are some that are much taller than we are. The unique thing that I would like to point out is the ones we did catalog were in fact humanoid.

This created a situation for the scientific community, they were trying to figure out why this would be the case, because if you thought life evolved with other planets that they would take on some type of other beings so to speak. Not necessarily look humanoid or like us, but apparently, we have quite a few species out there that are humanoid in appearance and that creates a question that has yet to be answered by science.[7]

Yes, that's a very good point. If evolution is true, then why are all these alien creature humanoids just like us? You would think, if it's supposed to be random, we'd get some blob or some random shape once in a while, if evolution is true, and that is where all of life came from and is based on some random chance event. But no! That's not what we get. Sounds pretty fishy to me!

But when you think about this, it starts to make you realize just how deceptive, just how seductive this lie in the last days really is concerning UFO's. When you put all the facts together you actually need the lie of evolution first in order to pull off this lie of aliens today. Which means, slowly, methodically, we have been conditioned to buy into the lie of evolution first, about 150 years ago with Charles Darwin. That's how long this thing has been in the works and now we're seeing the fruition of it in our days.

If you recall, in the section we already read, 'History of the UFO' sightings, these so-called encounters, and occurrences really began to take off when? In the late 40's and throughout the 60's and that just so happens when evolution began to make its entryway into our minds at least here in America. That is when it became more and more dominant in our country. If you put all this together, the timing, I don't think it's by chance, it's impeccable! First get us to buy into the lie of evolution so that eventually, once that's ingrained into our brains, then that's the ultimate set-up then you're set up for lie #2, the lie of UFO's. Do you get it? In fact, it's a lie that's been custom tailored for our last days technological society. One researcher, Dr. Walter Martin states about this technological lie in the last days.

Dr. Walter Martin , *"The big problem is not what they are but who they are. The key to it is their theology. They're all saying the same thing, and all of it is bad-mouthing the Bible. This tells me that what the Bible says was going to take place is taking place.*

What you're dealing with is another dimension of reality which the Bible frequently mentions. It's called 'the realm of the prince of the powers of the air'. In other words, this is a supernatural manifestation which Christianity calls demonic."

"Look," Martin says, "I don't think that there's a devil behind every bush and tree. I'm just saying, what would we expect at the end of the age in our advanced culture? We would expect a manifestation that would fit into our time frame. What better way to attract us than with intergalactic visitors? We're obsessed with them!"[8]

And boy is he right, thanks in large part to the media. You know, like in Star Wars or Star Trek that tells us we're evolving into higher intelligent beings and can explore other galaxies and encounter other higher evolved beings as we travel through space. Yet, if nothing can evolve, and it can't, it's a lie, then this whole identity of UFO's being occupied by evolving aliens is a lie, a fantasy just like Star Wars and just like Star Trek. Therefore, this tells us that we are dealing with something deceptive here. We're dealing with something that is lying to us and that is completely characteristic of demons, because that's what demons do! They lie! And satan, the Bible says, is the father of all lies!

Chapter Eight

The False Teachings of UFO's

The **2ⁿᵈ reason** why UFO's are clearly demonic in origin is because they not only lie but they **Teach Like Demons**. So let's now take a look at what they teach and discover who their source is. They supposedly come from the edge of the universe and what are they doing here? They promote Occult/New Age teachings and debunk true evangelical Christianity. Sounds kind of fishy to me. In fact, it sounds like something a demon would teach. And that's exactly what this researcher had to say as well.

John Ankerberg *"In light of the messages given by the UFO entities, how credible is it to think that literally thousands of genuine extra-terrestrials would fly millions or billions of light years simply to teach New Age philosophy, deny Christianity, and support the occult?*

Why would they do this with the preponderance of such activity already occurring on this planet? And why would the entities actually possess and inhabit people just like demons do if they were really advanced extra-terrestrials? Why would they consistently lie about things which we know are true, and why would they purposely deceive their contacts?"[1]

Good question, that sounds like what a demon would do. Teach lying stuff just like that. But that's just the tip of the iceberg. Let's now observe some of their other lying messages, the things they teach, and you tell me if it's not demonic as well.

Lie #1: All of us are little gods. God and man or the creation are part of the same divine essence. Or in other words, old-fashioned pantheism. Yet the Bible says there is only one God, not many. Here's a transcript of a various people channeling these entities who are speaking through them teaching this blaspheous lie that we are all gods.

"Some channeled entity, some Christ, some priest, some preacher, some deity, some prophet is our redeemer that excuses us from living life, we have missed the message.

Why don't we learn to think on our own and find new benefactors for that greatness? Genius you know is not mediocracy, it's not predictable, is not funded, it's not hired, it's that which can dream beyond the paradise. You have the ability to be a genius. Did you know that every dream that you dream should never be put aside as imagination? Every dream is the next step of your evolution.

The one that gives us permission first tells us, 'you are god, so let's get about learning how to be that'. Religion is no longer sacred. Everyone questions the church. They should. Everyone questions the meaning of life. And everyone questions the direction that science is taking and when you do that it's the age of enlightenment.

You cannot have, enlightenment does not come on the heels of the black plague. No, that is not enlightenment. Enlightenment comes on the heels of plenty. Because only when you are gluttonous to everything and question everything, you are right to know what you have never known.

So, forget about the past and live today on the wisdom and the virtue of what you gain. You don't have to feel guilty about your life any more. I would love for someone to stand up and say, God doesn't live outside of you, God is you.

While J.Z. Knight is among the more successful mediums she is certainly not alone. A nearly identical doctrine is preached from a series of channelers that believe that they are in communication with extraterrestrial spirits from other planets and galaxies.

In the documentary UFO's and Channeling the late actor Telly Savalas reveals that the purpose of channeling these alien entities is entirely consistent with the New Thought, New Age Movement, to change the thinking of mankind.

Telly Savalas: *"Tonight we are going to show you some film that will change the way you think about life."*

Next, we are introduced to a woman who channels a spirit who calls itself, Leah.

Leah: "Good afternoon, Phillip, how are you today?"

Phillip: "Very good, how are you?"

Leah: "Fine, thank you, so, what is it you wanted to know?"

Phillip: "Where are you from?"

Leah: "I am from Venus."

Phillip: "I don't think anyone is going to believe that you or anybody else could be from Venus. Can you explain to us how you could be when everybody knows it is uninhabitable?"

Leah: "They think it is uninhabitable because it is not inhabitable by any physical life forms, we have bodies of light."

While Leah rambles on about fantastical ideas she soon compels the audience with global unity, a message found throughout the New Age Movement.

Leah: "And what occurs here, on this planet, will affect the rest of the universe. Can you, with all of your different ideas, and your different races, come together as one planet and one people? We have dedicated millennia upon millennia to this idea. The earlier experiments with Penh and Lemuria and Atlantis were not successful but this one will be."

Now the interviewer asked the woman to exchange spirits and to channel another spirit that calls itself the Tibetan. Tibet is an often referred to hotspot for new age empowerment. Hitler's Nazi occultist went to Tibet thinking to find their ancient Aryan ancestors. Listen carefully to the Tibetans message as he refers to the great I am, the name God reveals in in the Bible to describe himself.

The Tibetan: "I am the Tibetan and I come during this time continuing to discuss with you the idea of the only question in the universe and that question is what the answer is, I am. For all things that are created, that were created, and what shall be created, fall under the question what is, you and each and every one of you are that answer, and that answer is, I am. I am, is also the name of the creator of this universe. That is all I relinquish control to the entity Leah."

As the entity Leah returns she confirms that you are God message and refers to the new race that will arise through the New Age Movement. Most new agers today do not realize that this new race is identical to the master race prophesied by Adolf Hitler, a race of so-called supermen who will be their own gods, having rejected the one true God of the Bible.

Leah: "This New Age Movement is where there will be a race on the planet and throughout all galaxies and the name of that race will be peace. It's been wonderful spending some time with you. As you take this little piece of information with you, know that you are never alone. You are all connected to the creative source of this universe and nothing can stop that flow except your denial that you are God. We thank you, good day."

Another man channels the spirit calling itself Bashar who seems to hold his audience spellbound as he tells them they are equal to the creator of the universe.

Bashar: "That we are all made in the image of the infinite creator and what that means is you are all infinite creators, we find you."

Jack Pursel has become one of the more popular channels possessed by a spirit named Lazaris.

Lazaris: "It is indeed a pleasure to be talking with you, shall we begin where you'd like to begin."

Lazaris tells the listener that God is already within man and that if man wants to find God he needs only to find himself.

Lazaris: "Now the problem is the people look out there. They're looking all over the place as if their God was somehow tired of them. It's with every spiritual reference, be it fundamental or be our own God, speaks of that spirit within and it would suggest that it's therefore your task in this physical life time really isn't to find God because God's everywhere, He's God is all it is, everything, all over the place. Your task in any physical incarnation is to find yourself."[2]

Jane Roberts was a new-age pioneer who channeled a spirit known as Seth. Roberts sold more than a million copies of her books and inspired many in this vocal recording. We hear her channel the spirit of Seth.

Seth: "I've seen these many times, I say it a million times, here in this class and in my book, you form your reality, then what is the YOU that forms this spectacular reality that you know? When will you be willing to admit the greatness that is within each of you, and not cower? And not say in this realm of reality: it is not possible? But encounter the greatness within yourselves."

Rick Stack, Teacher of "Seth" philosophy: "Clearly the main message that Seth is trying to say is people are gods in training."

Some may find it interesting that the name Seth is synonymous with the Egyptian god Seth Megszolal and in the realm of the occult Seth Megszolal is one of the infernal names of satan.[3]

But not only that, what's also very interesting is that this desire to be like God was what caused the very fall of satan.

Isaiah 14:12-15 "How you have fallen from heaven, O morning star, son of the dawn! You have been cast down to the earth, you who once laid low the nations! You said in your heart, 'I will ascend to heaven; I will raise my throne above the stars of God; I will sit enthroned on the mount of assembly, on the utmost heights of the sacred mountain. I will ascend above the tops of the clouds; I will make myself like the Most High. But you are brought down to the grave, to the depths of the pit.'"

And that's precisely why the Bible is very emphatic that there is only one God, not many.

Deuteronomy 4:35 "You were shown these things so that you might know that the LORD is God; besides Him there is no other."

Deuteronomy 4:39 "Acknowledge and take to heart this day that the LORD is God in heaven above and on the earth below. There is no other."

1 Kings 8:60 "So that all the peoples of the earth may know that the LORD is God and that there is no other."

Isaiah 44:8 "Did I not proclaim this and foretell it long ago? You are my witnesses. Is there any God besides me? No, there is no other Rock; I know not one."

Isaiah 45:5 "I am the LORD, and there is no other; apart from me there is no God."

But hey, it's a good thing that nobody's falling for this obvious lie. Actually, the lie is spreading fast, to almost all corners of society.

Environmentalism "The philosophy of environmentalism is based in the religious belief of pantheism, that god is in all and all is god; that earth is our mother (Gaia); that all living things have equal value and that mankind has overstepped its bounds, even being a cancer on the rest of nature. As ardent environmentalist, Al Gore states, "God is not separate from the Earth."

Hinduism says that all is god. "Hinduism worships multiple deities: gods and goddesses and that all reality is a unity. The entire universe (including you and me) is seen as one divine entity just in different facets, forms, or manifestations, and is worthy of worship, as seen in the following excerpt.

As an old white-haired man, is walking down the street in what looks like the crowded streets in India he is telling us, "Guru is our best friend, philosopher and guide and he shows the way to God. So, we in our India acknowledge him as a divine power just equivalent to God."

Male Follower: "If anyone could be near the beloved master and witness the love, the passion, the humility, the peace, the generosity, no one in his right mind would not know that this is a walking, talking, living god on earth."

Female Follower: "In our scriptures you will find that the master is the god incarnate power working on earth."

Male Follower: "You people that interviewed this gentleman today, I don't think you know who you interviewed, you interviewed god."[4]

Mormons even say you can become a god. "After you become a good Mormon, you have the potential of becoming a god. Then shall they be gods, because they have no end; therefore, they shall be from everlasting to everlasting, because they continue; ten shall they be above all, because all things are subject unto them. Then shall they be gods."[5]

So-called **spirit guides** say we are god. "Feel the millions of souls; the divine spark within each of them. We are here in your moment of realization in the moment you come to meet with your divinity; in the moment when you finally accept that which you truly are."

Even supposed messages from the **Virgin Mary** say we're god. "God is all that is. Therefore, we are prime creator expressing itself as us. We are not striving for perfection as we are already perfect. What we are striving for is to remember our perfection. We are not divided into parts. Since God is us, therefore, we are God."

Messages from the **angels** say we're god. "It is nice to come and break bread, the bread of truth. God gives all of His creation freedom of choice to find themselves. To find their true ancestry of God-Goddess within them."

And finally, **New Ager's** say we are god. One of the most ardent New Ager's, Shirley Maclaine, not only says she's god but she even made a movie encouraging everybody to do the same.

Actress Shirley Maclaine was Time Magazine's poster girl for the New Age movement in the 1980's. Maclaine starred in the biographical mini-series 'Out on a Limb' based on her journey into New Age belief. The series has been called the "most talked about mini-series of all time." The title 'Out on a Limb' refers to the risk involved in seeking the fruit of the tree of knowledge. In the mini-series she is being told, "Mayan told me to tell you one thing if you had a hard time with this, she said in order to get to the fruit of the tree you have to go out on the limb."

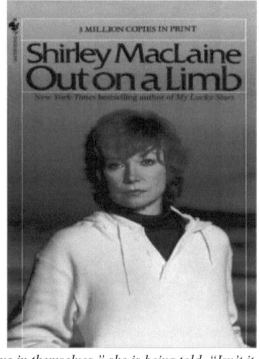

Mayan is a spirit guide sending a message to Maclaine, a message that is repeated throughout the series.

Here is a clip from that series:

"It's like saying that they don't believe in themselves," she is being told. "Isn't it hard to love somebody that doesn't love himself?" "Yeah," she answers, "It's like they don't know who they are, you know, I mean if you don't know who you are you can't love yourself."

He asks her, "Don't you ever get frustrated when you feel like you're not really being yourself?" She answers, "Yes, all the time." He then tells her, "That's what all the masters have tried to help us with." "What masters?" she asked. "You know, Christ, Buddha, the Indian avatars, they are really just master politicians who went right to the root of the problems in society, the individual.

Some of them said that if everybody believed that he was a part of God and the kingdom of heaven was within and if we took responsibility for that we wouldn't get so frustrated with ourselves, with ourselves or anybody else. But it seems like it takes multiple lifetimes to come to that simple realization." She replies, "That's mind boggling, David, I mean when you think of what that really means."

He asks her, "You want to know a good exercise that helps you get in touch with the realization that we each have inside of us?" "Exercise?" she asks. "Here's what you do. Just stand up, hold your arms out like this, and say the kingdom of heaven is within. I love myself." She stands and holds out her arms and repeats, "The kingdom of heaven is within, I love myself." Then he tells her, "Now better than that, say I and God are one." She spreads out her arms and gets ready to say that when he stops her. "I know one better than that," he says, "I got the best one, this is the best one.

Just say I am God." She turns to him and says, "David, I can't say that." He replies, "See how little you think of yourself, you can't even say the words." She thinks about it for a minute and then turns and stares out at the ocean, raises her arms one more time and says, "I am God. I am God." He then tells her, "A little louder please, with maybe a little more conviction."

Again, she turns to the ocean and raises her arms. She then proclaims, "I am God!!! I am...if I'm God then who does that make you?" He answers, "What we see in others we always see in ourselves. I am God." At that point they face each other, they both hold out their arms and recite together, "I am God! I am God! I am God! I am God!"[6]

Even **Wicca**, which is a new term for the old-fashioned **Witchcraft** also says we're god. "The existence of a supreme divine power is known as 'The One,' or 'The All'. 'The All' is not separate from the universe but part of it and from 'The All' came the god and goddess and they are manifested in various forms in the universe. Divinity is within."

And of course, here's where it all comes from, the **devil** says we can become god.

Genesis 3:5 "For God knows that when you eat of it your eyes will be opened, and you will be like God."

Lie #2: The occult is good: UFO entities teach that in order to contact them, one should refrain from certain foods and practice meditation. They also say that you need to develop your psychic abilities and seek direction directly from "the spirit world" via a psychic, a channeler, a palm reader, astrology, so-called angels, or even dead relatives. Now, the first obvious question is, "Why do I have to use occult techniques in order to contact a supposed alien, if they're supposed to be a higher evolved technological race? You would think I'd be able to use a walkie talkie or some other normal scientific communication device. Why is it only through occult techniques that contact can be made? Well, it just so happens that the Bible calls this type of communication a demonic deception and an abomination to God.

Deuteronomy 18:9-14 "When you enter the land the LORD your God is giving you, do not learn to imitate the detestable ways of the nations there. Let no one be found among you who sacrifices his son or daughter in the fire, who practices divination or sorcery, interprets omens, engages in witchcraft, or casts spells, or who is a medium, spiritist, or who consults the dead. Anyone who does these things is detestable to the LORD, and because of these detestable practices the LORD your God will drive out those nations before you. You must be blameless before the LORD your God. The nations, you will dispossess, will listen to those who practice sorcery or divination. But as for you, the LORD your God has not permitted you to do so."

And just like you'd expect if you violate this Biblical rule and seek direction from demons instead of God, you get lied to like in the following example:

Joe Fisher, was a researcher in metaphysics for many years before encountering the world of channeling. In his book Fisher tells how he was invited into the home of a woman called Aviva, who claimed that there were entities from another dimension speaking through her. A small group of people gathered weekly to witness the various voices that would take control of Aviva.

Joe Fisher: "I was so impressed with accents, the personalities, the different languages that were produced by Aviva in her tranced state that I said to my friends, among them several journalists, you have got to see this, you've got to see this for yourself. Which they did, and the group, by me introducing people and them introducing other people and other people introducing other people, the group swelled to over 30."

Alan Williams, "Sandford Ellison", Hungry Ghosts: "He said I found this group that meets on Friday night and it's just great and you have got to come and see what's happening. I think the information was, almost a secret society."

Joe Fisher: "So you can imagine, there was Aviva, lying down on her chesterfield, with little pink slippers pointed towards the ceiling, going into trance and she would switch from one voice to another, that was different guides speaking through her. As each different person in the room would speak, they would go around the room, and they would never introduce themselves. The voice would go out and immediately the voice she was producing would change in accordance with the voice that asked the question."

Alan Williams: "And all of these entities, beings, were what we would call inside of her physical body. We would see a lot of changes that would take over. There weren't just the voices but in being relatively close to her as these beings were coming through. I could see the difference. I could see the characteristics of these entities as they came through. Her body and particularly her face would change."

Image Credit: Joe Fisher

Joe Fisher: "Her eyes would close, she couldn't see this. I don't know how it was done to this day. I have many questions about just how this was going on. All I know is that, Lawrence Olivia, on his finest day, could never have produced this array of different voices and inflections and languages within a space of an hour."

Alan Williams: "Each one of us had a major, major guide. Russell was her guide and Tuctay was mine."

Joe Fisher: "And I spoke to the entity that came forward and he described himself as a sheep farmer in the last century. That was his last incarnation. He proceeded to tell me that I had a guide too, who was looking after me on the earth-bound plane. The guide that was in the disembodied realm. Her name was

Filipa, she was Greek, she and I had been together in Greece in the 18th century. That is now her responsibility in this other realm to oversee my spiritual development while I was on earth."

Fisher was intrigued by the entity claiming to be Filipa, his spirit guide. While it was talking through Aviva he taped it and took the recording to a linguistic expert at the University of Ontario to verify its authenticity.

Joe Fisher: "This man's name was Mr. George Thanual, and he's a native-born Greek himself. I thought this is perfect. A linguistic expert that is Greek by birth. He listened to two tapes of Filipa speaking and he said in part this is a native born Greek woman speaking. So, I thought there is proof that Aviva is not concocting this, she hadn't been to the library, read some Greek and then is making it up for me. And even if she were to learn Greek she would be unable to speak with a voice of a native-born Greek."

With such impressive evidence Fisher embarked on a journey to validate the claims of the guides. Had they lived previous lives?

Alan Williams: "Joe's involvement became quite enhanced. He decided at that point that this was something unique and marvelous and he was going to write a book on Channeling. And bring out all this wonderful information that we were given and actually go and source these various entities. You have to realize that there were 25 to 30 people at this time that were involved and each one of them had a guide. Each one of these guides had lifetimes and backgrounds and he was going to find proof of Russell's existence and proof of his guides existence and that was going to be part of the book and that would substantiate this wonderful information."

Fishers first trip took him to England where Aviva's spirit guide, Russell Parnick, claimed to have lived in the 18th century as a sheep farmer.

Joe Fisher, "He spoke about living near the village of Heathsville, in Yorkshire. I visited it and it was there, just as he had described. Just a few houses and a little church, that sort of thing. Russell spoke about the druid stones nearby that were a half a day's ride on horseback. Touchingly evoked in last centuries language and that was there just as he said.

He said he had a 22-acre farm, I wasn't able to find the farm, but he said the farm abutted up to a Bern gill that was a little stream that ran into the river. The stream and the river were there. However, when I came to the litmus test again searching for Russell, I searched high and low in the records, in the church records, and government records and he was nowhere to be found."

Another guide, Earnest Scott, had claimed to be a bomber pilot who had been with the Royal Airforce in the 99th squadron in WWII. Once again, Fisher went to great lengths to prove this claim, including interviewing members of the squadron only to leave disappointed.

Joe Fisher: "Most of the historical and geographical information he provided was accurate, it was there. The only problem was that Earnest, the bomber pilot did not exist. I couldn't find him in the records. So, I came back to Toronto and I told them I was much impressed with the fact all the information was there, but there was just this one problem. I couldn't find him. Then he went into a great song and dance about karma, that he has a charge sitting in his room who he must look after.

And he had realized too late that the information he was giving me might be detrimental to the welfare of the charge on the earthbound plain. So, he decided to change the information and backtrack. Now I argued with him at great length, I said you could have told me this before I left, if you felt this. And even so, you started off by giving me your name before you had this change of mind and the name that I was looking for was just not in the records.

And he weaseled and whined and invoked the higher laws. So, he got out of it. But the question remained with me. Was Earnest telling the truth, was he not. I will have to check out other guides to find out whether this is true or not."

The obvious choice of guides to investigate was his own guide, Filipa, who he had come to trust because of his personal effort to make contact.

Joe Fisher: "Initially Filipa encouraged me to contact her and rather than to go through a medium, the best way to contact your guide is directly and she said if I concentrated on her every day for 15 minutes or more that I would be able to make this contact after a period of time. So, every morning I would go up to my study and I would train my mind on making contact with her.

Nothing happened for weeks and weeks and weeks but eventually an image of a woman walking towards me in a white wrap was presented to my inner vision and I was convinced that this was Filipa and my response was to weep. I cried for several minutes. Again, when I went back to the group, I didn't have to say anything, Filipa said, you see we have made contact. And again, this was another brick in the wall. "

Alan Williams: "So, he said he was going to go off and, his guide who loved him dearly, certainly would not deceive him. She gave him all this information. He had maps and research and he was going to go and find her. He couldn't find Russell, that entity had never been born in that parish or lived in that place but enough of it fitted. He knew about that general area, same as Earnest knew WWII bombers and things like that. But Joe knew he could never be deceived by his guide."

Joe Fisher: "Now, I then went to Greece looking for Filipa. And a similar thing happened. I was looking for the village of Therus which, she said, was a five day walk from the Black Sea. Again, touchingly evoked from the ancient language. She made me believe her initially. I went to the town of Alexandropoulos in Northeastern Greece.

And it was there that the edifice on which her testimony was based on was crumbling because of the failure of her colleagues to pan out. I had expected Alexandropoulos to be an ancient city based on Alexander the Great. When I went there I found out that it wasn't, in fact Alexandropoulos was only built at the beginning of the century. And Filipa was talking about it having existed in her day. This could not have been. So, I carried on my search there looking for more clues of her existence but Filipa, even though her Greek had been veritable, Filipa too went that way and it was a very wrenching disillusion for me."[7]

No wonder God bans this practice. He doesn't want people to be lied to and deceived by demonic presences, which again, UFO occupants just happen to encourage.

Lie #3: Christianity is bad UFO entities teach that Christianity is the biggest culprit in destroying the earth by teaching that man had dominion over the earth when the earth is actually a living being. And they say we need to worship her and change our ways or we will be destroyed. Well, first of all, this is none other than old-fashioned pagan false teaching called Gaia worship. But it's a good thing that nobody's falling for this lie. Unfortunately, mother earth worship is spreading fast to almost every corner of society. Here's just a few different examples from various sectors of society.

As the video starts we hear crying and moaning. As the camera slowly moves closer to the earth there are people laying on their stomachs and sitting in an almost fetal position, all crying.

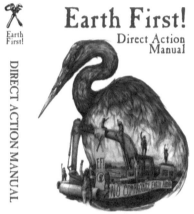

Earth First!
Direct Action Manual

Third Edition

DIRECT ACTION MANUAL

Earth First!

Reporter: Deep in the woods of North Carolina an extremist eco-group called 'Earth First' bewails the violation of American nature.

One of the worshipers exclaims: "We want the old trees, we don't want them to die! That we are some people here that do care. We want you to know trees. That we care!"

Sydnee L Ome Grace, Earth First: "I think that we are deeply hurting in America. I think we are deeply craving answers. I think we have lost our identity as we have evolved into technology, into an industrialized society. Bring me to this cathedral (as she waves her hand round to the trees). Bring me to those guys, the trees, bring me to this rock that has the most incredible life. That makes me feel alive."[8]

Caryl Matrisciana Reporter: "Why should we care about mother earth?"

Actor James Coburn: "Mother earth is our mother. She's the mother goddess. She's the one we should be praising, not raping. All of these people here today are here for one reason.

Because they are concerned about what is happening to the earth, what mankind is doing to the earth. I mean the negative emotion we carry around is another contributor. It all feeds the moon.

We have to be true to ourselves and true to mother earth. She is going to be bountiful, she is going to give us everything we need. She has for a long time. We have lost our way. The pagans used to know how to do it. The Indians used to know how to do it. Some of them still remember how to do it. The earth is a living organism. We are killing the one we love the most and she loves us. We have to praise our mother goddess."[9]

"The women's movement today is called the 'Women's Spirituality Movement' in great part and that is because it's not just concentrating on areas of social and political reform but it's looking hard and fast at spiritual reform. Women are gathering today in circles just like their 1960 counterparts did.

But now they're not just knocking down the doors to a man's world, asking for entrance, instead they are looking at the myths, spiritual beliefs, religions, values, everything that runs our culture. Everything that feeds our souls. We're going to take a look at the women's spirituality movement as it has been called by the women participating in it, weaving new stories, returning goddess, they believe she is back on the planet alive and well. And she can do a lot for you."

"The goddess is alive, magic is afoot, the goddess is alive, magic is afoot. Women are chanting and dancing around in a circle, beating drums, and ringing bells.

Comments from different members: "What the goddess means to me is wholeness and peace." "What the goddess means to me is my internal strength. She has come to me and shown me the beauty that is within myself." "The goddess is my voice. She is my self-empowerment, she is my self-respect. As a result, my life has really undergone some major transformations, not only creatively but in the pathway, I have started to take. And I have the works of Zsuzsanna Budapest to thank for that."

"The goddess is alive, magic is afoot, the goddess is alive, magic is afoot. Women are chanting and dancing around in a circle, beating drums, and ringing bells.

Comments from different members: "What the goddess means to me is wholeness and peace." "What the goddess means to me is my internal strength. She has come to me and shown me the beauty that is within myself." "The goddess is my voice. She is my self-empowerment, she is my self-respect. As a result, my life has really undergone some major transformations, not only creatively but in the

pathway, I have started to take. And I have the works of Zsuzsanna Budapest to thank for that."

Now we have little kids from the Mount Madonna School who are singing the pledge of allegiance, but it goes like this, "I pledge allegiance to the earth that cares for land and sea, and if we cherish every living thing with peace and justice everywhere. I pledge allegiance to the earth to care for land and sea and if you cherish every living thing with peace and justice everywhere, with peace and justice everywhere."[10]

"We stand at a critical moment in earth's history. A time when humanity must choose its future. The dominant patterns of production and consumption are

causing environmental devastation. Injustice, poverty, and violence are wide spread and the cause of great suffering."

Advertisement: "Fundamental changes are needed in our values, institutions, and ways of living. 'Your Earth' charter provides an ethical foundation for building a more sustainable world respecting nature, universal human rights, economic justice and a culture of peace.

The creation of the Earth Charter was achieved through a decade long, worldwide, cross cultural dialogue on commonly shared values, beginning with the 1992 'Earth Summit' in Rio De Janeiro, Brazil. The 'Earth Charter' drafting process continued gaining momentum at the 1995 'Earth Charter International' workshop in the Netherlands."

"This unique participatory and inclusive process continued over the next five years, The National and Regional workshops worldwide. 'Earth Charter' commissioners carefully considered the outcome of this international concertation as they worked in the final drafting of the charter. A new phase began in the year 2000 with the official launching of the 'Earth Charter'.

Speaker: "We make this gift of service to all our brothers and sisters in the human family, especially to the children, to those who suffer in poverty and oppression, and the future generations. We make this gift of service to the greater community of life."

Jan Roberts, Summits Organizer: "And today, we came together, and we launched in the United States, and make no mistake about this, we launched the 'Earth Charter', our declaration of interdependence."

And this idolatrous behavior is precisely why the Bible says God's wrath is being revealed from heaven. People have the audacity to worship created things (even the earth) instead of the Creator of the earth.

Romans 1:18-25 "The wrath of God is being revealed from heaven against all the godlessness and wickedness of men who suppress the truth by their wickedness, since what may be known about God is plain to them, because God has made it plain to them. For since the creation of the world God's invisible qualities – His eternal power and divine nature – have been clearly seen, being understood from what has been made, so that men are without excuse. For although they knew God, they neither glorified him as God nor gave thanks to him, but their thinking became futile and their foolish hearts were darkened. Although they claimed to be wise, they became fools and exchanged the glory of the immortal God for images made to look like mortal man and birds and animals and reptiles. Therefore, God gave them over in the sinful desires of their hearts to sexual impurity for the degrading of their bodies with one another. They exchanged the truth of God for a lie and worshiped and served created things rather than the Creator – Who is forever praised. Amen."

Lie #4: Christianity is outdated UFO's teach that Christianity is false and outdated. They say there is no such thing as sin and we do not need to be saved. Not so surprisingly, that's not what the Bible says.

Romans 3:23; 6:23 "For all have sinned and fall short of the glory of God. For the wages of sin is death, but the gift of God is eternal life in Christ Jesus our Lord."

Lie #5: Christianity is Wrong Orthodox Christianity has it all wrong UFO's declare. Jesus' real message they say was to teach us that each one of us could become "Christs." Again, shocker, that's not what the Bible says. In fact, Jesus warned about this lie in the passage we saw earlier.

Matthew 24:4-5 "Jesus answered: "Watch out that no one deceives you. For many will come in my name, claiming, 'I am the Christ,' and will deceive many."

Lie #6: The devil is good Believe it or not, UFO's even go so far as to say that the devil or lucifer is actually a good guy who has come to free us. Really? Here's just a few of the names the Bible uses to describe the character of satan. He's the Accuser, the Deceiver, the Evil one, the Father of lies, a Murderer, the Power of darkness, the Ruler of demons, the Tempter, a Thief who comes to steal, kill, and destroy, and of course, the Wicked one. Doesn't sound like a "good guy" to me!

Lie #7: All religions are the same UFO entities would have you and I believe that all religions (except orthodox Christianity) are of equal merit. They teach that we are at the threshold of a New Age of occult enlightenment and that extra-terrestrial entities are now present to assist mankind into leaving 'old ways' and adjusting to the New Age of spiritual advancement, which includes acknowledging that Jesus is but one of many great teachers such as Buddha, Muhammad or Confucius. They even state that these "teachers" all come from the ET's to assist mankind in our next step of evolution.

Now first of all, notice how once again the lie of evolution is needed to get us to believe in this next lie. First, the UFO's say we evolved physically but now, with their help, we will be evolving spiritually. Furthermore, all religions being one cannot be true because here's what Jesus Himself clearly taught.

John 14:6 "Jesus answered, "I am the way and the truth and the life. No one comes to the Father except through Me.""

John 14:7-10 "If you really knew Me, you would know My Father as well. From now on, you do know Him and have seen Him." Philip said, "Lord, show us the Father and that will be enough for us." Jesus answered: "Don't you know Me, Philip, even after I have been among you such a long time? Anyone who has seen Me has seen the Father. How can you say, 'Show us the Father'? Don't you believe that I am in the Father, and that the Father is in Me? The words I say to you are not just My own. Rather, it is the Father, living in Me, who is doing His work."

Now I'd say that's just a little bit different than Buddha, Muhammad or Confucius. Especially when you consider the fact that Jesus rose again from the grave and is still alive, but those guys are still dead. Major difference. So once again, it's a good thing that nobody's listening to this lie from the UFO occupants! Well, unfortunately just like other lies, this one too is gaining ground. Here's just a small proof of that from various outlets.

URI *"Peace, it should be natural order. Peace, why is it so hard to find? Peace, why do people try so hard to prevent it? Why do so many people divide, split and fracture, the one face of humanity? Is there something you can do to heal the violence? Religiously motivated violence can end. This is your invitation to be a Peace Builder.*

In the year 2000 a unique global community took the initiative to end religiously motivated hate and violence by founding the 'United Religions Initiative'. Because of URI Indians and Pakistanis of diverse faiths are looking beyond the boundaries that divide them. Because of URI Christians and indigenous peoples of Latin America are creating a new world of mutual respect. Because of URI Jews, Muslims and Christians in the Middle East are learning that the only real security is peace.

In just a few short years the 'United Religions Initiative' has spread to 50 countries on 5 continents. In a few short years former enemies have stopped seeing each other as 'the other' and started seeing each other as themselves. Bahai, Christian, Muslim, Jew, Buddhist, Sikh, Zoroastrianism, Hindu, all around the world URI is helping people experience the shared human face behind the different human faiths.

Achieving on a deep personal, spiritual level, what the governments and organizations have been unable to accomplish before. Now more than ever this initiative must become a shared initiative. One community, one neighborhood, one region at a time."[12]

Oprah Winfrey: *The mistakes that human beings are making is believing there is only one way to live and that we don't accept that there are diverse ways of being in the world. There are millions of ways to be a human being and many paths to what you call God, as she points to another woman, she says, her path may be something else. And when she gets there she might call it the light. But her loving, and her kindness, and her generosity may bring her, or if it brings her to the same point as you, it doesn't matter if she calls it God along the way or not."*

A lady in the audience says, "The danger in that, it sounds great at the onset, but if you really look at it from both sides…" Oprah interrupts her, "There couldn't possibly be only one way." Another woman in the audience asks, "What about

Jesus?" Oprah answers, "What about Jesus?" She then answers, "There is one way and only one way, and that is through Jesus!" Oprah then says, "There couldn't possibly be only one way." The lady in the audience then says, "Just because you say it, you intellectualize it, and say that there isn't, doesn't make it true. If you all don't believe it, you are all buying in to the lie."[13]

The Nevada Legislature is opened with a prayer from a Hindu statesman but is interrupted. The announcement is made that the session will open by NRI Hindu Chaplain Rajan Zed. As he steps to the desk to start his pray, before he can start speaking he is interrupted by a voice in the audience. "Lord Jesus forgive us Father, for allowing the prayer of the wicked which is an abomination in your sight." "The Sergeant at arms will restore order in the senate." "We shall have no other God's before you. You are the one true..." "The Sergeant at arms will restore order in the senate."[14]

ABC America Exclusive reports: *"Let me ask you some questions about faith, which is a tough subject to talk about. Do we all worship the same God, Muslim and Christian?"*

President Bush: "I believe we do. We have different routes of getting to the Almighty."

Interviewer: "Do Christians and Non-Christians and Muslims go to Heaven, in your opinion?"

President Bush: Yes, they do we have different routes of getting there."

The Vatican *"The Vatican and the Roman Catholic Church, this Pope is leading the greatest ecumenical movement in history in order to unite all religions under Rome's leadership. In 1986 Pope John Paul II gathered in Assisi, Italy, the leaders of the worlds major religions to pray for peace.*

There were snake worshipers, fire worshipers, spiritists, Buddhas, Hindu, Muslims, North American witch doctors.I watched in astonishment as they walked to the microphone to pray. The Pope said they were all praying to the same God. And that their prayers were creating a spiritual energy that was bringing a new climate for peace.

John Paul II allowed his good friend the Dali Lama, to put the buddha on the alter at St. Peters Church at Assisi, and with his monks have a worship ceremony there while Shinto's chanted and rang their bells outside. The Prophesied world

religion is in the process of being formed before our eyes."[15]

CNN Live reports: *There is a major effort taking place to curb free speech in this country, irrespective of our constitution and the bill of rights and free speech advocates say the United Nations has come down on precisely the wrong side.*

The United Nations has adopted what it calls a resolution combating defamation of religions. The United Nations now want to make that anti-blasphemy resolution binding on member nations including of course our own. That would make it a crime in the United States, if the United Nations were to have its way, to criticize religion."[16]

Lie #8: Antichrist is good UFO entities would even then teach that we should not neglect the fact that we need to submit to some drastic forms of authoritarian social control because it is necessary to assure the survival of this planet. They say that mankind needs to unite into a one world government and a one world religion or we will be destroyed. That lie too is making great headway.

CNN reports: *De-classified US government documents and witness testimony from former or retired US military personnel confirm beyond any doubt the reality of ongoing UFO incursions at nuclear weapons sights. When I say UFO, the witnesses have described these craft as disc shaped, or cylindrical shape, or spherical. These objects are capable of hovering, and high velocity flight usually completely silent.*

Over the past 37 years I have personally located and interviewed over 120 of these former or retired military personnel and all of whom report UFO incidents at one or more of the following locations; nuclear missile sites, nuclear weapons storage areas, and nuclear weapons test sites in Nevada and the Pacific during the era of atomic atmospheric testing.

I really believe, and these gentlemen believe, that this planet is being visited by beings from another world, who for whatever reason have taken an interest in the nuclear arms race which began at the end of WWII. Regarding the missile shutdown incidents, my opinion and their opinion, is that whoever is aboard these craft are sending a signal to both Washington and Moscow, among others, that we are playing with fire. That the possession and threatened use of nuclear weapons potentially threaten the human race and the integrity of their environment.

Then they further speculate that in order for the world to be at peace and harmony there must be a New World Order, universal monetary system, a world authority on food, health, and water, universal tax, one world leader, and the abolishment of Christianity. First of all, why once again do you pick on just Christianity to the point where you want to eradicate it? Secondly, surely nobody's falling for this ridiculous lie. Well, actually, leaders in the government think it's precisely why UFO's are here, to save us from certain destruction.

History Channel reports: *"I was abducted by aliens. These terrifying words have been spoken by people who claim to have had close encounters with little grey men."*

"Some of these greys have a very dark agenda."

"The greys are allegedly an alien species that have been reported countless times. It's been going on for thousands of years."

"There are multiple species and we have been visited on multiple occasions. We have had descriptions of greys for over 40 years."

"There was the Roswell incident, Outer limits, close encounters of the 3rd kind."

"We're going to meet with Miriam Delicado, who encountered greys."

Miriam Delicado: "It was October 1988, we were driving in Northern British Columbia, and all of a sudden out of nowhere these lights appeared behind the car. It was almost as wide as two lanes, we actually thought it was a big truck or something. The lights started popping on and off. The girl driving was beginning to get really afraid. Then all of sudden out of absolutely no where I said to her, 'pull over the car it's not you they want it's me.'"

Interviewer: "What possessed you to say that?"

Miriam Delicado: "I really didn't know at that point. We walked on board this craft and they sat me down on this chair and then in front of me came a screen from out of thin air. They started showing me all these different Images."

Tall Blonde Extraterrestrial

Interviewer: "What kind of images were these?"

Miriam Delicado: "Catastrophes on the planet. Earthquakes, solar flares, war, and I saw all these that I would interpret as time lines and paths that humanity could take, and I was explained how, if we could come together as a species, we could be able to avoid any and all of these events."

Interviewer: "So, what was the purpose of this? What were they trying to do?"

Miriam Delicado: "It was explained to me that they are the caretakers of this earth and that their purpose of being here is to enlighten us and make us aware of who we are and to make sure that we do not destroy ourselves or the planet."

Interviewer: "Well, this was very interesting what Miriam was telling us about the greys showing her pictures of us in war, harming the planet. Sounds to me like they are bringing a benevolent message that they are trying to help us. It doesn't sound to me like they wish us harm."[17]

Oh, but that's not all. Others say that the aliens are not only here to save us from blowing ourselves up, but they say they've also come to free us from the evil grip of corporations that are hindering us from experiencing global peace and prosperity and creating our own utopia.

*"**Foster Gamble**: I have spent nearly a lifetime trying to figure out what happened that could account for the staggering agony and degradation on this planet. I set out on a journey seeking to answer questions like, is it even possible for humans to thrive. I found a code. A pattern in nature that has been embedded in arcs and icons throughout the century."*

***Astronaut Edgar Mitchell, Appollo 14**: "Yes there has been crashed crafts and bodies recovered."*

***John Callahan, Senior FAA Official**: "But who do you tell that you were involved in a UFO incident without them looking at you like you ain't wrapped too tight?"*

***Osirian Temple Abydos, Egypt:** "It's not etched into the rock, it's not carved, it's burned into the atomic structure in some extraordinary way."*

"I believe that they are giving us a model for accessing energy, clean, safe, limitless way, that can completely revolutionize the way all people live."

***Adam Trombly, Phjysicist, Inventor:** "Right here in this strobe there is enough energy to transform the entire earth. That's not just a theoretical statement, it's literally true."*

Steven Greer, M.D.: *"Energy is extracted from the fabric of the space around us which means that it cannot be metered. That is a direct threat to the single largest industry in the world. Energy."*

"The suppression of the UFO phenomena goes hand in hand with the suppression of the so-called free energy."

"An elite group of people and the corporations they run have gained control of not only our energy, food supply, education, and healthcare but over virtually every aspect of our lives."

Deepak Chopra, M.D: *"The way the system of medicine is set up, the medical education is funded by pharmaceutical companies."*

Bill Still, Writer, the Money Masters: *"We have a privately owned Central Bank System disguised as a government owned system"*

Alan Greenspan, Former Chairman Federal Reserve: *"There is no other agency of government which can overrule actions that we take."*

Catherine Austin Fitts, Former Assistant Secretary, U.S. Dept of H.U.D.: *"It gives them the ability to print money in a way that insiders are protected, and everybody is drained."*

David Icke, Author, the Biggest Secret: *"No matter where you go in the world, they control the money, they control the world."*

Now that might all sound well and good, and definitely politically correct these days, but little do people know that these suggestions from UFO's occupants to save our planet from nuclear threat and evil corporations and then submit ourselves to a one world ruler who will oversee a one world government, one world economy, and a one world religion, just so happens to be what the Bible describes as the antichrist's kingdom. This is the very evil satanic government that arises in the last days and gives birth to the 7-year Tribulation, which again, Jesus said would be mankind's greatest nightmare!

Revelation 13:5-9,11-17 "The beast was given a mouth to utter proud words and blasphemies and to exercise his authority for forty-two months. He opened his mouth to blaspheme God, and to slander his name and his dwelling place and those who live in heaven. He was given power to make war against the saints and to conquer them. And he was given authority over every tribe, people, language and nation. All inhabitants of the earth will worship the beast – all whose names have not been written in the book of life belonging to the Lamb that was slain from the creation of the world. He who has an ear, let him hear. Then I saw another beast, coming out of the earth. He had two horns like a lamb, but he spoke like a dragon. He exercised all the authority of the first beast on his behalf and made the earth and its inhabitants worship the first beast, whose fatal wound had been healed. And he performed great and miraculous signs, even causing fire to come down from heaven to earth in full view of men. Because of the signs he was given power to do on behalf of the first beast, he deceived the inhabitants of the earth. He ordered them to set up an image in honor of the beast who was wounded by the sword and yet lived. He was given power to give breath to the image of the first beast, so that it could speak and cause all who refused to worship the image to be killed. He also forced everyone, small and great, rich and poor, free and slave, to receive a mark on his right hand or on his forehead, so that no one could buy or sell unless he had the mark, which is the name of the beast or the number of his name."

Now, I don't think that's a coincidence. **UFO's** are helping to prepare people with their false teachings to accept the rise of the antichrist's kingdom. It truly is **The Last Days Great Deception**. Again, stop and think about it logically. Come on! You came all the way to earth just to promote the rise of the antichrist, support the Occult and demonic New Age teachings and debunk Christianity? Really? You'd think you'd share with us some secret technology or help us gain a cure for cancer or something beneficial like that since you're supposed to be so intellectually superior to us and much more highly evolved. But nope! You just came here to slam Jesus, Christianity, and the Bible, and promote the antichrist kingdom. That sounds demonic to me!

Lie #9: The 7-year Tribulation is good As if what we've seen so far isn't bad enough, UFO's and Aliens then have the audacity to also teach that the 7-year Tribulation that is coming is not something to be concerned about at all or even avoided like what Jesus said. Incredibly, they actually say it's something we should look forward to! Here's how the Bible describes that period. You tell me if there is anything in here we should be looking forward to!

Seal Judgments
1st Seal - White Horse – Global False Peace

2nd Seal - Red Horse – Global War
3rd Seal - Black Horse – Global Famine
4th Seal - Pale Horse – Global Death – 1/4th of Mankind Killed by…
Sword
Famine
Plague
Wild Beasts
5th Seal - Altar of Souls – Global Persecution
6th Seal – Beginning of Great Tribulation which unleashes…
A Global Earthquake
Sun Turns Black
Moon Turns Red
Asteroids Fall to Earth
Sky Recedes
Mountains/Islands Removed from Places
Global Fear of God's Wrath

Trumpet Judgments – Opened by the Seventh Seal – Silence in Heaven
1st Trumpet - Hail/Fire - 1/3rd of Earth/Trees & All Green Grass Burned Up
2nd Trumpet - Huge Asteroid – 1/3rd of Sea Dies & 1/3rd Ships Destroyed
3rd Trumpet - Blazing Comet – 1/3rd of Rivers & Fresh Water Bitter – Many People Die
4th Trumpet - Solar Smiting - 1/3rd of Sun, Moon & Stars Struck – 1/3rd Day & Night without Light
5th Trumpet - Satan Releases Demon Horse of Locusts – People with Mark Tortured 5 Months
6th Trumpet - Four Angels Loosed from Euphrates – 1/3rd Mankind Killed

Bowl Judgments
1st Bowl – Ugly Painful Sores on Receivers of the Mark
2nd Bowl – All the Sea Turns to Blood – All Sea Creatures Die
3rd Bowl – All the Rivers & Fresh Water to Blood
4th Bowl – Sun Scorches People with Fire – People Curse God
5th Bowl – Kingdom of Antichrist Plunged into Darkness
6th Bowl – Euphrates Dries Up
Prepares Way for Kings of East for Armageddon
Three Evil Frog-Like Spirits Deceive the World for Armageddon
Out of Mouth of Satan
Out of Mouth of Antichrist

Out of Mouth of False Prophet
7th Bowl – Final Pronouncement – IT IS DONE
Greatest of all Earthquakes
A New Look for Jerusalem - Split in Three
All Cities Collapse
A Cup of Wrath for Babylon
All Islands and Mountains Gone
A Massive Hailstorm – 100 lbs. each
Angel Harvest of the Righteous
Angel Harvest of the Unrighteous – Blood as High as Horses Bridle (4 feet deep) for 1,600 Stadia (200 Miles)

Now folks, I don't know about you, but I'd say that's not a pleasant time. That's not something we should be looking forward to. Yet, that's exactly what the so-called Space Brothers or UFO entities out there are saying! They say the Tribulation period is going to be wonderful because it will help us "evolve spiritually" so we can create utopia on this planet. Here's just a few examples of how they are trying to get us to buy into this ludicrous lie.

"Climatic shifts, droughts, floods, acid rain and pollution, earthquakes and volcanic eruptions. Although severe, these changes will pave the way for a cleansing of the earth and a new relationship between earth and man. This will be the Day of Purification. Trees will die. Cold places will become hot. Hot places will become cold. Lands will sink into the ocean and lands will rise out of the sea. All the suffering going on in this country with the tornadoes, floods and earthquakes is carried on by the breath of Mother Earth because she is in pain. This battle will cleanse the heart of people and restore our Mother Earth from illness, and the wicked will be gotten rid of."

Really? So, being left behind to face all these atrocities is a good thing and only those nasty wicked people will be gotten rid of? In fact, here's one of their promotional videos encouraging us to think this way.

As we listen to beautiful soft music of this video, the words 'The time has come, our Evolution has begun' appears on the screen. Then a picture of the earth comes on and a soft-spoken woman starts to speak. "All around the planet, people are awakening to the reality that humanity and the earth are now entering a heightened phase of activity on their inseparable journeys of growth and expansion.

This acceleration is marked by the increasing intensity of global events and by the rising temperature of nearly every planet in our solar system. While here on earth time itself seems to be speeding up and chaos mounting, as phenomenal shifts occur in our physical and perceptual realities with increasing rapidity. The simplest explanation behind this sense of speeding up is that our planets vibrational frequency is rising.

This event which many ancient cultures have prophetically termed 'the quickening' has begun. And it is the greatest opportunity of our times. We believe that by expanding our imaginations to explore possible future events we may prevent ourselves from reacting in fear should the previously unimagined become manifest. As a result of having already experienced these events in our minds we will be more centered and able to see the opportunities they present should they or something similar occur.

And so, with this understanding of the power of imagination as the means of which we can navigate the unknown this presentation will not only explore what sorts of events could occur between now and October that might lead to the end of the world as we know it. We will also look at how such events regardless of how challenging they may seem, could serve to bring humanity to a global experience of unity consciousness that would then lead us into a harmonious new existence and to our return to the long-prophesized experience of heaven on earth."

The speaking stops and the screen goes black. Then the words appear, 'Return to One'. Then she starts speaking again.

"This anticipated period of great change and purification which many believe will happen sometime between now and 2012 is referred to as the shift of the ages. And though there are those that believe that the shift is some grand event that is going to occur in the outer physical world or in the Cosmo at some point in the not too distant future bringing either salvation or destruction to the world, there are others who believe the shift is happening right now.

And in fact, that it has been and always will be happening. For these people believe that the shift can be experienced at any moment by anyone who is willing to make the internal shift back to one."

"I am ready for the next step in humanities evolution. The time has come to live for each other.

The Darkness Before the Dawn; *"Let us now consider how the events that are set to unfold the next few months could assist humanity in it's evolution from a purely material based perspective of existence to one more routed in spirituality. As mentioned before there are many people in the world today who because of their focus on material success and survival will not spare a second thought for their soul, or spiritual self until they are faced with death, suffering and the inevitable collapse of everything they have come to depend on in the material world.*

Thus, in accordance with the familiar phrase that it is always darkest before the dawn; it is our belief that in the coming months the world will be required to experience a level of death and destruction that will encourage its material obsessed inhabitants to return to a more spiritual based of existence.

Though it is understandable that the collapse of our material world and its existence could be quite a frightening experience, it is essential to understand here that those who learn to have faith in the spiritual purpose in these events will be given the tools and awareness that will allow them to face and flow through all of the challenges of the coming shift with relative grace and ease.

With this perspective, when they learn to move through the events of the coming months with a heart full of love and gratitude, rather than being consumed with hate and fear then it is the power of this faith to bring us peace that is being referred to in the Hopi prophecy of the blue and the red cochina's when it says, 'Life will get very perverted, and there will be little social order in these times. Many will ask for the mountains themselves to fall upon them, just to end their misery.

While still others will appear as if untouched by what is occurring. For they are the Ones who remember the original teachings, and who have reconnected their hearts and spirit. When the purifier comes, many things will begin to occur that will not make sense, for reality will be shifting back in and out of the dream state. Things unseen will be felt very strongly.

There will be many strange beasts upon the Earth in those days, some from the past and some that we have never seen. The nature of mankind will appear strange in these times we walk between worlds, and we will house many spirits even within our bodies. After a time, we will again walk with our brothers from the Stars and rebuild this Earth. But not until the purifier has left his mark upon the Universe. "[18]

So, wait a second, being left behind to face the horrible realities of the 7-Year Tribulation is actually a wonderful thing, a badge of honor, instead of what the Bible says that it is actually the hand of God, His judgment? Pretty slick if you put all that together. And that's exactly what this guy says.

Stuart Goldman, *a reporter, concludes his research on UFO's with these comments: 'The unpleasant fact is, fifty thousand people cannot be lying. Something is here – probing people, inspecting them, and planting thoughts in their minds, manipulating their bodies – treating them, in a sense, like so many cattle.*

Is it all simply a gigantic cosmic joke, or is there a more sinister plot at hand? Are we seeing the formation of a new and highly destructive cult, one whose view posits the elimination (the New Ager's call it 'spiritual cleansing') of people who are 'unfit' to exist in the coming New World?

Are there really demonic entities hovering about, searching for likely candidates whose brains and minds they can invade, filling them full of fairytales and lies, fattening them for the kill? "[19]

The answer would be yes. Why? Because they're demons and that's what they do! This is exactly what kinds of lies you would expect them to teach. Let's look at the text again from Jesus.

John 8:44 "You belong to your father, the devil, and you want to carry out your father's desire. He was a murderer from the beginning."

John 10:10 "The thief comes only to steal and kill and destroy; I have come that they may have life and have it to the full."

All these signs of the planet experiencing increasing turmoil and unrest and increasing in earthquakes and destruction have nothing to do with mankind getting ready to evolve spiritually into the Age of Utopia. They are the signs given by Jesus nearly 2,000 years ago to let us know when His return was imminent and that we better be ready when He comes back.

Luke 21:11 "And there shall be great earthquakes in diverse places, and famines, and pestilences; and fearful sights and great signs there shall be from heaven."

Disaster in Japan, people in their offices are falling, trying to hang on to their desks as the ceiling is falling around them because of a major earthquake.

Another earthquake hits New Zealand Christchurch February 22, 2011. People are running for their lives as the buildings are crumbling around them.

Honshu Japan, April 7, 2011, another earthquake and March 11, 2011 with a magnitude of 9.0. People are running out of the buildings in fear of losing their lives from the falling debris. The skyscrapers are swaying back and forth.

Newspapers report: "Earthquakes increase around the world." "Scientists find increase in microearthquakes after Chilean quake." "Strong Earthquakes increasing, disrupting planets magnetic field." "Huge quake hits Chili, prompting region-wide tsunami warning."

Isaiah 24:20 "The earth shall reel to and fro like a drunkard and shall be removed like a cottage; and the transgression thereof shall be heavy upon it; and it shall fall and not rise again."

Luke 21:25-26 "And there shall be signs in the sun, and in the moon, and in the stars; and upon the earth distress of nations, with perplexity; the sea and the waves roaring; Men's hearts failing them for fear, and for looking after those things which are coming on the earth; for the powers of heaven shall be shaken."

Signs in the Sun, Moon, and Stars

Massive CME solar flares February13, 2011: RED HORSE OF THE APOCALYPSE?

Total Lunar Eclipse June 15, 2011: LONGEST AND DARKEST IN A CENTURY

Newspaper report: "Longest, darkest lunar eclipse of the Century. New Delhi: The longest and darkest total lunar eclipse of the century will occur tomorrow giving sky enthusiasts all over the country an opportunity to witness the event. An unusually long lunar eclipse with the Moon immersed deeply inside the darker shadow of the Earth will occur tomorrow. Nehru Planetarium Director said."

"Blood moon rising as ash cloud tipped to alter eclipse." "Longest in a hundred years." "Century's longest lunar eclipse."

Newspaper report: "Moon, Saturn, Spicia, Australia August 2, 2011. Rare 'super moon' rising tonight. 'Super moon' describes a new or full moon occurring at the same time the Moon comes within 90 percent of its closest approach to Earth in a given orbit.

It's an event that happens 4-6 times a year but according to a NASA Science

News story tonight's full moon will nearly coincide with the moon's arrival at its closet point in its orbit around the Earth resulting in the biggest visible full moon in North America in two decades."[20]

"P/2010 A2: Hubble telescope image unlike any object ever seen before, Scientists baffled."

"Comet Elenin 2011, causing cosmic and atmospheric

"Extreme super moon March 19, 2011."

disturbances, effecting the magnetic poles are estimated to make one of its closest passes to earth on September 11 and the October and November months."

Russian Reports Warn: Comet Elenin under intelligent control. Elenin update: June 2011: Document reading of Russian reports on Elenin being under intelligent control also the Russian government wars 2012 may be too late for building 5000 bomb shelters."

Strange signs in the sky:

Montreal July 25, 2011, a large circular cloud hovers over the city.

March 2, 2001, 2 objects are hovering over 2 Suns China

A meteor flies through the sky over Wisconsin, seen over downtown Milwaukee.

Something strange that looks like a jellyfish is flying over Russia March 13, 2011

Revelation 6: 3-4: "When the Lamb opened the second seal, I heard the second living creature say, 'Come!' Then another horse came out, a fiery red one. Its rider was given power to take peace from the earth and to make men slay each other. To him was given a large sword."

Death of Animals

Portugal 2011, dead squid laying on the beach.

New Zealand 2011, Dead Whales on the beach.[20]

Arkansas 2011, Dead fish laying thick on the beach.

January 1, 2011, Beebe, Arkansas Mass wildlife deaths spread, thousands of dead black birds fall from the sky and 100,000 dead fish wash up in the Arkansas River.

Fox Reports: *"Birds, fish, and all kinds of creatures are dropping dead." "In Ireland, California, England, Middle East, Greece, Rio de Janeiro, Brazil, Portage County, Maryland, Chesapeake Bay, this is all the sign of the Apocalypse."*[22]

Hosea 4:3; "Therefore the land shall mourn; and everyone who dwells there shall languish, with the beasts of the fields and the birds of the air; even the fishes of the sea shall be taken away."

"Millions of locusts invade Russia June 9, 2011."

"China, 2011, South Eastern Australia 2011; Thousands of beetle's swarms Australian tourist mecca, stumping scientists. The Australian tourist mecca of Surfers Paradise has been swarmed by thousands of beetles a never-before-seen phenomenon that has stumped local scientists. The water beetle invasion captured on amateur YouTube footage shows the large black beetle swarming around lights and dropping to the footpath in Surfers Paradise in Queensland, about 70KM southeast of Brisbane last night, The Gold Coast Bulletin reports".[23]

"Plague of millions of frogs invade Greece. Highways shut down, experts clueless."[23]

"150 human animal hybrids grown in UK labs; Embryos have been produced secretively for the past three years."

"Human-animal hybrid created amid 'Frankenstein' warnings."

"Scientists create human-animal hybrids in secret research. Hybrids were produced in secret by researchers looking into cures for diseases."

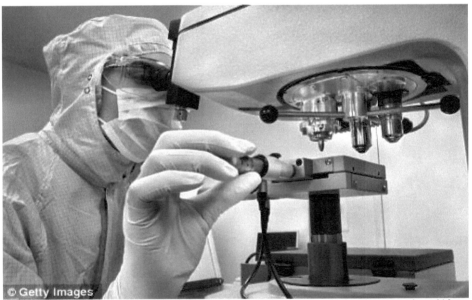

The Human Fertilization and Embryology Authority is currently considering whether donors can be paid for their services

"Part Human/Part Animal Hybrid Monsters Created by Scientists all over the Planet."[25]

Luke 17:26; "And as it was in the days of Noah, so shall it be also in the days of the Son of man."

"INGV Earth shifted 4 inches on its axis."

"Japan Earthquake shortened length of 24-hour day."

NASA: Japan quake appears to have shortened Earth days shifted axis."[26]

"Honshu Island shifted 8 feet."

"South's super tornado outbreak worst ever in US history: Storm forensics experts have begun to put into historical perspective the massive twisters outbreak that hit Alabama and six other Southern states. The Tuscaloosa twister alone may register as the most powerful long track tornado in US history."

"Record 226 tornadoes in 24 hours last week. Washington: Preliminary government estimates say there were more tornadoes in a single day last week than any other day in history. Government analysts say there were 312 tornadoes during last week's outbreak, including a record setting 226 in one day."[27]

A tornado moves through Tuscaloosa, Ala. April 27, 2011. A wave of severe storms laced with tornadoes strafed the South on Wednesday, killing nearly 200 people across the South.

"Mile-wide monster tornado rips Tuscaloosa, April 27, 2011."

"2011 tornado death toll tops 500 and season not over. Reuters: More than 500 people have been killed by twisters in 2011, making it the deadliest tornado year."

"Australia flooding of 'biblical proportions' It hasn't quite been 40 days and 40 nights of rain, but the Australia flooding has already been described as a 'disaster of biblical proportions', slashing coal exports, ruining crops and stranding 75,000 people in a coastal town turned island."

"Australian flood size of France, Germany."

"Chili volcano June 6, 2011."

"Volcanic Ash Blocks out Sun in Bariloche, Argentina. Ash cloud 6 miles high."

"Largest Hurricane in Australian History cat 5 Cyclone Yasi Hitting Queensland."

"Montreal July 25, 2011, made no sound remained stationary 1 hr. through wind."

"Hawaii volcano erupts March 6, 2011, lava spews 65 feet high"

"January 5, 2011, Pole shift confirmed by FAA. Shift of Earth's magnetic north pole moving 40 miles per year. Scientists say the magnetic north pole is moving toward Russia and the fallout has reached of all places, Tampa International Airport. The airport has closed its primary runway until Jan 13, to repaint the numeric designators at each end and change taxiway signage to account for the shift in location of the earth's magnetic north. The closure of the west parallel runway will result in more activity on the east parallel runway and more noise for residential areas of south Tampa."

Climate chaos: Rare June snow falls in desert of Namibia."

"7.8 mag Quake triggers tsunami in New Zealand."

"Blizzard of 2011 'a storm of historic proportions'."

"Las Vegas Review Journal, 4 homes wash away in Arizona, Dangerous flooding creates emergency."

Matthew 24:34; I tell you the truth, this generation shall not pass away until all these things have taken place.

Looks like the signs that Jesus is getting ready to come back are all around us. I sure hope you're ready!

Chapter Nine

The Travel of UFO's

The **3ʳᵈ reason** why UFO's are clearly demonic in origin is because they **Travel like Demons**. Kind of like the sign you see as you head out to Area 51, the Extraterrestrial Highway. I don't think it's actually their highway but let's take a look at how UFO and Aliens travel. It just so happens they travel in the same manner as demons do. But don't take my word for it. Let's see how demons travel according to the Bible and you tell me if they don't co-inside with the same things that these UFO occupants are able to do as well.

2 Kings 6:15-18 "When the servant of the man of God got up and went out early the next morning, an army with horses and chariots had surrounded the city. "Oh, my lord, what shall we do?" the servant asked. "Don't be afraid," the prophet answered. "Those who are with us are more than those who are with them." And Elisha prayed, "O LORD, open his eyes so he may see." Then the LORD opened the servant's eyes, and he looked and saw the hills full of horses and chariots of fire all around Elisha. As the enemy came down toward him, Elisha prayed to the LORD, "Strike these people with blindness." So, he struck them with blindness, as Elisha had asked."

So here we see the classic passage in the bible where the prophet of God Elisha was being hunted down and when his servant got up and saw an army coming against them, he freaked out and ran to Elisha. So Elisha knowing better, asked God to open his servant's spiritual eyes so he could see that there really was no reason to be afraid. God's angels far outnumbered the army that was opposing them. Now, here's the point in sharing that passage. This is just one of many passages in the Bible that tells us how angels travel, and demons are in that category because they are fallen angels. What we see is, according to this text, that they have the ability to appear and disappear to materialize and to dematerialize and to travel very rapidly. Wonder of wonders, that's precisely what these UFO's and their occupants also do.

Travel Indicator #1: UFO experts are saying that these beings are not so much physical in nature as they are spiritual and that because they clock them at speeds up to 15,000 mph making right turns which would instantly destroy anything physical.

History Channel reports:

Richard Dolan, Author: "The significant wave of sightings over Belgium in particular in 1989 and 1990 of triangular aircraft have yet to be identified to today."

On that first night the police were swamped with telephone calls from 150 witnesses. Soon sightings of the Eupen 'triangle', as it comes to be called, are reported throughout the country. The UFO phenomena there results in an unprecedented level of cooperation between various government agencies and private UFO investigators about UFO incidents.

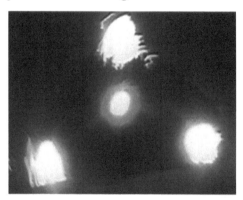

The Belgium air force quickly takes the lead and starts setting up a procedure for tracking this unidentified flying object. Colonel Wilfried De Brouwer, the Air Forces chief of operations coordinates a special task force to work with local and national police agencies as well as civilian UFO investigators.

On the night of March 30, 1990, the triangle is sighted again. Two Belgium F16 fighters are scrambled from Beauvechain Air Base. Despite flying for over an hour the pilots are unable to make visual contact with the UFO but do manage to record radar images of it.

The encounter leads some to speculation that the Eupen triangle is actually an American craft. If so the most likely culprit would be the F17A Stealth fighter. This secret triangular shaped aircraft is designed to have a minimal radar signature. But sophisticated analyses conducted on both ground based and on-board radar images of the Eupen triangle calls this theory into doubt.

According to the radar the UFO could within seconds accelerate from 170 to 1,100 miles per hour and drop from 11,000 feet to near ground level. Maneuvers like those would generate an enormous g-force far in excess of what military testing film show a human can endure. Thereby dismissing the possibility of the UFO as man or American made.[1]

And that's why researchers say they are massless by our physics, i.e. spiritual in nature. Demons are spiritual, aren't they?

Travel Indicator #2: UFO's are not only able to go faster than the speed of sound, but they make no sonic boom like a normal physical object does. Another clue, that they're spiritual in nature.

Travel Indicator #3: Radar has never recorded the actual entering of UFO's into our atmosphere.

Travel Indicator #4: Even with supposed millions of advanced civilizations in outer space, it would be almost impossible if just once a year for an extra-terrestrial craft to find us out here on the limb of our galaxy. Yet we are seeing literally tens of thousands of these so-called craft every single year.

Travel Indicator #5: The so-called "aliens" seem to be able to live in our atmosphere without the help of respiratory devices.

Travel Indicator #6: UFO's have been fired upon scores of times by American, Russian, and Canadian pilots, but these pilots have never been able to physically bring down a craft or capture it.

Travel Indicator #7: UFO entities seem to have the ability to materialize and dematerialize at will as if coming from another doorway or portal. Which just so happens to also be the ability that angels or angelic beings have, which of course the demons are, only of the fallen category that rebelled against God with satan. They too travel through dimensional doorways. In fact, the Bible tells us:

Genesis 28:10-12, 16-17: "Jacob left Beersheba and set out for Haran. When he reached a certain place, he stopped for the night because the sun had set. Taking one of the stones there, he put it under his head and lay down to sleep. He had a dream in which he saw a stairway resting on the earth, with its top reaching to heaven, and the angels of God were ascending and descending on it. When Jacob awoke from his sleep, he thought, "Surely the Lord is in this place, and I was not aware of it." He was afraid and said, "How awesome is this place! This is none other than the house of God; this is the gate of heaven."

And this is why many UFO experts are now saying that, based on decades of research, these beings aren't coming from outer space but inner space. They're coming from another dimension.

Jacque Vallee on UFO's: *"They're more like windows into another dimension."*

Spiritual Nature of UFO's: *It's this dimensional thinking that helps to explain some of the shape shifting and morphing abilities these UFO's seem to have. For instance, it would be like a 3-dimensional ball going through a 2-dimensional piece of paper. From the paper's point of view the ball would first appear as a small sphere as it entered and then gradually get larger as it continued to enter until the middle of the ball and then as it departed would get smaller and smaller until it totally disappeared. And that's precisely what some of the UFO's do as they enter and depart. Hey, wait a second. The Bible says demons come from another dimension called the spirit realm. Very interesting! So again, these beings and their so-called craft don't appear to be so much physical in nature as they are spiritual in nature.*

Flying Saucer Review UFO's: *First of all, this periodical supports an assemblage of over 50 experts and specialists worldwide who conduct major UFO encounter investigations and is just one of the few journals that has objectively and thoroughly evaluated the phenomenon worldwide for almost 40 years.*

Gordon Creighton, Editor: *"There seems to be no evidence yet that any of these crafts or beings originate from outer space."*

Brad Steiger: *"We are dealing with a muti-dimensional para-physical phenomenon which is largely indigenous to planet earth."*

Arthur Clark, famous science fiction writer: *"One theory that can no longer be taken very seriously is that UFO's are interstellar spaceships."*

So, as you can see, based on these findings, many researchers, secular even, believe that UFO and their supposed occupants are clearly of a "supernatural-spiritual" origin and not some natural in origin from Outer Space. And wonder of wonders, again, it just so happens to fit the profile of demons.

Chapter Ten

The Fear of UFO's

The **4ᵗʰ reason** why UFO's are clearly demonic in origin is because they **Instill Emotion** like demons. Let's see what happens when demons appear on the scene according to the Bible.

Mark 1:21-27 "They went to Capernaum, and when the Sabbath came, Jesus went into the synagogue and began to teach. The people were amazed at His teaching, because He taught them as One who had authority, not as the teachers of the law. Just then a man in their synagogue who was possessed by an evil spirit cried out, "What do you want with us, Jesus of Nazareth? Have you come to destroy us? I know who you are – the Holy One of God!" "Be quiet!" said Jesus sternly. "Come out of him!" The evil spirit shook the man violently and came out of him with a shriek. The people were all so amazed that they asked each other, "What is this? A new teaching – and with authority! He even gives orders to evil spirits and they obey Him.""

Mark 9:17-27 "A man in the crowd answered, "Teacher, I brought you my son, who is possessed by a spirit that has robbed him of speech. Whenever it seizes him, it throws him to the ground. He foams at the mouth, gnashes his teeth and becomes rigid. I asked Your disciples to drive out the spirit, but they could not." "O unbelieving generation," Jesus replied, "how long shall I stay with you? How long shall I put up with you? Bring the boy to Me." So, they brought him. When the spirit saw Jesus, it immediately threw the boy into a convulsion. He fell to the ground and rolled around, foaming at the mouth. Jesus asked the boy's father, "How long has he been like this?" "From childhood," he answered. "It has often thrown him into fire or water to kill him. But if you can do anything, take pity on us and help us." "If you can?" said Jesus. "Everything is possible for him who believes." Immediately the boy's father exclaimed, "I do believe; help me overcome my unbelief!" When Jesus saw that a crowd was running to the scene, He rebuked the evil spirit. "You deaf and mute spirit," he said, "I command you, come out of him and never enter him again." The spirit shrieked, convulsed him violently and came out. The boy looked so much like a corpse that many said, "He's dead." But Jesus took him by the hand and lifted him to his feet, and he stood up."

Okay, now that'll creep you out! And that's precisely the point. How many of you would say, according to the Bible, that when a demon is on the scene, it instills some serious pain, torment, and fear, etc.? Okay, just a little! And not just the person being possessed and set free by Jesus of the pain and torment, but imagine being one of those people who were there witnessing one of those encounters? That would be some serious fear, right? Well, wonder of wonders, one constant theme of the UFO entities is that they too instill massive fear and utter terror when they show up on the scene. But don't take my word for it. Let's listen to those who say they've had encounters with them.

Whitley Strieber is the author of the bestselling books 'Communion' and 'Transformation' about UFO encounters. Here is how he calls his own personal encounter. "I became entirely given over to extreme dread. The fear was so powerful that it seemed to make my personality completely evaporate. Whitley ceased to exist.

What was left was a body and a state of raw fear so great that it swept about me like a thick, suffocating curtain turning paralysis into a condition that seemed close to death. I died, and a wild animal appeared in my place. They had changed me, done something to me. I wondered if there was any relationship between my experience and the mystic walk of the shaman, or the night ride of the witch. The visitors persisted in my mind like glowing coals.

Whatever this was, it had been involved with me for years. I felt their presence. It was palpable. Most upsetting, I could smell them. Increasingly I felt as if I were entering a struggle that might even be more than life-or-death. It might be a struggle for my soul, my essence, or whatever part of me might have reference to the eternal.

There are worse things than death, I suspected. So far, the word demon had never been spoken among the scientists and doctors who were working with me. Alone at night I worried about the legendary cunning of demons. At the very least, I was going stark, raving mad. I felt an absolutely indescribable sense of menace.

It was hell on earth to be there in the presence of the entities, and yet I couldn't move, couldn't cry out, couldn't get away. Whatever was there seemed monstrously ugly, so filthy and dark and sinister. Of course, they were demons and I couldn't get away."[1]

Elaine Morganelli, *a guest at an L.A. meeting came up with the simple, yet chilling answer, as to why these entities would do this to people. "People can be duped by devils. A demonic spirit can tell you anything. They love to fool you. These people, the UFO abductees, are being taken over. The more you go along with it, the harder it is to get away from it." But to what purpose? "I think they're being used to get an anti-Christian movement going. What got me was when he, Whitley, referred to the Lord and His angel as the 'Nazis of the air'."*

Stuart Goldman, *newspaper writer we saw earlier and who has also talked with Whitley Strieber on several occasions says, "One could write Morganelli off as some sort of Christian fanatic. However, she's not the only one who's come to the conclusion that Strieber's visitors and in turn the beings who are abducting countless thousands of people are nothing more than good old-fashioned demons, doing what they do best, stealing souls."*

Is this evidence starting to add up or what? But that's still not all. Another characteristic of demonic appearances is that when people do have encounter with UFO's, they often end up doing one of three things.

1. Go deeper into the Occult/New Age, i.e. they are led further away from God, and Jesus, and the Bible.
2. Go insane or literally become demonically possessed exactly like what happened to this man.

On the evening of October 25, 1973, a young Pennsylvania farmer, Steven Polanski, and 15 other witnesses saw a bright object hovering over a field. Steven grabbed his rifle and went to investigate. It was then he noticed something walking along by the fence.

They were hairy and long armed with greenish yellow eyes and they smelled like burning rubber was present. Steven sensed that these creatures were not friendly and fired a tracer bullet over their heads. When they kept on coming he fired

directly at one of them. Then all the creatures disappeared into the woods and the glowing object disappeared from the field instantaneously. UFO researchers as well as a state trooper were called in to investigate. When they arrived the people there told them that Steven had been growling like an animal, flaying his arms, his own dog running towards him and Steven attacked the dog. Steven then collapsed and after a while began to come to his senses. The entire group commented on the nauseating Sulphur like odor that was present.[2]

Now, speaking of strange smells and specifically the smell of sulphur, not only did we see that same strange odor presence earlier in the history of UFO, but it's also quite common in both demon and alien encounters.

The 'Amittyville Horror' was based on a factual account of what happened to a family in Amittyville, New York. An irritating and nauseating odor seemed to accompany the presence of the ghost or spirit entity that entered from time to time. Whitley Strieber wrote of his abduction experience in his book 'Communion'. He said he could smell their presence. That it smelled like Sulphur.

Now here's the point. Little do most people realize that sulphur just happens to be the smell to describe the Lake of Fire.

Revelation 19:20 "But the beast was captured, and with him the false prophet who had performed the miraculous signs on his behalf. With these signs he had deluded those who had received the mark of the beast and worshiped his image. The two of them were thrown alive into the fiery lake of burning **sulfur**."

Revelation 20:10 "And the devil, who deceived them, was thrown into the lake of burning **sulfur**, where the beast and the false prophet had been thrown. They will be tormented day and night for ever and ever."

Revelation 21:8 "But the cowardly, the unbelieving, the vile, the murderers, the sexually immoral, those who practice magic arts, the idolaters and all liars – their place will be in the fiery lake of burning **sulfur**. This is the second death."

Not copper, not cheeseburgers, not stale milk, but of all things for aliens to smell like when they appear on the scene is sulphur, the very stench of hell, demons, and the lake of fire. I don't think that's by chance!

But that's not all. The third characteristic of demonic appearances is that when people have encounters with UFO's they not only…

1. Go deeper into the Occult/New Age, i.e. further away from God!
2. Go insane or become demonically possessed like this man did but they also,
3. Go commit suicide. They kill themselves.

And remember, that's exactly what demons do! Their leader satan is a murderer as we saw and has been one from the beginning. However, sometimes, and this is the tricky part, UFO's will appear on the scene with a different kind of emotion. They can also appear on the scene with a sense of euphoria. And this is important because some people who have encounters with UFO's and Aliens will invariably say something like the following.

"Oh, don't tell me these aliens were demons. I experienced nothing but beauty and light. I felt so much love emanating from them. It was totally pleasant and absolutely wonderful. They can't be demons. That's crazy!"

Not so. The Bible says angels, which demons are, only the fallen kind, can play good cop, bad cop and deceive you.

2 Corinthians 11:13-15 "For such men are false apostles, deceitful workmen, masquerading as apostles of Christ. And no wonder, for satan himself masquerades as an angel of light. It is not surprising, then, if his servants masquerade as servants of righteousness. Their end will be what their actions deserve."

And believe it or not, these guys that I'm about to share with you found out the hard way, just how deceptive these beings can be, including going to the extreme of playing this good cop, bad cop on you, masquerading as an angel of light!

Mike Mundel is a Canadian, entertainer and lecturer. For many years he was involved in various aspects of the occult including mediumship. Dozens of entities would speak through him on an on-going basis. "I became involved in what is now called channeling in the late 1960's. It was a spontaneous experience.

We had been trying astral travel and a group of other techniques to let our spirits leave our bodies to develop clairvoyant abilities and so on. When I say we, I mean a small group that had polarized together around an occult world view. By trying these different techniques, I inadvertently opened myself up and various entities began speaking through me. Initially speaking in my head and eventually taking over to such a degree they were using my vocal cords, speaking through me to my friends."

Steve Wahrer, former Occultist: "Mike could literally be talking to you like I am now and instantly in a moment change, be taken over, and someone else would be talking. His voice would literally stop being Mike and then be somebody else."

Mike Mundel: "Initially it seemed like it took quite a bit of effort to take control of me. And, it was more or less a voluntary thing. But as time passed it was getting much, much easier for them to slip in and out. We used to call it popping in. We used to say 'Oh, so-in-so just popped in'. And then they would be gone. Sometimes they would be around for hours and others for just a few minutes. Then we eventually realized that they were able to go in and out as they pleased, by the end of things.

We asked one of the entities, 'Why is it you can go in and out of Mikes personality so readily?' And they said something to the effect of all human beings have a door that will keep other spirit beings out and, in most peoples, cases the door is locked, barred, and stapled, shut, rope shut, and sealed and that in my case it was virtually off the hinges."

Steve Wahrer: They claimed to be distinctive entities. In other words, if they had a name, they would say their name, if they had a purpose they would tell you that in many cases. But the range would range from very low-level life forms that didn't really have any purpose except to be pranksters, that sort of thing, up to the human range, up to the ascended masters, the wise, benevolent, powerful type entities and the antisepsis of that, evil, powerful, intelligent, entities as well."

Mike Mundel: "They claimed to be ascended masters, highly advanced spirit beings from other planets, people from various astral planes, reincarnated and then gone on to perfection, Tibetan Buddhists, people from the past. I mean there was an entire realm they called themselves, but the common thread was that they were all spiritually pure and were contacting our little group specifically to help us evolve spiritually."

Wahrer often experienced strange occurrences. He feared the darker controlling entities, one of whom regularly threatened him with knives. Still he was fascinated with the spirits powers.

Steve Wahrer: "One evening when I was over at Mikes place we were just sitting talking when all of a sudden one of the entities popped in and became visibly angry with primarily myself. He began ranting and raving, I can't remember the exact words he was saying but he sort of stormed off and went into the kitchen.

My habit was to always follow Mike into the kitchen where there were knives present.

So, I just followed but I was very concerned with what was going on. As I got to the doorway of the kitchen, Mike was standing, and he picked up two coke bottles off the counter, two 26oz coke bottles, and held them both out in front of him and crushed them both simultaneously, one in each hand. Then unfortunately, the entity left, and Mike was not able to come back right away and in that delayed time Mike fell forward into the broken glass, cutting his hands, I don't know if they were cut then or if they were cut when he broke the bottles, but they were cut very badly.

He was obviously in shock when he came back. I got him up and moved him to the couch in the living room and again he was taken over by a different entity that seemed much gentler and more benevolent and held out his hands in a very almost pathetic sort of way, 'Do the wounds on my hands look familiar to you?' Now we had an entity who was claiming to be or imitating Christ."

Mike Mundel: "One of the things the entities used to do was they used to test us. It was as though we were being brain washed. We would be told to do something very bazaar immediately. Or we would be told to go at midnight to a certain forest that was very, very terrifying to us because there had been a number of manifestations there. We would be told to go alone at midnight, stay there for an hour and then come home.

They were testing our readiness to respond immediately to their commands and we were not to test them ever. Because they said proof comes to those who do not ask for it. Which sounds vaguely Biblical, but it isn't. I recall one time one of the entities was put to the test.

One of the particular people in the group suddenly spoke to it in German and the entity, without missing a beat stopped its sentence with the other person, turned and addressed that person in fluent German and then turned back and continued the conversation. None of us knew German, none of us had studied it at any time but the entity was able to switch in and out of the other language immediately."

Emanuel Swendenborg spent an entire lifetime associating with the spirit world, yet he warned, "When spirits begin to speak with a man, he ought to beware that he believes nothing whatever from them, for they say almost anything. Things are fabricated by them and they lie. They would tell so many lies and indeed with solemn affirmation that a man would be astonished. If a man listens and believes they press on and deceive and seduce in many ways."

Mike Mundel: *"They claim to be ascended masters but in reality, they were the exact opposite, end of the spiritual scale. There is no question in my mind now that they were demon spirits. If you would have asked me then I would have believed entirely that they were higher beings, a higher spiritual order of beings. I wouldn't have believed in demons. I didn't believe they existed. I thought they were an invention of the Christian Church. In retrospect now, I can see back with horrible clarity that they were malevolent, created, demonic, spirits intent on our destruction."*

"Some of these entities out here will say 'Oh yeah, there are bad spirits and there are good spirits', in fact the old mediums before the channelers came along, it was a little more complicated. The mediums would have a control, it's called a control spirit and the function of the control spirit was to keep the bad spirits away. To kind of line things up to make it work out as it should. And they would even say, "Oh that was just a lower entity".

Mike Mundel: *"In my own case I recall that some of the entities that we had to deal with were overtly violent, almost psychotic and the others were pure and altruistic and all they wanted to do was help us and they would warn us about things that the nasty entities were doing and they would give us teachings and methods of developing ourselves and so on.*

But in retrospect I'd like to say all the entities were equally evil. It was the clever way it was presented by showing this group as overtly evil made us readier to accept these guys as the good guys. In reality, they were all in it together. Whatever they say they are, Jesus Christ, Buddha, your Aunt Vera, whoever, they are not your true altruistic beautiful beings that they claim to be.

If you strip away the covering you will find a demon behind every one of these voices, behind every one of the spirits. In fact, one of their most clever ploys is what the Bible says. Even Satan disguises as a spirit of light. We are seeing these emissaries of evil that are dressing in the most wonderful packaging, so people are accepting them as genuine. People are seeing them as good and pure and in reality, even the good ones are demon spirits."

Sounds to me like demons are so sneaky that they can bait you into darkness by first appearing as an angel of light! Then their true colors eventually come out. Where have I heard that before? Speaking of their ability to masquerade and morph into different shapes, here's what one researcher said about this deceptive characteristic of UFO's.

John Ankerberg: *"Around the globe there are tens of thousands of reported 'UFO entity' cases, thousands involving human abduction reports. These entities range in size from just a few inches to almost 20 feet, but usually between four and seven feet. They appear in forms that are human or humanoid, robot or animal-like, bizarre or ghostly. Sometimes these entities exhibit deliberate hostility toward humans which has resulted in physical or psychological harm, and even possession by the entity.*

Most of the time they feign an aloofness toward man, or in contactee cases a genuine 'concern'. Sometimes, just like UFO's, these beings appear independently in three-dimensional space and time, while at other times they exist only in the experience of the 'observer'. The morphology or form of the UFO 'occupants' suggests ties to the earth, not outer space. Classification of the entities correspond broadly to creatures of historic folklore, mythology, demonology, and occultism in a wide variety of times and cultures.

The fact that the UFO entities fit historic patterns of previously existing morphological types from many occultic traditions argues for their being indigenous to this planet. Both Lawson and Vallee have done interesting and important work in this field. It is significant that Lawson himself observes. The devil 'is a polymorph and so can mimic any form imaginable or change his size at will.'

That's exactly what these UFO entities do and that's why many UFO researchers just flat out call them for what they are. They too believe they are demonic! But don't take my word for it. Let's take a look at their quotes.

Dr. Jacques Vallee: *"We are dealing with a yet unrecognized level of consciousness, independent of man but closely linked to the earth. I do not believe anymore that UFO's are simply the spacecraft of some race of extraterrestrial visitors.*

This notion is too simplistic to explain their appearance, the frequency of their manifestations through recorded history and the structure of the information exchanged with them during contact. An impressive parallel can be made between UFO occupants and the popular conceptions of demons. UFO's can project images or fabricated scenes designed to change our belief systems.

Human belief is being controlled and conditioned, man's concepts are being rearranged and we may be headed toward a massive change of human attitudes toward paranormal abilities and extraterrestrial life. (i.e. they're deceiving us). The medical examination to which abductees are said to be subjected, often accompanied by sadistic manipulation, is reminiscent of the medieval tales of encounters with demons.

The symbolic display seen by the abductees is identical to the type of initiations ritual or astral voyage that is imbedded in the occult traditions of every culture. Thus, the structure of abduction stories is identical to that of occult initiation rituals."[3]

Lynn Catoe, *UFO researcher: "A large part of the available UFO literature is closely linked with mysticism and the metaphysical. It deals with subjects like mental telepathy, automatic writing and invisible entities as well as phenomena like poltergeist or ghost manifestations and possession. Many of the UFO reports now being published in the popular press recount alleged incidents that are strikingly similar to demonic possession and psychic phenomena."*

Dr. Pierre Guerin, *an eminent scientist associated with the French National Council for Scientific Research: "UFO behavior is more akin to magic than to physics as we know it. The modern UFOnauts and the demons of past days are probably identical. What is quite certain is that the phenomenon is active here on our planet, and active here as master. (i.e. they're controlling things)"*

John A Keel, one of the most informed persons in the world on UFO's, author of the now-classic 'UFO's: Operation Trojan Horse': "The manifestations and occurrences described in this imposing literature on demonology are similar if not entirely identical to the UFO phenomenon itself. The UFO manifestations seem to be, by and large, merely minor variations of the age-old demonological phenomenon."

Ivar Mackay, former chairman of respected British UFO Research Association, "If one sets the three occult groups against the three classifications of UFO entities and their characteristics it is rather surprising how complementary to each other they appear to be, not only through their appearance, activities, and level of behavior but also in the quality of mental and especially, emotional reaction and response that has been noted to have occurred on contact."

Trevor James, a veteran UFO researcher: "A working knowledge of occult science is indispensable to UFO investigation."

Sociologist Stupple and McNeece stated, "Studies of flying saucer cults repeatedly show that they are part of a larger occult social world."

John Keel (UFO's Operation Trojan Horse) and Dr. Jacques Vallee, (Messengers of Deception) both believe that the UFO entities are deliberately programming their human observers with false information in order to hide their true nature and purpose. Dr. Vallee has actually addressed the UN on UFO's and was the model for 'Lacombe in Seven Spielberg's film 'Close Encounters of the Third Kind.' He has spent decades in serious UFO research and like veteran UFO researcher John Keel, he has put his intellectual finger on the lowest common denominator of UFO contacts, deception, and also on the most common parallel to UFO phenomena, paganism and demonology. Vallee also reveals that 'The UFO beings of today belong to the same class of manifestation as the occult entities that were described in centuries past.' (i.e. demons)

John Ankerberg: "No one can deny that even many non-Christian researchers have concluded that the UFO phenomenon is an occult one. If it can be established that the world of the occult is the masterpiece of the biblical Satan and his demons, then it is logical to conclude that UFO's constitute a demonic phenomenon with a hidden agenda. After 20 years the extent and depth of our research now constitutes for us a conclusion that has become a virtual certainty that UFO's constitute a spiritistic (demonic) phenomenon. We believe that such a conclusion may affect us all."[4]

Now, lest you think these demonic entities really don't have an evil murderous agenda when one makes the mistake of cohabitating and intermingling with them, let us now observe the unfortunate fate of the man who uncovered their deceptive deeds as we saw earlier. Apparently, they didn't like what Joe exposed.

"Joe Fisher, 53, author of The Siren Call of Hungry Ghosts, died on Wednesday, May 9, 2001, by jumping off a limestone cliff at Elora Gorge, near his hometown of Fergus, Ontario, Canada. Troubled by personal problems, as well as by the spirits he claimed to have angered in writing the Siren Call of Hungry Ghosts appeared to have pushed him over the edge.

That he would do so is all the more surprising considering what he had written earlier in The Case for Reincarnation: 'As much as the suicidal personality feels able to escape the world by getting rid of the body, reincarnation's revolving door ensures that all hope (of escape) is short lived. Those who learn that they have killed themselves in past lives are quickly brought to the realization that suicide, far from being an answer to life's problems is (instead) the violent breaking of the lifeline. If the (suicide) could only realize the resulting intensification of difficulty which must enter the life to come, (suicide) would never be (attempted).'

Joe Fisher was an investigative writer specializing in metaphysical topics. His books had sold more than one million copies in 22 languages.

He was born and educated in England and held dual citizenship with Canada, his home base since 1971. He regularly gave workshops and seminars based on his explorations into the supernatural.

A veteran broadcaster who gave more than 200 radio and television interviews on his work, Fisher started his career as a junior reporter on The Staffordshire Advertiser where he became, at 22 years of age, the youngest news editor in England. After emigrating to Canada, he worked as an investigative reporter and feature writer for both The Toronto Sun and The Toronto Star.

His journalistic stints were interspersed with excursions to Greece, Ireland, Ecuador, Morocco and Peru where he pursued personal writing projects. At Ecuador's Colegio Americano in Quito, he taught English and composed journals which were later edited for the book Cotopaxi Visions: Travels in Ecuador.

In 1981, Joe Fisher left daily journalism to concentrate on writing books and freelance articles. Since then, he has traveled widely (Australia and Antarctica are recent destinations) and contributed to periodicals ranging from Canada's national dailies, The National Post and The Globe & Mail, to magazines including Outpost, Equinox, Ocean Drive and Life & Soul.

Joe Fisher's books included the contemporary metaphysical classics The Siren Call of Hungry Ghosts, Life Between Life, The Case For Reincarnation and Predictions. While His Holiness The Dalai Lama wrote the preface to The Case For Reincarnation, film rights to Hungry Ghosts have been optioned to a Los Angeles film company which is moving towards production.

For five years, Fisher painstakingly investigated the claims of channelers and the mysterious voices that speak through them. The Siren Call of Hungry Ghosts, his last book, is his gripping journey into a realm of darkness and deception. The revised edition includes a new foreword by Colin Wilson, and an epilogue that updates events since the book was first published in the U.K. a decade ago.

In 1987, Fisher was presented with The Leask Award by The Spiritual Science Institute of Canada for 'making an outstanding contribution to the field of spiritual awareness.'

Many in the publishing community, as well as friends of Fisher's, are expressing shock at his death. A Fergus-area friend, writer Sheila O'Hearn said: 'He believed in giving of himself for other people. He felt, for him, that's what life was all about.' Her husband, Ray Krzyzanowski remarked: 'He's going to be really missed. He was my only real friend here. I'm going to miss him.'

In one of his last communications with his editor-in-chief, Patrick Huyghe at Paraview Books, Fisher noted that the spirits were still after him for having written his final book. Fisher's family have decided there will be no services."[5]

So sad! What a deadly deception going on here. It looks like these entities weren't too pleased with what Joe was exposing so they decided to take him out. Why? Because that's what demons do, they lie, they instill fear, and they kill if they need to. Wonder of wonders this is the same track record we see with UFO's and Aliens!

Chapter Eleven

The Actions of UFO's

The **5th reason** why UFO's are clearly demonic in origin is because **they Act Like Demons**. It just so happens that another strange feature or characteristic of UFO's is that they typically appear to people who have some history and/or involvement in occult practices. It's like once you engage in these occult demonic practices, wonders of wonders, you just opened the door for, of all things, UFO contacts to start coming in. This is exactly what these researchers are also saying.

One researcher stated: "An inordinately high percentage of the abductees have had previous experience with the occult. I remember when I was younger and into seances, necromancy, psychokinesis, and astral projection that one night I looked into the sky and saw a very bright light that moved at an extremely high rate of speed and made sudden and severe changes in direction during its flight. It moved extremely fast and accelerated out of sight as it moved high into the night sky and disappeared. I saw this with my own eyes.

But it doesn't stop there. During my occult days, I also saw many other unusual manifestations, heard voices and saw things move. I could go on but suffice it to say that I confirm the findings of those who experience UFO phenomena, and they are very often involved in the occult.

This is alarming and a major warning. My conclusion is that the UFO phenomena is occultic in origin and demonically based. I do not believe there is life on other planets, and I suspect that what has been manifested is nothing more than a great deception that is slowly enveloping mankind."

Other researchers state, "In fact, we know of no UFO contactee who is not basically a spiritistic medium."

Jacque Vallee says, "It is the rule, rather than the exception, to find significant UFO sightings preceded or followed by other anomalies, notably of the poltergeist variety."

So, you get involved in the occult and UFO's appear. Interesting. In fact, let me give you an actual testimony of two people that I personally know who have had major encounters with UFO's. One is a lady named Kristine in Oregon and who I talked with many times and personally interviewed on this issue. The other is another good friend named Bud from Arizona. I asked both of them to write down their background and here's what they shared.

Kristine's Occult Involvement

"My father, when he was in the military, got heavily involved with the occult. He said he was in a séance with some of his clan and the table started levitating and he heard voices.

They all ran out of the room and these phantom things followed.

He didn't say too much more about the experience. The weird thing is he says that a bald man sits by him at night and tells him what the kids are doing.

Then there was a Ouija board at our house from my father.

Somehow, we got hold of it and started playing with it.

We would hear scratching inside the walls of the house after that and to this day that house scares the heck out of me. There is something there not godly."

Bud's Occult Involvement

"Growing up I was always fascinated about the possibility of other life out there. I could not get enough about them. So, while surfing the net about them and ghost hunting, etc. I ran across a video that showed you how to make them show up on demand.

It worked so well, I would invite family and friends over on weekends to witness it and we would have BBQ's and play with this. However, it wasn't long before I started seeing dark shadows pass over me and around the yard. They were darker than the night but so dark you could see them. Hard to explain but true. I never said anything to anyone, so they would not get scared plus I really didn't know what I was seeing.

It wasn't until a few weeks later that my second oldest daughter asked me, 'Dad, what are those dark things that fly over us?' When I heard that I just got the chills and my eyes even started to water. It was such a strange feeling because I guess I was hoping that maybe it was just me. So, I caught my breath and said, 'So you see them also?'

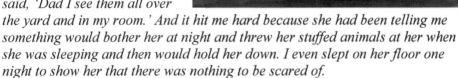

Then my youngest daughter said, 'Dad I see them all over the yard and in my room.' And it hit me hard because she had been telling me something would bother her at night and threw her stuffed animals at her when she was sleeping and then would hold her down. I even slept on her floor one night to show her that there was nothing to be scared of.

In fact, I set a video camera to prove to her that nothing happens while we're sleeping. Well, I couldn't show her that video because she was right, and I was wrong. Then one night my wife and kids took the puppies outside to let them run before bed and my daughter ran back in telling me mom said to come and look at this.

When I got outside I looked up and this huge reaper shaped thing was gliding in the air going around our house. It looked like silk flying in the wind, but it kept circling our house. So, I walked up to about 10 feet from it and it just stared back at me. I could not see a face, but the hood was facing right at me.

It was a windy full moon night and when I saw it fly in front of me I said, 'God, what is that?' We didn't talk much about it after that and still don't today. We no longer watch videos on ghost hunting, UFO's, or even scary movies, etc. We know who they are and what they want."

They want to mess you up because that's what demons do! So, is it really that surprising that once you start messing with the demonic occult issues, demonic practices, and demonic teachings, that it just so happens to open the door to demonic UFO activity? I don't think so. I think it's one and the same!

Chapter Twelve

The Possession of UFO's

The **6ᵗʰ reason** why UFO's are clearly demonic in origin is because **they Possess Like Demons**. As we saw earlier, the Bible clearly teaches how people can become possessed by demons. It's all over the Scripture. Well again, wonder of wonders, guess what these UFO occupants also do? They just happen to possess people just like demons. Shocker! In fact, so much so that even other researchers are seeing the obvious connection.

John Ankerberg: *"Perhaps there is no more striking hallmark of the occult than that of spirit possession. There are literally thousands of documented cases, many involving very ugly endings. But this phenomenon is similar if not identical to the possession of UFO contactees, as well as some Close Encounter UFO cases.[1]*

Whether in the occult or Ufology, the person is taken over by the invading entity, sometimes voluntarily, sometimes involuntarily, and controlled by the creature for whatever purposes it has in mind. Among UFO contactees or others who communicate personally with the alleged extra-terrestrials there are also literally 1,000's of cases of what can only be termed spirit possession.

Incidents of possession are mentioned by Keel, Steiger, Norman, Catoe, Vallee, Schwartz, Reeve, and a dozen other researchers. Indeed, a large number of UFO contactees had an occult or mediumistic background even prior to contact:

Adamski, Van Tassle, Menger, all the way up to Whitley Strieber. In fact, we have personally talked with several alleged abductees and/or contactees who have clearly been demon-possessed.

And many spirit-possessed mediums who are not even seeking UFO communications may end up being contacted and becoming channels for both 'the dead' and 'extra-terrestrials.' The fact that these supposedly advanced beings from outer space prefer to possess their contacts after the manner of demons is further evidence that we are dealing with an occult phenomenon."

Then, just like you'd expect with actual demonic possession, why is it that there's only one way on record to get rid of these beings when they do come your way. And that's when you command them in the name of **Jesus Christ** to leave and they do, every time!

Ephesians 6:12: "We wrestle not against flesh and blood, but against principalities, against powers, against the rulers of the darkness of this world, against spiritual wickedness in high places."

"This phenomenon was an actual phenomenon, this was actually happening to these people." "I was paralyzed." "It was luminescent." "It had grey skin." "What I saw a typical grey." "It had big black eyes." "They all were dealing with something that was very unusual from a human prospective. This was something that I felt we needed an answer to. For at this point in time there were no answers."

"My name is Joe Jordan. I am the state director of the Mutual UFO Network of Orange County Florida. I am also lead field investigator. When we get a call for an investigation, we take all the information we can over the phone and then we send investigators out, sometimes myself, sometimes other investigators go with me.[2]

We follow-up and make the investigative report. These people are sincere, they have sincere experiences and they are looking for help. They feel like we, as researcher and investigators, could be of some help."

"My name is Joyce Arens and I'm a floral designer. My husband and I were laying in bed. I was laying on my right side and all I could see when I opened my eyes was this red light about the window. I could see my husband's shoulder, but

I was paralyzed. Their skin looked like elephant skin. It had a round head with big wrap around eyes."

Joe Jordan: "As an honest researcher, I realized I couldn't just count these people out because the stuff that they had was so bazaar. Most of the researchers in this realm had said it wasn't possible. This type of experience. I called some of the leading researchers in the country and I said, 'Guys, I've got a very unusual case here.

This man, I'll use the name Bill, enduring his experience in fear, he calls out Jesus, Jesus, Jesus, Jesus please help me. By calling out, he abruptly stopped his abduction experience.' These entities can be stopped in the name and authority of Jesus Christ."

Joyce Arens: "After I accepted Jesus Christ, they tried to come. I kept saying 'No, no, no, you're not doing this,' and I took on the empowerment of Jesus Christ, and I stopped that."

Joe Jordan: "For we wrestle not against flesh and blood. These are spiritual entities."

Joyce Arens: "Taking on the empowerment of Jesus Christ put a stop to a lot of things and He has helped me a great deal. Thank you, Lord."

Colossians 2:15: He has spoiled principalities and powers; He made an example of them, triumphing over them in victory.

Of all things to do to stop an alien encounter or abduction is to rebuke them in the Name of Jesus Christ and they flee? That's exactly what demons do! They have to do what Jesus says. They have to obey Him!

Mark 1:23-27 "Just then a man in their synagogue who was possessed by an evil spirit cried out, "What do you want with us, Jesus of Nazareth? Have you come to destroy us? I know who you are – the Holy One of God!" "Be quiet!" said Jesus sternly. "Come out of him!" The evil spirit shook the man violently and came out of him with a shriek. The people were all so amazed that they asked each other, "What is this? A new teaching – and with authority! He even gives orders to evil spirits and they obey Him."

Mark 3:11-12 "Whenever the evil spirits saw Him, they fell down before Him and cried out, "You are the Son of God." But He gave them strict orders not to tell Who He was."

Mark 5:1-13 "They went across the lake to the region of the Gerasenes. When Jesus got out of the boat, a man with an evil spirit came from the tombs to meet Him. This man lived in the tombs, and no one could bind him anymore, not even with a chain. For he had often been chained hand and foot, but he tore the chains apart and broke the irons on his feet. No one was strong enough to subdue him. Night and day among the tombs and in the hills, he would cry out and cut himself with stones. When he saw Jesus from a distance, he ran and fell on his knees in front of Him. He shouted at the top of his voice, "What do you want with me, Jesus, Son of the Most High God? Swear to God that you won't torture me!" For Jesus had said to him, "Come out of this man, you evil spirit!" Then Jesus asked him, "What is your name?" "My name is Legion," he replied, "for we are many." And he begged Jesus again and again not to send them out of the area. A large herd of pigs was feeding on the nearby hillside. The demons begged Jesus, "Send us among the pigs; allow us to go into them." He gave them permission, and the evil spirits came out and went into the pigs. The herd, about two thousand in number, rushed down the steep bank into the lake and were drowned."

If there's one thing clear in the Bible it's that demons obey Jesus, they have to. Again, why is it that of all methodologies that will get rid of these UFO occupants if they do come your way, is when you command them in the Name of Jesus Christ to leave and they do? That's how demons respond! They have to obey the authority of Jesus as these next stories reveal.

***Testimony #1** Jennifer: "At first everything was normal, it appeared normal, there was nothing unusual."*

Reporter: 521 was the new home of the Moe family. Dean and Jennifer moved their nine children across the state of Oregon to Pastor a church.

Jennifer: "As time went on, after a couple of weeks our children started coming to me and asked me what I wanted. They would say, 'Why did you call me, mom?' Like I was calling their name, but it wouldn't be me that called them to me."

Charles: "I would get told to do stuff and I would do it. Like mom asked for ice water and we got her ice water. She would say, 'Thank you, but I didn't ask for it.'"

Reporter: Dean tried to protect his family from what he thought was a physical being.

Dean: "As time went on I would be laying in bed and hear what sounded like someone coming up the steps from the basement when we didn't have anybody down stairs. I was concerned first of all, that we might have an intruder in the house. I would jump up out of bed and go grab something and open the door to the basement and there wouldn't be anybody there."

Reporter: Fourteen-year-old Charles felt like he was being watched when he went down to the basement.

Charles: "I was putting a box of Christmas stuff inside there, the door slammed, and I was trying to get out. I couldn't get out, it was shut, and it wouldn't open."

Jennifer: "At that point I knew it was a demon present in our house. None of our kids would go downstairs without having the upstairs door open and you had to stand there at that door way and watch for them, so they could shout if they needed you in order to come back upstairs. They would sleep in our room, on our floor, or the living room floor, they wouldn't even go in their rooms to sleep, they wanted to be that close to mom and dad."

Reporter: Eventually Jennifer couldn't sleep at night either.

Jennifer: "I'd be asleep and usually there would be a flash of light, flashed into my face and that would wake me up. There would either be a face in my face or someone at the foot of my bed or somebody in the hall that I could see, or music. Just strange music that would play in the middle of the night."

Reporter: Dean and Jennifer fasted and prayed over this activity in their home.

Jennifer: "It left, but it had like a temper tantrum on its way out. It flung books around off of one of the bookcases. But it is gone, definitely the house has been set free."

Dean: "When I came home, everybody was more relaxed. The children were more playful. Everything in the house felt so much better. That tension had been released.

Jennifer: "I just want to reiterate the power of our God. Compared to satan, he's still, regardless of anything that he does, satan is definitely in subjection to our God. Greater is He that is in me than he that is in the world. Absolutely a true statement.[3]

Testimony #2 *Geeta Charmin: "When the evil spirit used to come into me I wanted to kill my husband."*

Reporter: Geeta Charmin knew she had been cursed by witchcraft. Demonic thoughts ran through her mind as she walked the crowded streets in New Delhi India. No one was safe, especially her husband.

Geeta: "I gave a lot of money to black magic for spells and drugs to try to get these evil spirits away from me, but nothing changed. I wanted to die, I wanted to kill. It was pure hatred. One day I even thought of killing everyone with poison then kill myself. "

Reporter: But Geeta turned on a TV program that taught that there was someone more powerful than black magic. His name, Jesus Christ.

Geeta: "I thought Jesus might be able to help me. So, I dialed the phone number and asked them to pray for me."

Reporter: The phone counselor prayed with Geeta and helped her to accept Jesus as her savior. Then Geeta turned faith into action.

Geeta: "I told the evil spirit you don't have any authority over me because I am a child of God."

Reporter: The evil spirit fled. A feeling of peace filled Geeta's heart and mind.

Geeta: "My life has completely changed. I speak with love to everyone, to my husband, my mother, and my brothers and sisters."

Demons flee in the name of Jesus and Aliens flee in the name of Jesus. Anybody seeing a connection here? In fact, it becomes even more obvious when you listen to the rest of Kristine's testimony.

"My twin sister and brother and I were left alone for the day on our farm in Oregon. I was eight years old and my brother was 12 years old. The day was hot, and we were playing in our front yard when we heard a strange humming noise and saw shadows come across the lawn.

At first, I thought it was airplanes, but my brother said, 'they are back,' I asked him what and he said these strange things that come and visit but you have to run and hide. Being in the front yard, there were trees and shrubbery but there really wasn't anywhere to hide. I don't know why we didn't go inside. It was only a matter of minutes when these objects landed in our field and another field right outside our own on the other side of the fence that grew grain.

My brother told, my sister and I to hide and we frantically tried finding a spot but couldn't, these creatures were everywhere. I mean they were in droves. We stopped at the mimosa tree and decided to let destiny fall where it may, not knowing anything else to do. While the other same creatures surrounded the house, three of them approached us.

They tried talking us into going with them and my brother told us not to because we would never return. How he knew that I don't know but I think something happened to him before. And he said they do sexual things to you. My brother said the only thing to get these creatures away is by saying, out loud, not thinking it, 'In the name of Jesus Christ I command you to leave.'

As soon as we said those words the three left immediately. One of them tripped on the gravel and left a scuff mark going to a pod that was in the other farms land. We watched all of them take off especially the one where the creatures boarded. The sound became intense like a whirling and then extreme heat and they took off, kind of mid-way stopped in the sky then shot off into the clouds. That's when I knew they hid in the clouds.

Now speaking of clouds in the air, isn't it interesting that the Bible says the following in regards to satan.

Ephesians 2:2 "The prince of the power of the air, of the spirit that is now working in the sons of disobedience."

Ephesians 6:12 "For our struggle is not against flesh and blood, but against the rulers, against the powers, against the world forces of this darkness, against the spiritual forces of wickedness in the heavenly places."

And then Kristine concludes with, "I can tell you that they obey God's Word." Just like a demon has to! But that's still not all. Kristine and the other people are not the only ones who experienced the rebuking of an Alien/demon with the name of Jesus. So, have many others. Check out what these independent researchers discovered.

One Gentleman: "Far from the abductee population including all those with religious beliefs, there is one group of people that, by and large, is notably absent. They are Christians, those who are often described as 'Christian Fundamentalists.'

Many people in the world claim to be a Christian; that is, they have Christian ideals or morality, and may even regard themselves as good people but I am talking about what are known as 'born-again,' Bible believing Christians. It is as if ET's tend to avoid this select group of people.

This reality has been largely ignored by many UFO researchers. Muslims, Buddhists, Jews, agnostics, all seemed to claim abduction experiences. As more case studies were examined, a puzzling trend emerged. The so-called Christians reporting the abduction experience tended to be people who intellectually espoused the existence of God but didn't apply it personally. i.e. not true Christians. But there seemed to be an obvious absence of devout, Bible believing 'walk the walk' Christians. Where were they in this equation?

One experience by a Mr. Bill D., took place at Christmas in Florida in 1976. His abduction started out typically, i.e., late at night, in bed. Earlier in the evening he saw some anomalous lights through his living room window over a forest north of his home. He assumed it was a police helicopter search for drug runners or something.

Whatever it was, it agitated his dogs for several hours thereafter. He eventually went to bed. He was lying in bed kept wide awake by the barking dogs when paralysis set in. He was unable to cry out. He could see nothing but a whitish grey, like a mist or fog, although he sensed someone, or something was in his room. His wife didn't waken.

The next thing he knew he was being levitated above his bed. By this time, he was alive with terror, but he couldn't scream. Here is where the story becomes very interesting. He states 'So helpless, I couldn't do anything. I said 'Jesus, Jesus, help me!'

When I did, there was a feeling or sound or something that either my words that I thought or the word that I had tried to say or whatever had hurt whatever was holding me up. I fell, I hit the bed, because it was like I was thrown back in bed. I really can't tell, 'but when I did, my wife woke up and asked why I was jumping on the bed.'

This was the first time that experienced field investigators had ever heard of an abduction being stopped, and this man did it by just calling on the name of Jesus.

Another experience stopping abduction with the name of Jesus Christ goes like this.

One man shared, "Back about 1973 my wife had a strange experience in the middle of the night. 'At the time we knew nothing about UFO abductions, so we had no category in which to place it other than extremely lucid nightmare.' It has many of the abduction 'components. The point is that she stopped the entities and the whole experience with the name of Jesus. It's vital to get this information out."

"In addition, the Christian Church is not equipped to deal with such reports because the UFO phenomenon has been largely misunderstood and dismissed by organized religions. Yet as the number of cases mounted, the data showed that in every instance where the victim knew to invoke the name of Jesus Christ, the event stopped. Period.

The evidence was becoming increasingly difficult to ignore. Gradually, things became a little clearer. They started to understand that these events were completely spiritual in nature and resembled ancient stories and descriptions of what the Bible called 'demons.' It seems amazing that the ET-believing Ufologists, and even skeptics, have noticed that modern alien abductions resembled ancient stories of demons. Yet they have ignored the world's most famous and best-selling book, the Bible, which explains their origins. Compare the spiritual nature of UFO sightings with the character of alien abductions and surely, we have to begin to realize that these entities are not real physical ET's from other planets.

They are from another dimension, just as Vallee, Keel, Mack, and so many other UFO researchers, from different sides of the fence have concluded, so, to find their source, one needs to wear 'spiritual glasses.' Unfortunately, most of these modern-day researchers have embraced a humanist-based view of this theory of evolution serving as the creator of both of them and the aliens. This opens them up to spiritual deception and, in turn, has blinded them to the claims of the Bible, which makes God the creator.

I suggest that the answers they have been looking for but do not want to hear may be, 'God is real, and the Bible is true.' This interpretation is further supported by the 'space brothers' single-minded obsession with undermining the Bible's account of the nature and mission of the only 'One' who appears to be able to stop them, Jesus."

Maybe it's just me, but it sure sounds like we're dealing with demons here! I mean, if it walks like a demon, and talks like a demon, and acts like a demon, and is rebuked in the name of Jesus Christ like a demon, then I'd kind of say, we're dealing with demons here! How much more proof do you need?

Chapter Thirteen

The Deception of UFO's

The **7th reason** why UFO's are clearly demonic in origin is because **They Deceive like demons**. If what we've seen thus far wasn't enough proof that we're actually dealing with demons here, little do people know that they're also being used to explain away the Rapture of the Church. It's the ultimate last days deception. Let's take a look at just one Biblical text talking about this next big prophetic event called the Rapture.

1 Thessalonians 4:15-17 "I can tell you this directly from the Lord. We who are still living when the Lord returns will not rise to meet Him ahead of those who are in their graves. For the Lord Himself will come down from heaven with a commanding shout, with the call of the archangel, and with the trumpet call of God. First, all the Christians who have died will rise from their graves. Then, together with them, we who are still alive and remain on the earth will be caught up in the clouds to meet the Lord in the air and remain with Him forever."

Here we see just one passage in the Bible that deals with the evacuation of the Christians from planet earth just before God's wrath is poured out upon the world in the 7-year Tribulation. Now, little do people know that the premise of extraterrestrials, Aliens and UFO's, are poised to become the ultimate excuse to explain away this event, the Rapture of the Church. I think this for obvious reasons. Put yourself in satan's shoes. Here you have an event that you cannot deny, you can't spin it away, it really happened. Millions of people, all around the world, suddenly disappeared, and it's specifically and only Christians. So, the logical normal response to those left behind would certainly be something like, "Oh no! Why didn't I listen to my Christian wife, brother, co-worker, neighbor, whatever? They were right! The Bible is true! I better get right with God now!" At that point, you'd think people en masse would get saved all over the world because of the shock of the Rapture. Therefore, if you were the evil one, theh devil, how would you try to put a stop to this? Simple. You do what you always do and what Jesus warned about. You lie, you deceive! You come up with the ultimate excuse to deny this event, the Rapture of the Church, so people won't connect it with God or Christianity. And that's precisely the ultimate deception behind the lie of Aliens and UFO's. They say it's not God coming to get his Church before He pours out His wrath on the planet. No! They're actually telling and prepping people right now to believe that it's the UFO's that are coming to save us. Don't believe me? Here's what your average UFO enthusiasts are being taught about this next event.

Barbara Marciniak, a famous New Age author and channeler: In her book 'Bringers of the Dawn', she documents what she claims extra-terrestrials from the star system of the Pleiades have told her. "There will be great shifting's within humanity on this planet. It will seem that great chaos and turmoil are forming, that nations are rising against each other in war, and that earthquakes are happening more frequently.

The Earth is shaking itself free and a certain realignment or adjustment period is to be expected. The people who leave the planet during the time of earth changes do not fit here any longer, and they are stopping the harmony of earth. When the time comes that perhaps twenty million people leave the planet at one time, there will be a tremendous shift in consciousness for those who are remaining."[1]

Thelma Terrell, who goes by her spiritual name "Tuella," wrote a book called 'Project World Evacuation' these are some quotes from that book. "Our rescue ships will be able to come in close enough in the twinkling of an eye to set the lifting beams in operation in a moment and all over the globe where events warrant it, this will be the method of evacuation.

Mankind will be lifted, levitated shall we say, by the beams from our smaller ships. These smaller craft will in turn taxi the persons to the larger ships overhead, higher in the atmosphere, where there is ample space and quarters and supplies for millions of people. We watch diligently for the threat of a polar shift for the planet in your generation. Such a development would create a planetary situation through which none could survive. This would necessitate an evacuation such as I have referred to. Earth changes will be the primary factor in mass evacuation of this planet.

There is method and great organization in a detailed plan already near completion for the purpose of removing souls from this planet, in the event of catastrophic events making a rescue necessary. The Great Evacuation will come upon the world very suddenly. The flash of emergency events will be as a lightning that flashes in the sky.

So suddenly and so quick in it's happening that it is over almost before you are aware of its presence. Phase 1 of the Great Exodus of souls from the planet will take place at a moment's notice when it is determined that the inhabitants are in danger. Do not be concerned nor unduly upset if you do not participate in this first temporary lift-up of souls who serve with us.

This merely means that your action in the plan is elsewhere, and you will be taken for your instructions or will receive them in some other manner. Do not take any personal affront if you are not alerted or are not a participant in this first phase of our plan. Your time will come later, and these instructions are not necessary for you at this time."[2]

Timothy Green Beckley: "Many of the New Age workers and instructors who feel that they will be taken will not be taken right away but left behind to help mankind survive through the cataclysmic period. That is their mission."

Kay Wheeler, known by her spiritual name Ozmana, describes herself as a Pleiadian star seed and channeler, published an article entitled, The Time is Now. "Souls of Light", who claim to be ET's from the Seventh Celestial Plane of Life who are concerned with helping earth evolve to full consciousness. She writes of the so called evolutionary purge.

"The Mother is desperately fighting for her life. Many of her vortexes have been drained. She is in critical condition at this time and must turn her thoughts to herself if she is to survive. That is why you see the many crises in the world. Many of these you do not hear about on your 'screen of lies.'

There is much happening on planet at this time. The Mother is cleansing. It is all she knows to do at this time to clear herself of the pollution that exists within her body. But you as light bearers can help your Mother cleanse in such a way that does not destroy all life on this planet.

Much of this is necessary. Many of these beings have appointments to leave at this time. Earth's population needs to be decreased to bring forth the necessary changes upon this planet to move into the fourth dimension. Your Earth is a fourth-dimensional being at this time. She has moved into this energy pattern, and those who plan to stay must be of this vibration.

Many of these beings who are leaving this planet at this time have completed that which they came to do. It is a time of great rejoicing for them. Do not feel sad about their leaving. They are going home. Many are waiting to be with them again. Many beings must move on, for their thought patterns are of the past. They hold on to these thoughts that keep Earth held back."

John Randolph Price, a famous New Age Intellectual and Promoter shares what his spirit guide told him. "The people who didn't go along with the New Age would be wiped off the face of the Earth during the coming cleansing."

Barbara Marciniak: "If human beings do not change, if they do not make the shift in values and realize that without Earth they could not be here, then earth, in its love for its own initiation, is reaching for a higher frequency, will bring about a cleansing that will balance it once again. There is the potential for many people to leave the planet in an afternoon."

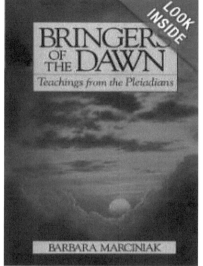

Various quotes from UFO channelers say,
"The cataclysms are all part of purifying this Earth back to a millennium. What is going to happen when you reach a certain point is that you will have the first wave of ascension. Those whose bodies cannot take this change will go in the first wave of ascension.

They will be taken up and their bodies will be changed in the twinkling of an eye. In the twinkling of an eye they will be removed from the physical completely into the new spiritual body. Those who remain will be changed through transfiguration in high places.

This will be the transfiguration of the bodies of those who are stronger that are on the Earth. There will be many visits from the galaxies by inter-dimensional beings, as from the Pleiades to assist and in some cases in your basin areas of large bodies of water to rescue people and take them into higher places. Those are the flying machines that you are seeing coming into your galaxies that have been preparing themselves for up to the last forty years.

They are coming in. Some never die on this earth, these missing persons have already been taken as their time was not up and they were not meant to go through a demise. They went through a lift-off in UFO's."

*The following supposed Alien Message from the Ashtar Command. "Greetings this is **Captain Solaris** speaking to you. Much has been said on the photon belt over the years on planet earth, what exactly is it? And why is it coming to earth? The photon belt is an extremely large belt of cosmic* *radiation that is bundled together, it is the father and mother combined of the ascension bringers.*

It is deadly to those who have not the vibration to stand with it, killing them instantly; we tend to take those who cannot stand up to the vibrations that are quite intense with the photon belt. We relocate them to another world until their souls are ready to move up.

For those who are ready and embrace the positive cosmic radiation they remain on earth. Once the earth is healed many people will be stunned as they feel their insides being changed. Many will scream as the last of their fear is taken away. The final step is the light which takes the world and all of its inhabitants including the moon to the fifth dimension where we will then land and introduce ourselves.

So, we ask each an every one of you to be patient, for the time is coming when the human race will ascend with the photon belt, now it's time for the second wave. Thank yourselves you are the ground crew who are going to change the earth." (i.e. help propagate the lie)

One researcher stated, "For almost 2000 years, the Christian belief has been that God will evacuate the earth of all born-again believers, prior to His pouring out of his wrath and Jesus' Second Coming to establish:

His reign and rule upon the earth, not to mention that whole final judgement of all souls, thing. But for many years now, many among the New Age movement have received messages from aliens and spirit guides that Mother Earth will soon cleanse herself by ejecting all those with bad vibratory patterns (i.e. the Christians) to another realm, allowing ascended masters and aliens to help us bring in a Golden Age upon the earth."

Really? Or maybe it's what the Bible calls man's worst nightmare, the 7-Year Tribulation. You talk about deception! Again, put this UFO evacuation talk instead of the Biblical Rapture in its context. It's the ultimate excuse. Imagine the day when tons of people worldwide are going to disappear from the planet via the Rapture of the Church. The whole world will be in a state of absolute panic and wondering, hoping, groping for some answer just to pacify their emotions. Human nature is that they'll gravitate towards any excuse just to maintain their sanity. But this isn't just any excuse. It's the ultimate excuse! The one that's been slowly methodically prepared for us over the last 150 years of evolutionary brainwashing. All it's going to take now is for somebody to get up and say, "Don't worry. Your loved ones are just fine. They've been beamed up by UFO's and are awaiting their time of rehabilitation when they can join us here back on earth safely as we, the chosen ones, now enter the Age of Utopia." That's not only plausible, but after all this prep work over the last several decades to get us to believe this lie, that's believable. It makes total sense. It's the ultimate last days deception! And the irony is that while many people would deny the event that the Bible calls the Rapture, it is this very event that the occult is waiting for to usher in the Antichrist's kingdom.

How Occult Sees Last Days

They believe that once all the world's religions come together (and they're expecting it soon) a religious leader will be chosen to be earth's religious spokesman and will then encourage all the people of the world to accept a new world leader, who will suddenly appear on the scene. Which sounds like the false prophet the Bible talks about, who convinces the world to worship the Beast or the antichrist. The occult is also in agreement that none of this can fully take place until the people who will never go along with this One World Religion are out of the way. Can you guess who that might be: In fact, they say that these people who are restraining or holding things up won't necessarily die but will somehow mysteriously disappear, or in their words, "elect to leave this dimension as if going to another room. And once these people leave this earth, the occult says the new world leader will take his rightful place over the world.

Then and only then will it be possible to build a combination Temple-Church-Mosque in Jerusalem. At the proper moment in history, a world religious leader will visit the combined Jewish-Christian-Moslem sector of Jerusalem to announce that all religions should be combined into one. This action will then finally break the Middle East log jam. Minutes before the antichrist arises, some supernatural sound will be heard and spiritually felt by everybody on the planet simultaneously. At no other moment in world history will so many people be impacted at once. This action is designed to get everyone looking around as to what caused this sound.

Now, what's really odd is there's a flurry of people around the world reporting that these strange noises are already being heard from the sky.

CTV News reports: There's been a lot of buzz reported over the last few weeks about strange sounds being heard in the atmosphere. People around the world and here at home have reported hearing some bazaar noises.

What appears to be the same strange noise reported on social media seems to be the same noise heard all around the world. According to posts on various websites similar noises have been reported for the past couple of years causing a dramatic increase of on-line searches.

Valley News Reports: Some strange noises have been heard around the world in the past few weeks, has people buzzing, especially on You Tube. Clips from Arizona to England all showing folks alarmed with what sounds like a noise right out of a science fiction flick. Valley news team tries to find out if there is any explanation for the strange sounds.

It's kind of like watching a scary movie. The background noise gives you the feeling that something terrible is about to happen.

At a baseball game the batter is about to swing when this sound come on in the back ground and the announcer says it is a haunting sound. As the batter hits a foul the announcers are asking each other, 'What can that possibly be? Someone shut the door, it sounds supernatural.' This sound is heard all over the world.[3]

Then with everyone's attention aroused, images of antichrist will appear simultaneously over the entire earth speaking to mankind, each in his own language. The 'sign and wonders' will have begun. The antichrist will appear as a man to a man and as a woman to a woman, He will appear as a white to white as a black to a black, as an Indian to an Indian, etc. It makes no difference whether you are viewing him in person or on Television. Thus, 'He will show that he is all things to all people.'

And, as one-person states, "I would not be surprised if this group is actually writing the Peace Treaty that the antichrist will sign with Israel at the proper time, which would be the fulfillment of Daniel's Prophecy of 9:27, which starts the 7-year Tribulation."

Another person states: "I believe the world stands at the crossroads. Today, Israel stands at the precipice of her war with her Arab neighbors a situation that seems like it will fulfill the satanic vision of 1870, which foresaw the need to wage three world wars to stage antichrist."

This demonic vision foresaw that the Third World War would start between Israel and her immediate Arab neighbors. Out of the dust, smoke and ashes of this world war, antichrist would come striding. Numerous New World Order authors have stated that the time period immediately preceding its actual implementation would contain the events found in Matthew 24, Wars, rumors of wars, famines and earthquakes in many places, multiplied lawlessness, etc. Society is planned to be wracked with great distress and disorder. UFO's may even appear on the scene. Authors have written about international crises and internal panic. The intended effect is to so panic the peoples of the world that they will accept the new governmental system of the New World Order and the antichrist as he makes his appearance. In fact, even previous presidents have hinted of how an alien presence or threat would instantly polarize us like this would.

President Ronald Reagan: *"Perhaps we need some outside universal threat. I occasionally think how quickly our differences worldwide would vanish if we were facing an alien threat from outside this world. I had a conversation privately with President Gorbachev.*

When you stop to think we are all God's children where ever we may live in the world, I couldn't help but say to him, just think how easy his task and mine might be at these meetings we just held if suddenly there was a threat to this world from

some other species from another planet outside of the universe.

We'd forget all the local differences that we have between our countries and we would find out once and for all that we really are all human beings here on earth together."

"Furthermore, the New World Order Plan envisions such total global panic that the peoples of the world

will be stampeded into accepting the loss of their democratic government, and their freedoms in exchange for a 'promise' to return to normalcy"

In fact, one New Age author tells what this total package of events will be like. "A very short but very deadly global war using nuclear weapons upon select population concentrations was contemplated and was not ruled out. Can you imagine what will happen if Los Angeles is hit with a 9.0 quake, New York City is destroyed by a terrorist planted atomic bomb.[4]

World War III breaks out in the Middle East, the banks and the stock markets collapse, Extraterrestrials land on the White House lawn, food disappears from the markets, some people disappear, the Messiah presents himself to the world, and all in a very short period of time?"

What's going to happen? People will panic and cry out for someone, anyone, to save them and yet the whole thing will be carefully staged. In fact, let's whet our appetite. Imagine if your day started off like this.

A little boy about 9 or 10 yrs. old is sitting on the bank of the river playing with his toy robots. The overcast is so heavy he can hardly see across the river. He starts hearing these loud sounds. It kind of sound like a roar coming from over his head. He starts looking up at the sky. Then the ground starts to shake and practically knocks him off the bench he is sitting on.

Now he is a little frightened, but he can't figure out where the noise is coming from or why the earth just shook. Then he sees what looks like a giant robot walking across the river. He starts to run towards the bridge, so he can get a better look. As he gets to the bridge and closer to the giant robot he looks up into the sky and sees flying saucers passing overhead.

Meanwhile, across town a man is driving his car down the road when he slams on his breaks to stop while three of these giant robot, or aliens, walk in front of his car. He stands there looking up and then he sees the alien ships flying over their heads. These huge robots are so big and so heavy that with each step they take, they tear up the earth. By now, everyone is seeing them.

The city has come to a stop as they watch to see what these things are going to do. The News now has come on the scene with their cameras. As the cameras are rolling and the newscaster is broadcasting what is happening. The huge monsters start shooting missiles out of what looks like their arms, tearing down buildings and destroying the city. The earth shakes, alarms go off, people are screaming and trying to run to safety. The alien ships are now flying lower into the crowds. These things are demolishing everything in their paths, whether it's people, cars, or buildings.

Suddenly airplanes show up trying to shoot these things out of the air. But it seems like the aliens have the upper hand. They are shooting the planes down. They don't have a chance. Then the giants stand still, they bend down and convert to a box like object. Suddenly they explode causing fire to consume what is left of the city and all of its inhabitants.

So, let's ask ourselves the common sense question. "If an event like that really happened, coupled with a stock market crash, nuclear bombs being dropped all over the world, earthquakes, wars, and a food shortage, just to name a few, what would people do? They will do what they have been conditioned to do. They will panic and cry out for someone, anyone, including an antichrist to save them and yet the whole thing will be carefully staged like this lady reveals.

Dr. Carol Rosin: *"When I was a corporate manager of Fairchild Industries in 1974 through 1977 I met the late Dr. Wernher Von Braun in early 1974. At that time Von Braun was dying of cancer, but he assured me that he would live a few more years in order to tell me about the game that was being played.*

That game being the effort to weaponize space, to control the earth from space, and space itself. Von Braun's purpose in life, during the last years of his life, his dying years, was to educate the public and the decision makers about why space weapons are dumb, dangerous, destabilizing, too costly, unnecessary, unworkable, undesirable idea.

The strategy that Von Braun taught me was that first the Russians were going to be considered the enemy. In fact, when I met him in 1974 they were the enemy. The identified enemy. We were told that they had killer satellites, we were told that they were coming to get us and control us, they were commies.

First the Russians were the enemy that were going to build space-based weapons, then terrorists would be identified, and that was soon to follow. We heard a lot about terrorism. Then we were going to identify third world countries crazies that we now call nations of concern.

But he said that would be the third enemy against whom we needed to build space-based weapons and the next enemy was asteroids. Now at this point he just kind of chuckled the first time he said it, ' asteroids were going to build space-based weapons.' So, it was funny then.

And the funniest one of all was against, what he called aliens, extraterrestrials, that would be the final card. Over and over and over during the four years that I knew him and was giving his speeches for him, he would bring up that last card. 'Remember Carol, that last card is the alien card.

"They're inventing enemies he (Von Braun) said, against whom they are going to build this space-based weapon system—the first of whom was the *Russians* which was existing at that time. Then there would be *terrorists*, then there would be *third world countries*, ...then there would be *asteroids*. And then he would repeat to me over and over 'and the last card, the last, the last card would be *the extraterrestrial threat*'... **aka FAKE ALIENS** - Dr Carol Rosin Asst. to Wernher Von Braun at NASA

Whistleblower: GOV'T INVENTING FAKE ENEMIES

We will have to build space-based weapons against aliens and all of it is a lie.' He didn't mention a time line, but he said it was going to be speeding up faster than anybody could possibly imagine. That the efforts to put weapons in space was not only based on a lie but would accelerate past the point of people understanding it until it was already up there, and it was too late.

The last card, the last card, the last card, would be the extraterrestrial threat. "[5]

Wow! What a set up! People not only have no idea what they're headed for, but they have no clue just how deep this demonic deception really goes.

UFO's not only help to try to explain away the Rapture of the Church, but they will help totally prepare hearts to receive the antichrist's kingdom. Once these things occur, people en masse will totally flip out and cry out "Please send somebody, we'll do whatever you want, you can do whatever you want, I don't care, just please bring back some sense of normalcy!" Yet, the whole thing has been carefully staged like a card game. What a lie!

But, what you've got to understand is that they're not just waiting for you and me to get mixed up into the occult or into New Age to come across this information and get indoctrinated into this lie, but it's now being promoted in the mainstream media. Once again, Hollywood to the rescue! Most people don't even realize how the modern-day media has been one of the biggest allies to this lie of UFO's and their demonic message. One man shares this.

How the Media Encourages UFO's

"Shortly after the first modern sightings of UFO's began in 1947, television programs were inspired to popularize the idea of UFO's, aliens, interstellar travel, etc. From Grade 'B' movies, to cartoon, to sitcoms, to all kinds of shows, themes of outer space and contact with alien life have fascinated millions of people including children who are now becoming adults."

And so, now, slowly, methodically, Hollywood is not only getting more and more blatant with the lie of UFO'S and aliens, they're conditioning us. In fact, they're really speeding the deception up right now, to help us visualize away the Biblical Rapture of the Church. Just to make sure our minds are pacified and we never make the connection of the Rapture of the Church with God or Christianity or the Bible, to cover all the bases they are manufacturing a multitude of different UFO scenarios in movies to explain why people suddenly disappear. For instance, one scenario is that the Aliens might be doing another good cop bad cop on us by pitting the good Aliens against the bad Aliens, and how the bad Aliens are the ones who seek to do us harm. In fact, even prominent scientists in the media are saying this would not be a good thing.

MSNBC News reports: Stephen Hawking is in the news tonight as one of the bonafied smart people on the planet. The renowned astrophysicist warned us about aliens from outer space this weekend. People tended to listen up. His new

Discovery Network Series, **Stephen Hawking** *says, "If aliens visit us here on earth the outcome would be much like when Columbus landed in America which*

didn't turn out well for the native Americans." Make a note, he indicates we should stay away from them at all costs. [6]

Well, there you have it! The late Stephen Hawking said it would be bad! So, what do we do? How do we prepare for this? Well hey, no worry! The so-called good Aliens are here to help us! But before the good Aliens could stop them, some people got lost in the fracas, you know, like a cosmic collateral damage. For instance, maybe the people got zapped and that's why they disappeared as this Hollywood movie helps us to imagine.

As the people are standing at the window looking at what is going on outside, balls of light are falling down from the sky. They are trying to figure out what exactly is going on when all of a sudden, one of the objects come flying through the glass and shatters the window.

The News reports, **"They are not from our world"** *as the picture shows police on the street trying to combat these aliens and being annihilated in the process.* **"They will not be stopped".** *They are absorbing all our power supplies, as the world goes dark. The scene of down town is traffic has come to a complete stop.*

"This is downtown Moscow, New York, London, Paris, Tokyo, all of them. They reported invisible invaders. They came here with a plan."

The Aliens plan, **Phase One: Seize the Planet.** *"They can see us, but we can't see them."*

Phase Two: Devour all Energy. *"What do they want?" "Energy, electricity." "Oh, my gosh!"*

Phase Three: Destroy All Life. *As the people watch, the dog barks at one of the beings and suddenly is zapped and disappears."*

So maybe that's what happened to your Christian loved one. The bad Aliens zapped them before the good Aliens could put a stop to it. But then again, maybe they didn't zap us, because that seems a little too harsh, maybe they just sucked us up into their spaceships and took us away like this movie helps us to imagine.

On August 28th, 2009, NASA sent a message into space farther than we ever thought possible in an effort to reach extraterrestrial life. A News report comes in on Channel 22: Stephen Hawking, an astrophysicist and one of the smartest people on the planet warned us about the possibility of aliens from outer space.

There is a flash of fire shot down from the sky into a skyscraper. Then another report comes on another channel: Stephen Hawking's warning on aliens: Do not try to contact them! If extraterrestrials visit us the outcome may be like when Columbus came to America, in other words it didn't turn out too well for the Native Americans.

As a result of trying to communicate with them, now they have come to our planet and are shooting their weapons down at the population of earth. **"Maybe we should have listened!"** *They are annihilating civilization. And they are sucking humans up into their aircraft.* **"Don't look up!"**

I don't think it's by chance that they specifically said don't look up because that's exactly the opposite of what Jesus says to do. He said when you see these things taking place, look up because your redemption draws near.

Luke 21:25-28 "There will be signs in the sun, moon and stars. On the earth, nations will be in anguish and perplexity at the roaring and tossing of the sea. Men will faint from terror, apprehensive of what is coming on the world, for the heavenly bodies will be shaken. At that time, they will see the Son of Man coming in a cloud with power and great glory. When these things begin to take place, stand up and lift up your heads, because your redemption is drawing near."

That's right. Don't worry. Just move along. Thanks to Hollywood you no longer need to be concerned if you see the Biblical Rapture with your very own eyes. Your loved ones, the Christians, they didn't leave the planet because God rescued them before He poured out His wrath upon the earth in the 7-year Tribulation. No! No! No! As you saw with the movies, their disappearance was caused by the Aliens, the bad ones that sucked them up! Ye, never fear, the good Aliens are here to help us restore order to the planet. Yeah right!

But just in case that excuse didn't work, thanks again to Hollywood, maybe the reason why your Christian loved ones disappeared was because the so-called good Aliens came to earth to take only certain people away in order to save mankind from certain destruction. You know, kind of like an environmental protection program. Because as we all know, we're under the constant threat of an asteroid or a comet plunging into the earth and we need to somehow keep the human race thriving like this next Hollywood movie shares.

Object 07/493 was first spotted just beyond Jupiter's orbit by the Space guard program. It was notable by the fact it was not moving in an astroidal ellipse but rather it had a hyperbolic orbit and it was shooting through our solar system. The object is moving at speeds up to 3 times ten to the seventh meter per second.

At first it was projected to pass millions of miles outside of earths orbit, however we soon discovered that the object was not following the gravitational free fall trajectory. As such its path was recalculated. It is coming directly to earth.

"Maybe they are just collecting specimens from our planet." The speaker says. In response a fellow researcher says, "It's not our planet. That's what he said to me in the hospital. An ark, it's an ark, so are all the other spheres. They are saving as many species as they can." He replies, "If the sphere is an ark, if what comes next is the flood."

Now, notice the twisting of the Biblical language there. That's not by chance. And neither is this next possible deceptive scenario with UFO's explaining away people's disappearance from the planet. The Bible says that the Christians are the chosen ones of God and He's coming again to take them again out of the horrible 7-Year Tribulation. But the aliens are right there with their counterfeit too. They too have their "chosen ones" only they're not the ones who believed God's message of salvation through Jesus Christ like the Bible says. No! Rather, their chosen ones are the ones who believed their message of how the Aliens are the

ones who have come to save us, not God, as this next movie regurgitates.

A lady goes into a convenience store. As she enters a warning comes on the TV. "This is not a test. This is an Emergency transmission." The message is, "The solar flares have caused more damage than what we originally thought. We recommend that people stay indoors until further notice. Keep your pets inside, stock up on extra water and if possible seek out underground shelter."

As the people hear this announcement they start to panic. The main character's son tells him, "They are taking us all, Dad. They sent a message ahead. Now they have come for us. It's time to go Dad. They have chosen us, so we can start over. So, everything can start over."

The alien comes down to take them, but the son looks at the alien and says, "What do you mean?" he turns to his dad and asks him, "Why is he saying that?" His dad asks, "What? What is he saying?" The son answers, "He's saying only the children must go. Those who heard the call." The Dad looks at the alien and begs, "Please!"

But as the children start to go onto the alien ship, the aliens transform into a brilliant light form with wings and then they too turn around to go. The dad looks on with tears in his eyes as his son walks on board the ship and it leaves along with all the other ships, taking all the children. The children then are taken to another planet where the air is clean, and everything is beautiful and safe.

The dad is now in his truck going back to his home and he sees what is coming behind him. Fire is engulfing the city. He makes it to his parents' home and holding each other they watch as the fire reaches them and destroys everything. The world is now totally destroyed.

Now, in this movie the so-called Aliens even appeared to have wings like angels. That's not chance. Once again evoking a quasi-Biblical reference. But who is it, according to this movie, that's coming to save us? Not God, but the Aliens. We are seeing for the very first time in mankind's history how people are being prepared right now to explain away the Rapture of the Church, via UFO's even to the point where people will actually think that being left behind is a good thing or even an honorable thing, instead of mankind's greatest nightmare like Jesus warned about.

Then, as if that wasn't bad enough, even when you try to explain this to the average Joe so to speak, thanks to this brainwashing from Hollywood, people today would rather listen to these demons and their demonic message about UFO's than the Bible! Yet, the Bible, the book that nobody wants to read or just scoffs at, actually told us that this very thing would happen, specifically in the last days.

1 Timothy 4:1 "Now the Holy Spirit tells us clearly that in the last times some will turn away from what we believe; they will follow lying spirits and teachings that come from demons."

How can you get any clearer than that? This is exactly what's going on right now with UFO's. These demonic entities are dishing out demonic teachings, and people are buying it! And it's these lies that Jesus warned about just prior to His Second Coming! Watch out that no one deceives you, beware of the false messiah's promising false hopes and false rescues. Don't let anyone deceive you. The Bible says in the last days that there will be a time of great deception marked by a lie so powerful that even the very elect could be deceived if that were possible. Again, I wonder what that lie is? UFO's maybe? Makes you wonder, doesn't it?

And so to me, the question at this point is this, "Why? Why would they do this?" Well, again, what does the Bible say? They're demons. What else do you expect? They are trying to deceive you and keep you from going to Heaven. That's what they do!

John Ankerberg: "Let us begin by asking another question: Why would demons want to do this? The answer for this ruse is deception. People are fearful of death and judgement and are more than willing to listen to alleged postmortem spirits who will soothe their fears and promise them that life after death is other than what the Bible teaches.

But while spirits may play on the fears of people in one instance, they may play on the hopes of people in another. Mankind has always been fascinated with the heavens, and even more so with the recent advent of the space age. Millions of people are longing for contact with a vastly superior civilization from space in the hope that it may solve the world's problems and end war, poverty, and everything else that no one likes.

This longing includes some of our leading politicians and statesmen. So, it is not surprising that demons, whose primary purpose is spiritual deception (leading people away from God) would take advantage of this hope and seek to pervert it. Consider the following. One of the most dominant cultural influences of UFO's is to undermine faith in the Bible.

UFO phenomena support the myth of naturalistic evolution and the idea that man can finally perfect himself apart from God. For many people, belief in UFO's has become a replacement for personal faith in God since the UFO entities encourage people to look to the skies (or the aliens) for their individual and collective salvation. UFO encounters also promote occultism and expand its territory under a novel and unexpected guise.

For other people, the UFO phenomenon makes the Bible outdated and undermines its authority by relegating it to a level of vastly more primitive earthbound literature. The UFO phenomena tend to belittle mankind's place in the universe from its biblical heights to something lower. Man is no longer the crown of God's creation and the one for whom Jesus Christ died. Instead, he is something of an almost infinitely lesser creature, one lower species among probable billions of more advanced species in the universe.

Thus, many extraterrestrial theorists place man as an infinitely small speck in an infinitely vast universe whose only genuine hope for survival is contacting a much more evolved form of life. But the end result, is to cheapen the value of man, his being made in the image of God, and the significance of the fact that God Himself became man in the incarnation to save His creation. This also tends to cheapen the concept of the atonement and Christian redemption."

In other words, they're doing this to deceive you into missing out on Heaven and instead end up going with them straight into the Lake of Fire. And contrary to popular belief, that place of punishment is real. The demons know it, and they want you to join them there too. Let's take a look at what the Bible says about Hell.

"Contrary to the Father of Lies, God's word describes Hell as the place where God pours out his wrath upon the wicked."

Romans 2:5-6,9 "But because of your stubbornness and unrepentant heart you are storing up wrath for yourself in the day of wrath and revelation of the righteous judgement of God, who will render to every man according to his deeds. There will be tribulation and distress of every soul of man who does evil.

Hebrews 10:26-31 "Certain terrifying expectation of judgement, and of raging fire which consumes the enemies of God, severer punishment, for we know Him who said, "Vengeance is Mine, I will repay.' It is a terrifying thing to fall into the hands of the living God"

Contrary to the Father of Lies, Hell will not be a place of friendship and rock music, but of misery, darkness and isolation. The only thing you will hear from others are their cries of torment.

Matthew 8:12 "The subjects of the kingdom will be thrown outside into darkness, where there will be weeping and gnashing of teeth."

II Peter 2:17 "The wicked, for whom the black darkness has been reserved."

God's word declares that there is no rest for the wicked in Hell.

Revelation 14:11 "And the smoke of their torment goes up forever and ever; They have no rest day and night."

Matthew 25:41,46 "Then He will say to those on his left, 'Depart from Me, you who are cursed, into the eternal fire prepared for the Devil and his angels'. Then they will go away to eternal punishment, but the righteous to eternal life."

II Thessalonians 1:7-9 "He will punish those who do not know God and do not obey the gospel of our Lord Jesus. They will be punished with everlasting destruction and shut out from the presence of the Lord and from the majesty of His power."

Every Moment a Soul Goes to Hell for Eternity

You can deny and scoff all you want, but the Bible is clear. Hell is real, and you really don't want to go there. The demons know this. That's why they've concocted this age-old lie about UFO's. They want you to go to Hell and then join them later in the Lake of Fire forever. That's how evil they are.

But the good news is, God doesn't want you to go to Hell. The Bible says Hell was originally created for the devil and his demons. Mankind was originally intended to be in paradise with God. But since we've all blown it, myself included, we've all become disqualified for heaven and instead have earned a place in Hell.

Romans 3:23, 6:23 "For all have sinned and fall short of the glory of God. For the wages of sin is death, but the gift of God is eternal life in Christ Jesus our Lord."

Again, this is the good news. God doesn't want us to go to hell. And so, out of love, He made a way out so that we could escape this horrible destruction. That way out, the only way out, is through His Son Jesus Christ and His death on the cross. He took the death penalty in our place. Please, before it's too late, call upon His Name, ask Him to forgive you of all your sins, believe in your heart that God raised Him from the grave, the Bible says you will be saved. He will come get you, not the Aliens, at the Rapture of the Church. It could happen at any moment, don't delay!

But if you'd rather listen to lying demonic teachings including the lie of UFO's over what the Bible says, then your fate is sealed. That's what this book is all about. That's the question I leaven you with, "Are you ready?" Will you be deceived? Will you fall for the lie? Will you continue to fall for **UFO's: The Great Last Days Deception**? Or will you listen to the truth and receive it before it's too late? Listen to the Words of Jesus.

Luke 12:35-40 "Be dressed ready for service and keep your lamps burning, like men waiting for their master to return from a wedding banquet, so that when he comes and knocks they can immediately open the door for him. It will be good for those servants whose master finds them watching when he comes. I tell you the truth, he will dress himself to serve, will have them recline at the table and will come and wait on them. It will be good for those servants whose master finds them ready, even if he comes in the second or third watch of the night. But understand this: If the owner of the house had known at what hour the thief was coming, he would not have let his house be broken into. You also must be ready, because the Son of Man will come at an hour when you do not expect Him."

Please be ready. The time is now. Call upon the Name of Jesus Christ and ask Him to forgive you of all your sins. Don't fall for the lie! Receive the truth! The Rapture is going to happen and it won't be from liftoff of UFO's. Will you be left behind because you chose to listen to the false teachings of a demon in the last days, just like the Bible warned about? I pray you won't! Please, don't fall for the lie! Don't be left behind like these guys. God Bless!

Everyone is going along with their daily activities. Walking their kids to the park, catching the train to get to work, husband and wife having coffee in the morning. It's just like any other day. It's kind of cloudy, maybe it will rain today. Suddenly, without any kind of warning, the guy walking behind you disappears, the child swinging is gone, and the swing comes back empty. The husband having coffee with his wife, while holding her hand, is left sitting at the table alone and the hand that was holding his wife's hand is now empty. When he opens his hand, he realizes that her wedding ring is all that is left of her. Where have they all gone?

Matthew 24:42 "Watch therefore, for you do not know the hour your Lord is coming."

Take the way out through Jesus Christ. Don't delay. Read the next page. I hope to see you in Heaven. God Bless!

How to Receive Jesus Christ:

1. Admit your need (I am a sinner).

2. Be willing to turn from your sins (repent).

3. Believe that Jesus Christ died for you on the Cross and rose from the grave.

4. Through prayer, invite Jesus Christ to come in and control your life through the Holy Spirit. (Receive Him as Lord and Savior.)

What to pray:

Dear Lord Jesus,

I know that I am a sinner and need Your forgiveness. I believe that You died for my sins. I want to turn from my sins. I now invite You to come into my heart and life. I want to trust and follow You as Lord and Savior.

In Jesus' name. Amen.

Notes

Chapter 1 *The Premise of UFO's*

1. *News Reports on UFO's*
(Various News Reports when searched from Youtube)
2. *Polling Data Revealing People's Beliefs on UFO's & Aliens*
(http://www.etupdates.com/2014/06/24/would-et-contact-challenge-religious-faith/)
(https://www.huffingtonpost.com/2012/10/15/alien-believers-outnumber-god_n_1968259.html)
(https://www.nytimes.com/2017/07/21/opinion/sunday/dont-believe-in-god-maybe-youll-try-ufos.html)
(https://www.newscientist.com/article/dn18437-religion-could-survive-discovery-of-et-survey-suggests/)

Chapter 2 *The History of UFO's Part 1*

1. *History of UFO's*
http://www.rense.com/ufo4/historyofufo.htm
http://wedentondoit.com/blog/2017/4/21/the-1897-texas-airship-invasion
http://thenightsky.org/hopeh.html
2. *Battle of Los Angeles*
http://www.latimes.com/visuals/framework/la-me-fw-archives-1942-battle-la-20170221-story.html
3. *Ghost Rockets*
http://www.bibliotecapleyades.net/ciencia/ufo_briefingdocument/1946.htm
4. *Angelholm Incident*
http://www.mufon.com/maury-island-incident---1947.html
5. *Kenneth Arnold*
http://www.bellinghamherald.com/news/local/article85417412.html
6. *Mantell UFO Incident*

http://www.mufon.com/mantell-case---1948.html

7. *Mariana UFO Incident*
https://sites.google.com/site/ufosandotheroddities/the-mariana-sighting

8. *McMinnville UFO*
https://ipfs.io/ipfs/QmXoypizjW3WknFiJnKLwHCnL72vedxjQkDDP
1mXWo6uco/wiki/McMinnville_UFO_photographs.html

9. *Lubbock Lights*
http://roswellbooks.com/museum/?page_id=166

10. *Washington D.C. UFO Incident*
http://www.openminds.tv/the-beginning-ufo-encounters-over-
washington-d-c/38413

11. *Kelly-Hopkinsville Encounter*
http://www.countryliving.com/life/a44064/eclipseville-hopkinsville-ky-
history/
https://en.wikipedia.org/wiki/List_of_reported_UFO_sightings

Chapter 3   *History of UFO's Part 2*

1. *Antonio Villas Boas*
http://www.conspiracyarchive.com/UFOs/boas-abduction.htm

2. *Dyatlov Pass Incident*
http://mysteriousuniverse.org/2012/01/mountain-of-the-dead-the-dyatlov-
pass-incident/

3. *Betty and Barney Hill Abduction*
https://www.thoughtco.com/the-hills-abducted-by-aliens-3293363

4. *Lonnie Zamora Incident*
https://www.youtube.com/watch?v=03uMtm6E5P0

5. *Exeter Incident*
https://www.huffingtonpost.com/2011/09/08/exeter-new-hampshire-ufo-
sighting_n_951064.html

6. *Kecksburg Incident*
https://www.atlasobscura.com/places/space-acorn

7. *Mothman Sightings*
https://www.chicagoreader.com/Bleader/archives/2017/08/09/theres-been-a-
record-number-of-flying-humanoid-sightings-over-chicago-this-year

8. *Wanaque Reservoir UFO*
https://www.ufoexplorations.com/witness-to-wanaque-great-mass-ufo

9. *Westall UFO*
   http://www.nationalgeographic.com.au/videos/invasion-earth/westall-ufo-sighting-4136.aspx
10. *Portage County UFO*
   https://www.clevescene.com/scene-and-heard/archives/2016/04/14/50-years-ago-a-small-town-ohio-policeman-chased-a-flying-saucer-into-Pennsylvania-and-it-ruined-his-life
11. *Falcon Lake UFO*
   http://www.cbc.ca/news/canada/manitoba/falcon-lake-incident-book-anniversary-1.4121639
12. *Shag Harbor Incident*
   http://nationalpost.com/news/canada/we-saw-something-something-came-down-the-shag-harbour-ufo-sighting-50-years-later
13. *Schirmer Abduction*
   https://kevinrandle.blogspot.com/2008/10/schirmer-abduction.html
14. *Minot Incident*
   http://minotb52ufo.com/introduction.php
15. *Jimmy Carter*
   https://www.politico.com/story/2013/09/this-day-in-politics-096937
16. *Pascagoula Abduction*
   https://www.youtube.com/watch?v=BW3DCv4tfbk
17. *Walton Abduction*
   https://www.youtube.com/watch?v=DRinOL7KjtA
   http://www.travis-walton.com/
18. *Allagash Abductions*
   https://www.historicmysteries.com/the-allagash-abductions/
   https://en.wikipedia.org/wiki/List_of_reported_UFO_sightings

Chapter 4 *History of UFO's Part 3*

1. *Colares Brazil*
   https://ufo-blogg.blogspot.com/2012/04/colares-brazil-ufo-invasion-1977.html
   https://ufologie.patrickgross.org/htm/colareshollanda.htm
2. *Malboeuf Incident*
   https://ufologie.patrickgross.org/ce3/1977-01-06-canada-montreal.htm
3. *Valentick Disappearance*

https://www.historicmysteries.com/frederick-valentich/
4. *Kaikoura Lights*
http://strangesounds.org/2014/11/mysterious-kaikoura-lights-%C2%91unexplained-ufo-sightings-over-new-zealand.html
5. *Val Johnson Incident*
https://www.mprnews.org/story/2015/08/26/minnesota-deputy-squad-car-ufo-mystery
6. *Robert Taylor Incident*
http://www.ufocasebook.com/taylor1979.html
7. *Manises UFO Incident*
https://www.ufo-spain.com/2014/01/06/manises-ufo-incident-spain/
8. *Hudson Valley UFO Sighting*
http://www.unmuseum.org/triufo.htm
9. *Japan Flight 1628*
http://ufodc.com/page%2024.html
10. *Voronezh UFO Sighting*
http://www.nytimes.com/1989/10/11/world/ufo-landing-is-fact-not-fantasy-the-russians-insist.html
11. *Belgian Triangle*
https://www.outerplaces.com/science-fiction/item/3607-revisiting-the-belgian-ufo-wave-of-1990
12. *Montreal UFO*
http://www.thinkaboutitdocs.com/1990-the-place-bonaventure-incident-montreal-quebec-canada/
13. *NASA*
https://www.express.co.uk/news/science/627966/UFOs-caught-camera-NASA-scientists-NOT-explain-away-aliens-space-shuttle
14. *Kelly Cahill*
https://www.ufoinsight.com/kelly-cahill-incident-encounter-shadow-people/
15. *Meng Zhaoguo Incident*
https://www.huffingtonpost.com/michael-meyer/chinese-lumberjack-alien_b_6986618.html
16. *Varginha Incident*
https://www.disclose.tv/three-sisters-found-an-injured-alien-in-brazil-the-varginha-incident-313339
17. *NASA Columbia space shuttle*
https://www.youtube.com/watch?v=lHsNmgOiZnY
18. *Phoenix Lights*

http://www.aliensthetruth.com/ufo-sightings/phoenix-lights/
19.*Mexico City Skyline*
   https://www.youtube.com/watch?v=9H6sEbDLb1o
20.*Somerset Incident*
   https://www.youtube.com/watch?v=JQMIRKttXHQ
21.*UFO over Southern Illinois*
   https://www.youtube.com/watch?v=618Uqte_g1I
   https://en.wikipedia.org/wiki/List_of_reported_UFO_sightings

Chapter 5   *The History UFO's Part 4*

1. *New Jersey Turnpike Incident*
   https://www.youtube.com/watch?v=0McZOARbh3o&feature=related
2. *Tinley Park Lights*
   https://www.youtube.com/watch?v=7nwTVtUdXu4
3. *Leaked footage – O'Hare Airport Incident*
   https://www.youtube.com/watch?v=AlhiAFHHTM4
4. *Islington Incident*
   https://www.youtube.com/watch?v=7CagrSs305o
5. *Alderney Sighting*
   http://news.bbc.co.uk/2/hi/europe/guernsey/6591365.stm
6. *Istanbul Incident*
   https://archivosovni2.blogspot.com/
7. *South India Incident*
   https://www.unexplained-
   mysteries.com/viewvideo.php?id=_TubIwaV1Sg&tid=127974
8. *Hole in the Sky in Moscow*
   https://www.youtube.com/watch?v=nT2jwkCirP0
9. *Spiraling White light in Australia*
   https://www.youtube.com/watch?v=9pgaw6qFbdk
10.*Morphing Spaceship*
   https://www.youtube.com/watch?v=iEgJpATCCWQ
11.*Zhejiang Incident*
   http://www.dailymail.co.uk/sciencetech/article-1293395/UFO-China-closes-
   Xiaoshan-Airport-spotted-flying-city.html
12.*Jerusalem UFO sighting*
   https://www.youtube.com/watch?v=EKmSf-7Nd-M

https://en.wikipedia.org/wiki/List_of_reported_UFO_sightings

13. *Fox interviews Stephen Bassett*
https://www.youtube.com/watch?v=GLNeWTFsg0g

14. *News coverage and Secret Pentagon UFO Research*
https://www.youtube.com/watch?v=bnii4P3N24Q

15. *Art Bell Area 51: The Frantic Caller*
https://www.youtube.com/watch?v=ee3bld4lTG0

16. *Benjamin Crème*
https://www.youtube.com/watch?v=9JihYJhfAs4

17. *Vatican & UFO's*
https://www.youtube.com/watch?v=4Uu4zX8S2Kc

18. *Vatican Behavior*
https://www.youtube.com/watch?v=V0Y1Qg10pys

19. *Pope Francis to Baptize Aliens*
https://www.youtube.com/watch?v=rObvz3U_pTo
https://www.youtube.com/watch?v=pCjPJlc4ds0

20. *Bill Clinton on UFO Landing*
https://www.youtube.com/results?search_query=bill+clinton+kimmel+ufo

Chapter 6   *The Bible and UFO's*

1. Derived from personal Research by Billy Crone

Chapter 7   *The Lies of UFO's*

1. *Christian View*
https://answersingenesis.org/astronomy/alien-life/are-ets-ufos-real/

2. *Logic of the Honey Bee*
http://www.wiseoldgoat.com/papers-creation/hovind-seminar_part4c_2007.html#honeybeenasa

3. *Logic of Mt Rushmore*
https://creation.com/mount-rushmore-evidence-of-design

4. *We came from a Rock*
https://www.apologeet.nl/en/evolutie-

schepping/hovind_transcripts/seminar_3_transcript/
5. *Odds of Single Protein*
   https://www.allaboutthejourney.org/miracle-of-life.htm
6. *Odds of Single Bacteria*
   https://www.jashow.org/articles/general/the-evolution-of-life-probability-considerations-and-common-sense-part-3/
7. *Humanoid Aliens*
   https://www.youtube.com/watch?v=TqahF0nb7rM
8. *Walter Martin*
   https://www.youtube.com/watch?v=-AlZJFnYhnk
   John Ankerberg & John Weldon, *The Facts on UFOs and Other Spiritual Phenomena* (Eugene, OR: Harvest House Publishers, 1992).

Chapter 8   *The False Teachings of UFO's*

1. *John Ankerberg*
   http://christianworldviewpress.com/are-aliens-demons/
2. *Lazaris*
   https://www.youtube.com/watch?v=kElxIukxDfY&list=PLHRqBO6Gb4xR9xRvcB8MkyqATCypAWGoj
3. *Jan Roberts channels Seth*
   https://www.youtube.com/watch?v=LWDZoKNRsAk
4. *Hindu*
   http://www.hinduwebsite.com/gurus.asp.
5. *Mormons*
   https://en.wikipedia.org/wiki/Exaltation_(Mormonism)
6. *Shirley Maclaine*
   https://theintermediateperiod.wordpress.com/2013/11/12/metaseries-out-on-a-limb-at-the-dawn-of-the-new-age/
7. *Joe Fisher*
   http://monkeywah.typepad.com/paranormalia/2011/02/dabbling-in-the-occult.html
8. *Earth First*
   https://en.wikipedia.org/wiki/Earth_First!
9. *James Coburn*
   https://canadafreepress.com/article/earth-day-and-total-transformation-for-a-

post-christian-world
10.*Women's Spirituality Movement*
https://canadafreepress.com/article/earth-day-and-total-transformation-for-a-
post-christian-world
11.*Earth Charter*
https://earthcharterfuture.blogspot.com/
12.*United Religions Initiative*
https://www.jashow.org/articles/guests-and-authors/carl-teichrib/blending-of-
the-gods-the-united-religions-initiative-global-charter-signing/
13.*Oprah Winfrey*
https://www.youtube.com/watch?v=noO_dCWtB1E
14.*Hindu Prayer in Nevada Senate*
http://www.nriinternet.com/NRIhindu/Rajan_Zed/Prayer_in_Senate_
Disrupted.htm
15.*Pope Francis*
https://www.youtube.com/watch?v=tnUCgWydg2A
16.*United Nations*
https://www.un.org/press/en/2004/hrcn1082.doc.htm
17.*Miriam Delicado*
https://www.youtube.com/watch?v=lelwpASvhPQ
https://www.youtube.com/watch?v=ClPPPRjoMYU
18.*The Return to One*
https://www.youtube.com/watch?v=bkTccU8x7a4
19.*Stuart Goldman*
https://somecurrentissues.blogspot.com/2011/02/aliens-from-outer-
space.html
20.*Extreme Super Moon*
http://fgb.domosir.xyz/
21.*Whales on the Beach*
https://www.youtube.com/watch?v=nOzdmixtapURio de Janeiro Brazil,
2011,
22.*Beebe Arkansas*
https://www.youtube.com/watch?v=ZmnwVhCqEvs
23.*Beetles*
https://www.youtube.com/watch?v=ZmnwVhCqEvs
24.*Frogs*
https://www.youtube.com/watch?v=6DhWKtxRXJU
25.*Hybrids*
https://www.youtube.com/watch?v=1IIWcdo9aw0

http://www.dailymail.co.uk/sciencetech/article-2017818/Embryos-involving-genes-animals-mixed-humans-produced-secretively-past-years.html
26. *Japan Quake*
http://content.usatoday.com/communities/ondeadline/post/2011/03/quake-shifted-japan-coast-about-13-feet-knocked-earth-65-inches-off-axis/1
27. *226 Tornadoes*
https://www.cbsnews.com/news/noaa-record-226-tornadoes-in-24-hours-last-week/
John Ankerberg & John Weldon, *The Facts on UFOs and Other Spiritual Phenomena* (Eugene, OR: Harvest House Publishers, 1992).

Chapter 9   *The Travel of UFO's*

1. *1989-1990*
   https://www.youtube.com/watch?v=d9PVBL2MkKk
   John Ankerberg & John Weldon, *The Facts on UFOs and Other Spiritual Phenomena* (Eugene, OR: Harvest House Publishers, 1992).

Chapter 10   *The Fear of UFO's*

1. *Whitley Strieber*
   http://www.ufocasebook.com/1985strieber.html
2. *Pennsylvania Farmer*
   http://members.tripod.com/~task_2/Wave-Scary.htm
   https://wwwmacsufonews.blogspot.com/2012/01/1973-pennsylvania-ufo-bigfoot-encounter.html
3. *Jacques Vallee*
   http://www.thejinn.net/jacques_vallee_interview.htm
   http://www.topsecretwriters.com/2016/03/jacques-vallee-continues-begging-for-serious-ufo-research/
4. *Comments*
   http://www.chesterfieldparanormalresearch.com/quotes-concerning-ufo--alien-deception.html
5. *Death of Joe Fisher*
   http://www.anomalist.com/milestones/fisher.html

http://www.paraview.com/fisher/index.htm
John Ankerberg & John Weldon, *The Facts on UFOs and Other Spiritual Phenomena* (Eugene, OR: Harvest House Publishers, 1992).

Chapter 11   *The Actions of UFO's*

1. John Ankerberg & John Weldon, *The Facts on UFOs and Other Spiritual Phenomena* (Eugene, OR: Harvest House Publishers, 1992).

Chapter 12   *The Possession of UFO's*

1. *John Ankerberg*
   https://www.crossroad.to/Quotes/spirituality/aliens.html
2. *Joe Jordan*
   http://www.alienresistance.org/stop-alien-abduction/
3. *Jennifer and Dean*
   http://www1.cbn.com/700club/moe-familys-haunted-parsonage
   John Ankerberg & John Weldon, *The Facts on UFOs and Other Spiritual Phenomena* (Eugene, OR: Harvest House Publishers, 1992).

Chapter 13   *The Deception of UFO's*

1. *Barbara Marciniak*
   https://video.search.yahoo.com/search/video;_ylt=Awr469z._6Zax1
   cA1Q9XNyoA;_ylu=X3oDMTEyNzR0aHVuBGNvbG
   8DZ3ExBHBvcwMxBHZ0aWQDQjQ4NTNfMQRzZWMDc2M-
   ?p=barbara+marciniak&fr=tightropetb
2. *Tuella*
   http://www.sanandaseagles.com/gai/pages/tuella.html
   John Ankerberg & John Weldon, *The Facts on UFOs and Other Spiritual Phenomena* (Eugene, OR: Harvest House Publishers, 1992).
3. *Loud Noises around the World*
   https://video.search.yahoo.com/search/video;_ylt=AwrSw7wK

AqdaC0gAtRv7w8QF;_ylu=X3oDMTBsOWdjMmRnBHNlYw
NzZWFyY2gEdnRpZANWSURDMQ--
;_ylc=X1MDOTY3ODEzMDcEX3IDMgRhY3RuA2NsawRiY2s
DZXV1cnRsNWRhZGJiNiUyNmIlM0QzJTI2cyUzRHRzBGNzcm
NwdmlkA2tJVHlQVEV3TGpMdmUzMnBXcWF0Wmd3c01qQXdN
UUFBQUFFVzNsdmsEZnIDdGlnaHRyb3BldGIEZnIyA3NhL
WdwBGdwcmlkA29SU1dfc01qUmE2Q0lnN1RyQ1dxc
EEEbXRlc3RpZANVSTAxJTNEVklEQzEEbl9yc2x0AzYw
BG5fc3VnZwMzBG9yaWdpbjN2aWRlby5zZWFyY2gue
WFob28uY29tBHBvcwMyBHBxc3RyA2A2xvdWQgbm9pc2
VzIGhlYXJkBHBxc3RybAMxNwRxc3RybAM0MgRxdW
VyeQNzdHJhbmdlIGxvdWQgbm9pc2VzIGhlYXJkIGFyb3
VuZCB0aGUgd29ybGQEdF9zdG1wAzE1MjA4OTQ1MDk
EdnRlc3RpZANWSURDMQ--
?gprid=oRSW_sMjRa6CIg7TrCWqpA&pvid=kITyPTEw
LjLve32pWqatZgwsMjAwMQAAAADW3lvk&p=strange+loud
+noises+heard+around+the+world&ei=UTF-
8&fr2=p%3As%2Cv%3Av%2Cm%3Asa&fr=tightropetb#id
=1&vid=3ec521aa6cdde75f254702d98289aeb5&action=view

4. *Reagan and Gorbachev*
   https://video.search.yahoo.com/search/video?fr=tightropetb&p=ronald
   +reagan+speech+of+world+coming+together#id=2&vid=b30dc5342
   da7dd9ee8c749d3d5c1dbb1&action=click

5. *The Last Card*
   http://www.theeventchronicle.com/galactic/the-last-card-is-the-aliens/#

6. *Stephen Hawkings*
   https://video.search.yahoo.com/search/video?fr=tightropetb&p
   =stephen+hawkings+says+we+should+stay+away+from+aliens#id
   =5&vid=d5e2599130727ededb6a322c21680610&action=view